# Chopin

## HIS LIFE & MUSIC

Jeremy Nicholas

# Chopin

## HIS LIFE & MUSIC

Jeremy Nicholas

**sourcebooks mediaFusion**

An Imprint of Sourcebooks Inc.®
Naperville, Illinois

Published by Sourcebooks MediaFusion, an imprint of Sourcebooks, Inc.
P.O. Box 4410, Naperville, Illinois 60567-4410
(630) 961-3900
Fax: (630) 961-2168
www.sourcebooks.com

Originally published in the UK by Naxos Books.

Printed and bound in the United States of America.
BVG   10 9 8 7 6 5 4 3 2 1

# Author's Acknowledgments

First and foremost, I owe a huge vote of thanks to Harriet Smith. It is always a comfort to have a trusted friend as your editor – and she has fulfilled that role with her customary erudition and genuine affection for the subject. It's not always one's editor who initially suggests the author to the publisher. Genevieve Helsby at Naxos took the plunge and, having given me a detailed brief, simply let me get on with it. Another lucky break. I am enormously grateful to her for her guidance and encouragement whenever I needed it.

I have also been fortunate in the friends who have helped me with sundry queries and various aspects of this biography, usually responding to my requests in the blink of an email: Alison Waggitt who has, as with all my previous books, provided the first-rate index; Michael Quinn; Ludwig Madlener; Kacper Miklaszewski, Tony Gray, Sophie Gray and Slawek Danek; Roger Vignoles; Andrew Mussett; Jo Carpenter; and, of course, Jill and Rosie for their usual generosity and forbearance whenever Chopin had to come first.

# www.naxos.com/chopinlifeandmusic

Visit the dedicated website for *Chopin: His Life & Music* and gain free access to the following:
- Hours of extra music to listen to
- Music by many of Chopin's contemporaries
- A timeline of Chopin's life, set alongside contemporary events in arts, culture, and history

To access this you will need:
- ISBN: 1843791153
- Password: Mazurka

## About the Life & Music Series

The Life & Music series presents fully rounded, accessible portraits of composers through an ideal mix of media: words, pictures, and the music itself. With its extensive catalogue of classical recordings, its experience of the classical music world, its expertise in the use of the Internet, and its growing reputation for educational material, Naxos is ideally placed to provide richly illustrated and authoritative biographies of the great musical figures in the western tradition.

## About Sourcebooks MediaFusion

Launched with the 1998 New York Times bestseller *We Interrupt This Broadcast* and formally founded in 2000, Sourcebooks MediaFusion is the nation's leading publisher of mixed-media books. This revolutionary imprint is dedicated to creating original content—be it audio, video, CD-ROM, or Web—that is fully integrated with the books we create. The result, we hope, is a new, richer, eye-opening, thrilling experience with books for our readers. Our experiential books have become both bestsellers and classics in their subjects, including poetry (*Poetry Speaks*), children's books (*Poetry Speaks to Children*), history (*We Shall Overcome*), sports (*And The Crowd Goes Wild*), the plays of William Shakespeare, and more. See what's new from us at www.sourcebooks.com.

# Contents

# Preface

*'Chopin proposes, supposes, insinuates, seduces,*
*persuades; he almost never asserts.'*

André Gide

Chopin is among the most universally beloved of all composers. For those to whom the contrapuntal rigors of Bach, the Olympian utterances of Beethoven and the Teutonic splendor of Brahms are overly severe companions, Chopin proves an understanding friend. He shares your confidences and reflects your dreams, anxieties and joys. His music has its own distinct voice, immediately identifiable and almost completely original.

He differs from most other so-called 'great composers' in two main respects: he wrote no symphonies, no operas, no ballets, very little chamber music and no church music (except for a setting of Veni Creator, now unfortunately lost); and every single composition, regardless of form, involves the piano. For Chopin it was his entire musical raison d'être.

Many people know Chopin only through a handful of overplayed works with simplistic nicknames – the 'Revolutionary' Study, the 'Raindrop' Prelude, the 'Military' Polonaise – without having the vaguest idea of who he was or what he was like. For others, however, Chopin represents a great deal more. Not only was he one of the greatest and most original pianists in history, he used that experience in his own compositions, creating something entirely new in the process. His music made a significant contribution to the development of the piano's potential – and this at a time when the instrument itself was developing in much the same way that home computers today are constantly being upgraded and improved.

His name has other resonances too: a symbol of Polish patriotism; the dandified musical aristocrat of Parisian salons; the tragic lover of George Sand; a sensitive consumptive who died young like the hero of the archetypal Romantic novel. And for others – lost to this writer, it must be admitted – Chopin is a somewhat effete composer of short piano pieces who was limited in his range and made a minimal contribution to music.

Although he composed a relatively modest amount of music – which pales alongside the output of, say, Bach, Haydn or Liszt – a huge proportion of it is still regularly played and recorded. And it has never fallen out of favour as did, for instance, the works of Vivaldi, J.S. Bach and Mozart. Vivaldi was virtually unknown until the 1930s and few of Mozart's sublime piano concertos were in the regular repertoire of pianists until a century after his death. Yet Chopin's music has remained a favorite among both musicians and listeners. One reason for this is the extraordinary fecundity of ideas (melodic, harmonic, rhythmic and structural), tempered by hypersensitive self-criticism. Very few works that he allowed to be published fall below his own high standards.

This is reflected in the fact that many of Chopin's Waltzes, Studies, Preludes and Nocturnes have been recorded literally hundreds of times. The pianists who do not include his music in their repertoire are very much the exception. Who, in short, could love the piano and fail to respond to Chopin's music?

But what of the man? Ah – now therein lies the mystery. That he was a genius in the truest sense of that overworked description, there can be no doubt. He changed the rules; he composed what he had to with total conviction in a unique and novel way. Like many other men and women of his mindset, he was a complex and contradictory character. In Chopin's case he was a reserved, private individual whose emotions and innermost feelings were expressed, consciously or not, in his music. And, of course, like anyone who does not easily reveal himself, he becomes ipso facto infinitely more alluring.

What sort of person, what kind of experiences, what kind of emotional make-up are behind such startling originality? From where did the heart-wrenching **Mazurka in A minor**, Op. 17 No. 4 come? Or the Romanze from the E minor Piano Concerto, or the C minor Nocturne, Op. 48 No. 1? How could these come from the same miraculous source that produced the ecstatic last movement of the B minor Sonata and the dramatic conflict of the G minor Ballade?

This book, I hope, will answer a few of these questions and throw some light on a composer whose music is so much part of the fabric that its creation is taken almost for granted. Above all, may it inspire you to listen to Chopin's music and persuade you, in the words of his friend, the poet Heinrich Heine, that 'since he is neither Polish, nor French, nor German, he reveals his higher origin; he comes from the country of Mozart, Rafael and Goethe. His true country is the country of Poetry'.

**Jeremy Nicholas**

# Chopin

## HIS LIFE & MUSIC

Jeremy Nicholas

# Chapter 1

## From Farmhouse to Palace, 1810–1822

# From Farmhouse to Palace, 1810–1822

No one is quite sure exactly when Fryderyk Franciszek Chopin was born. The year is not in question: 1810. The place, too, is certain: a single-story farmhouse with whitewashed walls and earth floors on the estate of Count Skarbek in Żelazowa Wola, a small village on the Utrata River about twenty miles west of Warsaw. The register of baptism in the nearby church of Brochow gives his birthday as 22 February, but, as was often the case with such records, the date might well be that on which the birth was entered, often several weeks after the event. Uncertainty arose because the composer's family and Chopin himself always maintained that he was born on 1 March. Chopin scholars favor this date over 22 February in the proportion of roughly two to one, though there is no concrete evidence for either.

Chopin was Franco-Polish by birth. His father, Nicolas, had arrived in that Polish farmhouse by a circuitous route and for a long time there was uncertainty about his exact origins. Frederick Niecks, in what was for many years the standard authority on Chopin, stated that Nicolas Chopin was born on 17 August 1770 at Nancy, Lorraine, and dismissed the claims that 'he was the natural son of a Polish nobleman who followed King Stanislaus Leszcinski to Lorraine'. Now, though, there is little doubt that Nicolas Chopin was in fact born into a French peasant family on 15 April 1771 in Marainville, a village in the Vosges region of northeastern France. Young Nicolas came to the notice of a Pole, Jan Adam Weydlich, the administrator of the nearby estate of a Polish nobleman, Count Michal Pac. It is possible that the Pac family moved to the area when King Stanislaus was made Duke of Lorraine in 1735. At any rate, Nicolas Chopin was familiar with Poles from an early age and when, in 1787, Weydlich decided to return to his native country, Nicolas went with him, some say to escape conscription into the French army. For the next five years Nicolas worked in Weydlich's tobacco factory as a clerk in Warsaw.

The city must have presented quite a sight to the French country boy. A Mr. Coxe, who visited Warsaw not long before Nicolas Chopin arrived there, offered his impressions:

> *The streets are spacious, but ill-paved; the churches and public buildings large and magnificent, the palaces of the nobility are numerous and splendid; but the greatest part of the houses, especially the suburbs, is mean and ill-constructed wooden hovels.*

What must have impressed Nicolas Chopin more were the crowded streets and squares of Warsaw enlivened by a melting pot of Poles, Lithuanians, Russians, Germans, Muscovites, Jews and Wallachians. J.E. Hitzig, the biographer of E.T.A. Hoffmann knew Warsaw well, and painted a lively picture of the place:

> *The streets of stately breadth, formed of palaces in the finest Italian taste and wooden huts which at every moment threatened to tumble down on the heads of the inmates...*

*Long-bearded Jews, and monks in all kinds of habits; nuns of the strictest discipline, entirely veiled and wrapped in meditation; and in the large squares troops of young Polesses in light-coloured silk mantles engaged in conversation; venerable old Polish gentlemen with moustaches, caftan, girdle, sword, and yellow and red boots; and the new generation in the most* incroyable *Parisian fashion. Turks, Greeks, Russians, Italians, and French in an ever-changing throng; moreover, an exceedingly tolerant police that interfered nowise with the popular amusements, so that in squares and streets there moved about incessantly Pulchinella theatres, dancing bears, camels, and monkeys, before which the most elegant carriages as well as porters stopped and stood gaping.*

In 1792 Poland was divided up between Russia, Prussia and Austria, leading to the closure of the tobacco factory. Fate once again took a hand. Nicolas Chopin might well have returned to France to find work had he not fallen ill. By the time he had recovered, the insurrection of March 1794 – a reaction to the Second Partition of Poland – was underway. He joined the Warsaw National Guard, rising to the rank of captain, but was wounded. Following the defeat of the Polish forces six months later by Russia and Prussia, he once more found himself unemployed. It was his native tongue that proved to be his savior. French was at that time the lingua franca of the aristocracy and cultured society in Russia and Poland. It was fashionable for such families to have a French-speaking tutor for their children, and in 1794 Nicolas Chopin was fortunate to find such a post with the wealthy Laczynski family near Warsaw. So here was a Frenchman who, having turned his back on his native France, was making his living by teaching French to Poles. Like many other immigrants, Nicolas adopted the habits, culture and language of his new

*The Chopins' family home in Żelazowa Wola*

homeland with a greater fervency than native-born citizens, becoming more pro-Polish than the Poles themselves. He even changed his name from Nicolas to Mikołaj. Having severed the last remaining links with his homeland, in later years he kept from his children all knowledge of his French birthright and humble origins.

Six years later, when the children had finished their education, the Laczynskis recommended Mikołaj to their relatives the Skarbeks on their estate in nearby Żelazowa Wola. It was here that he met Tekla Justyna Krzyżanowska, a distant and impoverished relation of Count Skarbek who had been sent to live with the family as a young girl. She had since become companion and housekeeper for Countess Justyna. She was twenty-six when she and Mikołaj were married in 1806. Their first child, Ludwika, was born the following year and the couple moved out of the main Skarbek residence into the far less comfortable dwelling in the grounds of the estate. Here, three years later, the Chopins' second child – and only son – was born. He was named in honor of his godfather, Count Fryderyk Skarbek (the son of Mikołaj's employer), and his paternal grandfather, François.

Old Count Skarbek, meanwhile, had fallen on hard times and could no longer support the Chopin family. Once more the upwardly mobile life of Mikołaj Chopin was dealt another good card from a seemingly bad hand. The Count decamped to Paris to escape his debtors, but not before introducing his children's erstwhile tutor, through his role as a university official, to the Warsaw Lyceum. Napoleon, in liberating much of central Poland from the Russian–Prussian–Austrian axis, had formed the Grand Duchy of Warsaw in 1807 as a French puppet state. As a result, teachers of French were at a premium. Mikołaj Chopin took his family to Warsaw to begin a new career. Żelazowa Wola remains to this day a

*Chopin's parents, drawn by Ambrozy Miroszewski*

shrine for Chopin pilgrims, though in reality he lived there for only the first seven months of his life.

The Warsaw Lyceum, where Mikołaj taught French language and literature, had only recently been founded as a boarding school for the sons of the gentry. It was housed in the magnificent Saxon Palace which was large enough to provide spacious living quarters for teachers, who could also increase their income by taking on five or six boarders. It suited Mikołaj and Justyna perfectly: Mikołaj as director of studies, Justyna as house mother to half-a-dozen boys. Their own family grew in number too, with Izabela in 1811 and Emilia in 1812.

It is not immediately obvious where the music came from. Chopin's father played the flute a little but could hardly be called a musician and, indeed, does not seem to have regarded music as particularly important.

This was the background to the composer's earliest years. It is not immediately obvious where the music came from. Chopin's father played the flute a little but could hardly be called a musician and, indeed, does not seem to have regarded music as particularly important. From what we can gather he

7

was a somewhat prosaic man, described by one of his pupils as 'a rather ceremoniously grave personage with a certain elegance of manner'. Chopin's mother, on the other hand, had learned to play the piano to a respectable standard. The instrument by then had become a symbol of gentility and to play it was a necessary accomplishment for any well-bred young lady. Justyna gave her son his first lessons; by the age of six, it was clear that his abilities required a proper teacher. The family turned to an old friend of Mikołaj Chopin, an eccentric sixty-year-old Bohemian violinist named Adalbert Żywny who claimed to have been a pupil of a pupil of Johann Sebastian Bach. On the surface, he was not ideal for a budding keyboard prodigy: he was not a pianist, knew only the basics of fingering and hand movements and was quickly outpaced by his gifted pupil. But in fact, Żywny turned out to be an inspired choice and an important influence on Fryderyk's development. He was a charismatic tutor and a fine musician, and Chopin adored him. Because of his very limitations as a piano teacher, Żywny allowed Chopin to develop his own method of playing without relying on the preconceived ideas of standard exercise books. He encouraged Chopin's evident talent for improvisation, and did not interfere with the boy's natural facility. It would be wrong to think of Chopin as an autodidact but it is striking that such an unconventional apprenticeship led to such independence of thought and originality. Later, a similarly unstructured pianistic upbringing led to the same questing, unrestricted approach to the piano from two more creative thinkers of the keyboard: Leopold Godowsky and Ferruccio Busoni.

Żywny's other significant achievement was to give Chopin keyboard training centered on the German classics rather than current favorites such as Clementi and Cramer. He instilled in Chopin a lifelong love of Bach, Haydn and Mozart – and a healthy scepticism for Beethoven. Hummel and Moscheles were the only contemporary composers whom Żywny admired, while he actively disliked the music of Weber, Rossini and Spontini. Bach's music especially was to be a profound influence on Chopin's musical thought. Żywny was also a passionate Polish patriot and we may be sure that he encouraged his protégé to investigate the music of his fellow countrymen. This was readily heard in the drawing-rooms of Warsaw where the most popular form of piano music was the polonaise. Legend has it that this courtly dance had its origins in a processional ceremony celebrating the accession of Henry III of Anjou to the throne of Poland in 1573. It is quite likely that an existing national peasant processional dance, the Polski, was elaborated and danced for the occasion. It is a stately dance in 3/4 time that attracted composers such as Telemann, Bach (in the First 'Brandenburg' Concerto and Second Orchestral Suite) and Mozart (Piano Sonata, K.284) – not that there is anything recognisably Polish about these particular examples. In the decades immediately preceding Chopin's birth there was a resurgence of interest in the polonaise from Polish composers, and by the time of Chopin's studies with Żywny it had become a popular and clearly defined genre of piano music. Minuets and contredanses were also in vogue, but it was the waltz – another 3/4 dance – that really captured the imagination of Europe and America. Chopin's quick ear and an innate ability to improvise meant the young pianist quickly won a wide circle of admirers.

Two years after his first lessons with Żywny, Chopin's first composition was published. It was privately printed by a friend of the Chopin family, probably paid for by his godfather who had recently returned from his studies abroad to take up a post at Warsaw University. Nevertheless, there it was: 'Polonaise in G minor, dedicated to Her Excellency Countess Victoria Skarbek, composed by Frederick Chopin, a musician aged 8'. At about the same time, Chopin made his first public appearance as a pianist. Though not a Wunderkind of the same order as Mozart, his extraordinary gifts were a talking point in Warsaw.

These achievements prompted the first mention of his name in the press. The *Warsaw Review* of January 1818 asserted that:

> *Fryderyk... is a real musical genius [who] not only performs the most difficult pieces on the piano with the greatest ease and extraordinary taste, but is also the composer of several dances and variations that fill experts with amazement, particularly in view of the author's youth. If this boy had been born in Germany or France, his fame would probably by now have spread to all nations...*

With Professor Żywny's extensive contacts, Chopin soon became a sought-after attraction of the salons of the city. Countess Zofia Zamoyska had founded the Warsaw Benevolent Society and it was through her auspices that her 'little Chopin' appeared in the Théâtre Français, part of the former Radziwiłł Palace, on 24 February 1818. He played a concerto by Adalbert Gyrowetz (1763–1850), at that time a revered Bohemian composer of operas, symphonies, string quartets and much else, all of which enjoyed great popularity but are now completely forgotten. This landmark event in Chopin's life was not attended by his mother for some reason – perhaps she was ill or tending to the sickly Emilia – but Fryderyk wore a wide lace collar that Justyna had made especially for him. When he returned home after the triumphant evening and his mother asked him what the audience had liked best, it is said that he replied, 'My new lace collar'. True or not, it is an anecdote that is prescient of Chopin's lifelong diffidence concerning his public concerts. Whatever faults Mikołaj may have had, he never allowed his son's celebrity to go to the boy's head and, to his eternal credit, never permitted Fryderyk to be exploited as a child prodigy. On the other hand, he never allowed his Polish patriotism to compromise his son's advancement. His position meant that socially he was quite well connected. This was due in large measure to his ability to cultivate the right people and avoid offending anyone in a position of authority.

The concert opened the doors to the upper echelons of Polish society, including Prince Sapieha, Count Potocki, Prince Czerwertynski, Viceroy Zajączek, Prince Lubecki, Prince Radziwiłł, General Sowiński and, especially, the Czartoryski family. Chopin would remain in contact with many of them for the rest of his life (indeed, Princes Adam and Alexandre Czartoryski were pall-bearers at his funeral). The Czartoryskis were a useful family to know: Prince Adam enjoyed a close friendship with Tsar Alexander and, since the Congress of Vienna had established the Tsar as the ruler of the Kingdom of Poland, was a man of influence. The most feared man in Warsaw, though, was its ruler, the Tsar's brother, Grand Duke Constantin Pavlovich. This power-crazed schizophrenic summoned the young pianist to the famed Belvedere Palace. Here, incredibly, Chopin's playing not only seems to have soothed the tyrant's tantrums and led to many future such commands, but it also meant that he was frequently asked back to play with the Grand Duke's illegitimate son. Later on,

So, from an early age, we find Chopin moving easily in the highest society, disarming people with his playing and his personality.

he became friendly with the governor of the Principality of Poznan, Prince Radziwiłł of Antonin, himself a composer.

So, from an early age, we find Chopin moving easily in the highest society, disarming people with his playing and his personality. Time and again, later in his life, there are contemporary descriptions of him having 'a natural air of distinction', 'a prince-like charm', 'aristocratic bearing' and the like. But Chopin's talents gave him a passport to all sections of Polish society – one which was not as rigid as in England, for instance, where such universal acceptance was far less common. His natural milieu was that of his own family and friends, the far humbler middle class with its more nationalistic spirit. Mikołaj's fellow teachers, the local intelligentsia, poets, musicians from the Conservatoire were all frequent guests in the Chopin household. Here, where there was much discussion of all things uniquely Polish, the young musician was seen as a product of Poland and promoted as such. Another stratum of society became available when the Lyceum moved from the Saxon Palace to the seventeenth-century former royal residence, Casimir Palace. Among the boarders that the Chopins took under their wing were several boys with whom Fryderyk made close friends, notably Tytus Woyciechowski, Dominik Dziewanowski, Jan Białobłocki, Jan Matuszyński and, later, Julian Fontana. It was during several summer holidays at the country estate of Dominik Dziewanowski in Szafarnia, away from the polite drawing-rooms of Warsaw society, that Chopin experienced for the first time Polish folk music in its authentic rural setting. He was captivated by the dance rhythms and the astringent harmonies of the mazurka and krakowiak – and their symbolic importance to his people.

It was, to say the least, an interesting start in life. In little over twenty years, Chopin's staid, industrious father had risen from being a roughly educated clerk to become a respected teacher in the country's leading academy; a humble farmhouse had made way for a spacious apartment in a former royal palace; he had acquired a nobly born, if impoverished, wife; his son had been hailed as 'a genius', a 'new Mozart'; and he and his family had been welcomed into the homes of the most powerful men in the land.

*Józef Elsner*

In 1818, the Empress Maria Fyodorovna, mother of the Tsar and Grand Duke Constantin, visited Chopin's class in the Lyceum and was presented with two Polonaises by the eight-year-old composer. Yet, in Mikołaj Chopin's mind, there was no question of Fryderyk ever becoming a professional musician: it was no career for a gentleman. So when it became clear that Żywny had no more he could teach the boy and another musician was given the task of guiding his musical education, music lessons were seen merely as an addition to the curriculum. Once more, however, the Chopins made a fortunate choice in their son's musical mentor. He was a Silesian composer of German descent, Józef Elsner (1769–1854). With the assistance of Countess Zamoyska, he had founded in 1815 a society in Warsaw for the encouragement of music which, in 1821, became the Warsaw Conservatoire. Elsner was a gifted teacher, if mediocre composer, and gave Chopin lessons in musical theory and harmony. If Żywny was Chopin's only piano teacher, Elsner was to be his only teacher in composition. By and large, Chopin was allowed to develop in his own way. That he was able to do so was largely due

> By and large, Chopin was allowed to develop in his own way. That he was able to do so was largely due to the perspicacity of his tutors.

to the perspicacity of his tutors. When someone reproached Chopin for his disregard of conventional musical rules and customs, Elsner replied:

> *Leave him in peace. His is an uncommon way because his gifts are uncommon. He does not strictly adhere to the customary method, but he has one of his own, and he will reveal in his works an originality which in such a degree has not been found in anyone.*

# Chapter 2

## Warsaw and Vienna, 1823–1829

# Warsaw and Vienna, 1823–1829

Until he was thirteen, Chopin was educated at home along with his father's boarders; but in 1823 he became a full-time pupil at the Warsaw Lyceum. He already knew several of his classmates: Tytus Woyciechowski, Dominik Dziewanowski, Jan Matuszyński, Jan Białobłocki and Julian Fontana. Tytus in particular was to become an important figure in Fryderyk's life.

*While he had acquired the social graces that made him equally at home in the ballrooms of the aristocracy and on the country estates of the gentry he was by all accounts quite a comedian as a young man.*

One aspect of Chopin's character that emerged – and which is distinctly at odds with the general perception of him as a reticent, somewhat aloof individual – was that of prankster and mischief-maker. While he had acquired the social graces that made him equally at home in the ballrooms of the aristocracy and on the country estates of the gentry – Ferdinand Hiller later described him as being 'as supple as a snake and full of charm in his movements' – he was by all accounts quite a comedian as a young man. His gift of mimicry, both verbal and musical, his fondness for telling jokes, and his talent for caricature made him popular among his peers. It was said that he could transform his features so convincingly when imitating one of the form teachers or a well-known public figure that he was hardly recognizable.

It was a talent on which George Sand, Liszt, Balzac, Hiller, Moscheles and others would comment in later years, though it is hard to equate with the picture of dignity and rectitude that Chopin presented in public. He was the life and soul behind the theatricals in his parents' home. A well-known Polish actor, Albert Piasecki, who was stage-manager on these occasions, opined that 'the lad was born to be a great actor'. He was not alone. When he met Chopin many years later, the celebrated French actor Pierre-François Bocage (1797–1863) went so far as to say that he thought Chopin had wasted his talents by becoming a musician. Being the classroom jester is not such an uncommon role for a teenage boy. Neither are indolence and putting off school work until the last possible moment. Concerts, the opera and party-going meant that he was rarely in bed before the early hours of the morning.

While Franz Liszt, a year younger than Chopin, was being groomed as a virtuoso concert pianist, Chopin remained at school in the comparative cultural backwater of Warsaw, secure in the bosom of his staunchly middle-class family, with his parents' commitment to self-improvement, sound morality and a good education. During the summer holidays of 1824 and 1825, he enjoyed being outdoors in the boisterous company of his friends on their modest estates. He spent his spare time experimenting with mazurkas, waltzes and polonaises, and playing at charity concerts. At one, in April 1825, he played for Tsar Alexander I. After another, on 27 May, the Warsaw correspondent of the Leipzig *Allgemeine musikalische Zeitung* reported that:

> *The Academist Chopin performed the first* Allegro *of Moscheles' Pianoforte Concerto in F minor [sic, but most likely to be No. 1 in F major], and an improvisation on*

*the aeolopantaleon [an instrument introduced in Poland in 1825]. This instrument... combines the aeolomelodicon [another Polish invention, apparently resembling a harmonium] with the piano-forte... Young Chopin distinguished himself in his improvisation by a wealth of musical ideas, and under his hands this instrument, of which he is a thorough master, made a great impression.*

There was also a major musical event of a different kind at around this time. On 2 June 1825, Brzezina & Co. published Chopin's Rondo in C minor, Op. 1 – the first commercial publication of one of his works. It is dedicated to Madame de Linde, wife of the Warsaw Lyceum's rector, with whom Chopin often played duets.

In September 1825 Chopin began his final year at the Lyceum. To his school work and frequent appearances in the drawing-rooms of Warsaw was added the role of organist of the Visitandine Church every Sunday. When his schooldays ended in July 1826, he passed his exams with an honourable mention. At the end of that month Fryderyk travelled with his mother and Emilia to the resort of Bad Reinerz in Silesia. It was hoped that the spa would cure the tuberculosis afflicting his younger sister. When he returned, a compromise with his father and the persuasive powers of Żywny and Elsner meant that he was allowed to enter the Warsaw Conservatoire to study harmony and counterpoint while agreeing to attend lectures at the University on such subjects as history and literature.

In the event, Chopin managed to adapt this arrangement to his own needs. The only lectures that he attended were on Polish literature and those connected in some way with music, while his course of study at the Conservatoire, which he joined in September 1826, was confined to just six lessons in counterpoint per week with Elsner. This influential figure in Chopin's development is characterized by the biographer of Chopin, Friedrich Niecks, as:

*A man of considerable musical aptitude and capacity, full of nobleness of purpose, learning, industry, perseverance, in short, possessing all qualities implied by talent, but lacking those implied by genius.*

He wrote in all genres – oratorio, opera, symphony, piano variations, rondos, dances and a once-famous setting of the Passion. Perhaps there was something of the free spirit in Elsner that he recognized in his pupil, for we read of one critic who, while praising Elsner for the general excellence of his style:

*...forgives him readily the offences against the law of harmonic connection that occur here and there, and the facility with which he sometimes disregards the fixed rules of strict part-writing, especially in the dramatic works, where he makes effect apparently the ultimate aim of his indefatigable endeavours.*

When the people at Breslau praised Elsner's 'Echo Variations' for orchestra, Chopin exclaimed: 'You must hear his "Coronation" Mass, then only can you judge of him as a composer'. An anonymous visitor to Warsaw in 1841 described Elsner thus:

*The ancestor of modern Polish music, the teacher of Chopin, the fine connoisseur and cautious guide of original talents... When all the people of Warsaw thought Frederick Chopin was entering on a wrong path, that his was not music at all, that he must keep to Himmel and Hummel, otherwise he would never do anything decent – the clever Pan Elsner had already very clearly perceived what a poetic kernel there was in the pale young dreamer, had long before felt very clearly that he had before him the founder of a new epoch of pianoforte-playing, and was far from laying upon him a cavesson [a nose-band for a horse], knowing well that such a noble thoroughbred may indeed be cautiously led, but must not be trained and fettered in the usual way if he is to conquer.*

History may remember Elsner only as 'the teacher of Chopin' but for such an enlightened teacher we must be doubly grateful.

Chopin's first year at the Conservatoire was overshadowed by the tragic death of his beloved younger sister Emilia. In April 1827 at the age of fourteen she suffered a massive tubercular hemorrage. The most gifted of the three Chopin daughters and already a promising poet, she literally coughed herself to death. Fryderyk's own 'weak lungs' had been noted from his sixteenth year. Though never robust, his health was generally good; but his sister's fate haunted him. The family moved to a new apartment in one of the wings of the Krasiński Palace. Chopin had been given his own room while in the sixth form, his piano piled high with scores. Among these was the music of Hummel, Kalkbrenner, Ries, Moscheles and Field – and, of course, his beloved Bach, Mozart and Haydn. In April 1828, the great Hummel himself came to Warsaw, a visit of particular significance.

During the second half of 1827 and early 1828, Chopin had composed his first work for piano and orchestra. This was a set of **variations on 'Là ci darem la mano',** the famous duet from Mozart's Don

Giovanni, which, two years later, was to be published as
Chopin's Op. 2 Both the Op. 1 Rondo and these Variations
are transparently indebted to Hummel as far as the piano
writing is concerned and, in the case of Op. 2, the minimal
orchestral contribution. But then Hummel was the model for
every young pianist at the time and, besides, every genius,
however independent, begins by unconsciously imitating
his favorite composers. Despite Hummel's influence, both
pieces are unmistakably by Chopin. They already bear the
composer's stamp, his unique voice. It was probably these
works and his recently completed First Piano Sonata that
Chopin played to Hummel (who had himself studied with
Mozart). At any rate, Hummel was duly impressed. Such
praise would have meant a great deal to any seventeen-year-
old composer.

The summer of 1828 was spent with family friends on
their estate in the Mazovian countryside. Here Chopin
worked on a new Rondo in C major. Originally conceived
for solo piano, he soon changed his mind and arranged it for
two pianos. 'Today I tried it with Ernemann at Bachholtz's,'
he wrote to his friend Tytus on 9 September, 'and it came
out pretty well.' By mid-September, we find him in Berlin,
the first time he had experienced the rich cultural life of
the Prussian capital. The trip was made possible through
Professor Jarocki, a friend of Mikołaj Chopin, who was
taking part in a scientific congress in the city and invited
Fryderyk to come with him – all expenses paid. In the event,
Chopin came home disappointed. The buildings, the women
and the scientific company were all found wanting. He was
disappointed by the operas he saw. Only Handel's *Ode for St.
Cecilia's Day*, which he heard at the Singakademie, impressed
him as 'nearer to the ideal that I have formed of great music,'
he wrote to his family. Finding himself on one occasion in

the same room as Spontini, Zelter and Mendelssohn, he was too shy to introduce himself to any of them.

Back in Warsaw, he applied himself once more to composition. While Conservatoire students were obliged to write Masses and oratorios in Latin as part of their course, Elsner allowed Chopin to work on his own music. From this period come two further works for piano and orchestra (the Fantasy on Polish Airs and the 'Krakowiak' Rondo), the Piano Trio in G minor and the Rondo à la mazur in F major.

The biggest musical event in Warsaw that year was the appearance of the most celebrated and certainly most charismatic musician of the age: Nicolò Paganini. Already a legendary figure, Paganini had in fact only left his native Italy for the first time the previous year. His triumphant progress through the capitals of Europe has been well documented. He arrived in Warsaw on 21 May and immediately gave his first recital there, evidently determined to make his presence felt by 24 May – the date for the coronation of Tsar Nicholas, as King of Poland, in Warsaw Cathedral. Indeed, he played at the royal banquet that evening, for which he was rewarded with a diamond ring from the Tsar. In all, Paganini played ten concerts between May and July and Chopin attended every one of them.

Paganini had a mesmeric effect not only on the general public but on many greatly gifted musicians, such as Schumann, Berlioz and Liszt. Chopin was also bowled over by the dazzling technique and stage presence of the Italian violinist, but Paganini's effect was to give him a new confidence in his own ability rather than stylistic inspiration. In the case of Liszt, Paganini's music and personality stimulated works that reproduced on the keyboard the same electrifying effects that Paganini achieved on the violin. To Chopin, almost everything Paganini represented was alien and his direct influence is not reflected in any of his music (certainly not in the insipid set of 'Souvenir de Paganini' Variations written at the time). But within weeks he had begun work on the first of the **Études**, and by the end of the year he had completed four (Nos. 8–11) of what would become his Op. 10 – landmarks in the literature of the piano. With these, Chopin showed for the first time that it was possible to combine exercises addressing different areas of virtuoso technique with

music of profound poetic expression, and that the two were not mutually exclusive.

*Chopin aged nineteen*

The impression left by Paganini was of one kind; that left by a beautiful, dark-haired soprano was of another. Konstancja Gladkowska was a student at the Conservatoire, but it appears Chopin was unaware of her until she sang in a concert with her fellow pupils. He fell for her with all the confused passion of any nineteen-year-old, too shy to let her know how smitten he was, beside himself when he saw rivals flirting with her. This coincided with the conclusion of his student days. Elsner's final report read simply: 'Chopin, Fryderyk; third year student. Outstanding abilities; musical genius.' Immediately after the exams on 21 July, Chopin left Warsaw with a party of friends en route to Vienna via Cracow.

CD 1
tracks 6-9

www.naxosbooks.com

*The Kärntnerthor Theatre, Vienna*

They reached the Austrian capital ten days later. Here, Chopin was as bold as he had been bashful in Berlin. He called on the publisher Haslinger, to whom he had sent his Variations on 'Là ci darem' and the C minor Sonata following Hummel's visit; Haslinger promised Chopin that he would publish the Variations if Chopin played them in public. Various other friends from Warsaw introduced him to the two foremost piano-makers in Vienna, Stein and Graf, as well as the director of the Kärntnerthor Theatre, Count Gallenberg. More by luck than good management, less than a fortnight after arriving in Vienna, Chopin found himself giving a triumphant concert in the Kärntnerthor Theatre. The following day, 12 August 1829, he wrote excitedly to his parents:

Yesterday, Tuesday evening at 7, in the Imperial-and-Royal opera house, I made my entry into the world!... When I finished, they clapped so much that I had to come out and bow a second time.

*Yesterday, Tuesday evening at 7, in the Imperial-and-Royal opera house, I made my entry into the world!... As soon as I appeared on the stage, the bravos began; after each variation the applause was so loud that I couldn't hear the orchestra's tutti. When I finished, they clapped so much that I had to come out and bow a second time.*

He followed the Variations with a 'free fantasy' on themes from Boiëldieu's opera *La Dame Blanche*, a last-minute substitution for the 'Krakowiak' Rondo which the orchestra had refused to play at the rehearsal because the parts had been so untidily written by the composer. After that, something Polish was called for, so Chopin launched into an improvisation on various folksongs which, he recalled:

*...electrified the public, as they are not used here to such songs. My spies in the stalls assured me that people even jumped on the seats... All the same, it is being said everywhere that I played too softly, or rather, too delicately for people used to the piano-pounding of artists here. I expect to find this reproach in the paper as the editor's daughter enjoys nothing better than a good thump at the piano. It doesn't matter, there has always got to be a 'but' somewhere, and I should rather it were that one than have people say I played too loud.*

In the end, even the disgruntled orchestra joined in the storm of applause as Count Dietrichstein, the Emperor's director of music, came on stage to congratulate the young pianist. 'This,' continues Chopin, 'my first appearance has been as fortunate as it was unexpected. [One of his Warsaw companions, Romuald] Hube says that no one ever attains anything by ordinary methods and according to a prearranged plan; that one must leave something to luck. And it was just trusting

to luck that I let myself be persuaded to give the concert...
Today,' he concludes, 'I am wiser and more experienced by
about 4 years.' How is it, he was asked, that he had managed
to grow into such a fine musician in Warsaw? 'With Messrs
Żywny and Elsner even a half-wit would learn,' was his
generous reply.

A week later, on 18 August, Chopin gave a second
concert, this time playing the 'Krakowiak' Rondo with legible
parts and offering the 'Là ci darem' Variations as an encore.
Another triumph. For the first time in his life, Chopin's music
and his playing had been acclaimed by public and critics to
whom he was a stranger. 'I don't know what it is,' he wrote
again to his parents, 'but all these Germans are amazed by
me, and I am amazed at their being so amazed.'

The *Wiener Theaterzeitung* of 20 August 1829 identified
the chief characteristics of Chopin's playing in a perceptive
review:

*[Chopin] surprised people because they discovered in him
not only a fine but a really eminent talent; on account of
the originality of his playing and compositions one might
almost attribute to him already some genius, at least in so
far as unconventional forms and pronounced individuality
are concerned. His playing, like his compositions... has a
certain character of modesty which seems to indicate that to
shine is not the aim of this young man, although his execution
conquered difficulties the overcoming of which even here,
in the home of pianoforte virtuosos, could not fail to cause
astonishment... His touch, although neat and sure, has little
of that brilliance by which our virtuosos announce themselves
in the first bars; he emphasised but little, like one conversing
in a company of clever people, not with that rhetorical aplomb
which is considered by virtuosos as indispensable. He plays*

*very quietly, without the daring élan which generally at once distinguishes the artist from the amateur.*

A second review in the same journal on 1 September 1829 was even more gratifying:

*He is a young man who goes his own way, and knows how to please in this way, although his style of playing and writing differs greatly from that of other virtuosos, and indeed chiefly in this; that the desire to make good music predominates noticeably in his case over the desire to please.*

For the first time in his life, Chopin's music and his playing had been acclaimed by public and critics to whom he was a stranger.

With the words of the Viennese critics ringing in his ears – 'a true artist', 'a master of the first rank', 'the stamp of great genius' – Chopin left the city, not before paying visits to Ignaz Schuppanzigh, the leader of Prince Razumovsky's private quartet that had performed all Beethoven's chamber music under the master's eye, and the composer-pianist Carl Czerny ('more sensitive than any of his compositions', observed Chopin). He arrived home early in September 1829 via Prague, Dresden and Breslau.

# Chapter 3

## A Polish Prodigy, 1829–1830

# A Polish Prodigy, 1829–1830

It was clear that Warsaw could not hold Chopin for much longer. He had graduated from the Conservatoire and his friends had left to go their own separate ways; he was unable to profit from his Viennese success – he saw how severely provincial the Polish capital was by comparison, and here he was not fresh news; the political situation in Poland had changed drastically since the death of Tsar Alexander in 1825 – his successor, the autocratic Nicholas II, had turned the country into a police state, spies were everywhere, and the cafés and universities were rife with mutterings of subversion and revolution. Chopin, though a patriotic Pole and outraged at the injustices of the government and the suppression of individual rights, was not a political activist. He was not going to man any barricades. This sense of isolation from his peers, the uncertainty about his future and his frustrated feelings over his emotional life cast him into a depression. 'You wouldn't believe how dreary I find Warsaw now,' he wrote to Tytus in September. 'If it weren't for the family making it a little more cheerful, I shouldn't stay.' And in April 1830: 'What a relief to my intolerable boredom when I get a letter from you.'

Chopin's letters to Tytus Woyciechowski during this

Chopin's letters to Tytus Woyciechowski during this period provide an illuminating insight into his emotional and creative states.

period provide an illuminating insight into his emotional and creative states. His outpourings to his confidant are certainly real and intense. Enshrined on the page, they are historical documents of some significance, but their literary merit is slight – the nineteenth-century equivalent of phone conversations or emails that he might have sent had he lived today. After the premature death in 1828 of Chopin's school friend Jan Białobłocki, Tytus became the composer's principal confidant (he had dedicated the Variations on 'Là ci darem' to him). So freely does Chopin express himself, and with such passion, that some commentators have suggested there was a physical attraction between them. 'My dearest life!' Chopin invariably begins, and then 'I have never missed you as I do now'; in another letter: 'No one else except you shall have my portrait. There is only one other person to whom I would give it, and even then to you first, for you are my dearest'; and a third: 'It's no use, I know that I love you and want you to love me always more and more, and that's why I scribble all this.' Though to us today this may read like the language of love, there is no evidence that Chopin ever had any homosexual tendencies, and it has to be borne in mind that he was not unusual for his time in finding it easier to share his emotions with men than women. His letters to Tytus reveal an emotionally insecure young man relying on a slightly older, more self-assured friend. To him, Chopin poured out the frustration and wallowing self-pity typical of any lovestruck teenager.

For his holiday that year, Fryderyk went to Strzyzewo, the property of his godmother Madame Wiesiołowska. While there, he accepted an invitation from Prince Radziwiłł to visit him at his country seat, Antonin. Apart from his social prominence as governor of the Grand Duchy of Posen and being related by marriage to the royal family of Prussia,

*Chopin playing at* *the Radziwiłłs'* the Prince was a genuinely gifted composer, a good singer and a competent cellist. Chopin wrote an Introduction and Polonaise brillante for him and his daughter, Princess Wanda, to play. The latter provided a distraction from Konstancja. 'She's young (seventeen), pretty,' he wrote to Tytus, 'and it's a real joy placing her little fingers on the keys.'

By the following March Chopin had completed his Concerto in F minor and gave its first performance in his family's apartment in a reduced chamber version. Unexpectedly, some of the Polish press covered this private event. The reviews were, to say the least, gratifying, and enthusiastic enough to persuade him to play the work in a concert at the National Theatre. This took place on 17 March, with Chopin's friend Karol Kurpiński conducting. It was a sellout – 800 people, his largest audience to date. Along with music by Elsner, Kurpiński and Paër, Chopin played the new Concerto and his Fantasy on Polish Airs. The evening was a resounding success, though there were comments (among them from Kurpiński) that the piano had been too soft-toned and that many of Chopin's effects had been lost – precisely the criticism that had been voiced in Vienna. A second concert was quickly arranged for 22 March. For this, Chopin did not play on his own instrument but was lent a stronger-toned Viennese piano ('better than Hummel's,' he said). This time the reaction was uniformly ecstatic; he played his F minor Concerto (its Adagio was particularly admired), followed by the 'Krakowiak' Rondo and an improvisation on some Polish folksongs. These two concerts marked Chopin's first commercial successes as a pianist.

Everyone clamored for a third but he declined. The reasons for his refusal to capitalize on his triumph say much about Chopin's personality, and show traits that would color his future career. The attractions of earning some much-needed money and further acclaim paled alongside the tortuous process of choosing which musicians should play, which composers should be heard alongside him, even down to which friends should be given reserved seats. Chopin was afraid of inflaming petty jealousies among the closely knit musical establishment and of opening himself up to further criticism – and, equally, to more fulsome (as he saw it) praise. His first experience of the repercussions of great public success had frightened him. His confidence in his own creative ability was high but his self-confidence was low. This was also true of his dealings with other people, and although he was socially gregarious and made friends easily he found it difficult to establish close relationships. Fear of rejection, suspicion of others' motives, and the possibility of being placed in an embarrassing position meant that he tended to keep people at arm's length. No wonder he could not express himself to Konstancja Gladkowska and relied so heavily on the advice of Tytus, his most trusted friend.

> His first experience of the repercussions of great public success had frightened him. His confidence in his own creative ability was high but his self-confidence was low.

Nurturing his feelings for the singer, he set about composing a second Piano Concerto, this one in the key of E minor. (In the event, this was published before the earlier F minor Concerto and thus became Chopin's **Piano Concerto No. 1.**) 'I don't know whether it is because it was with you that I learned to feel,' he wrote to Tytus on 10 April 1830, 'but whenever I write anything, I want to know whether you like it, and I think my second Concerto in E minor will have no value in my judgement till you have heard it.' Three weeks later, on 15 May, he reports:

*The Adagio of the new concerto is in E major. It is not meant to be loud, it's more of a romance, quiet, melancholy; it should give the impression of gazing tenderly at a place which brings to the mind a thousand dear memories. It is a sort of meditation in beautiful spring weather, but by moonlight. That is why I have muted the accompaniment.*

Chopin was enraptured. 'It seems as if she breathed some perfume of the freshest flowers into the hall,' he reported to the absent Tytus.

We can take this, which would become the Romanze (slow movement) of the E minor Concerto, as a love-letter to Konstancja. It was one of the rare instances in his career that Chopin ever offered a specific meaning to any of his music.

His stifled passion for Konstancja was put on hold at the beginning of June when the celebrated German soprano Henriette Sontag visited Warsaw. Born in 1806, she had created the title role in Weber's Euryanthe in 1823 (she would die in the cholera epidemic of 1854 while on tour in Mexico City). Chopin was enraptured. 'It seems as if she breathed some perfume of the freshest flowers into the hall,' he reported to the absent Tytus. 'She caresses, she strokes, she enraptures, but she

seldom moves to tears.' Prince Radziwiłł introduced the two *Konstancja* of them. Chopin was infatuated but tongue-tied; Sontag *Gladkowska* was in any case unavailable, having married in 1828 Count Rossi, the Scandinavian ambassador to the Dutch court. So Konstancja remained Chopin's romantic ideal, even though, just two months later, he wrote to Tytus about another girl whom he could not take his eyes off; and a week or so after that yet another caught his eye.

The political situation and the completion of his E minor Concerto seem to have raised Chopin from his lethargy and galvanized him into action. 'If only my health lasts,' he wrote presciently to Tytus in September 1830, 'I hope to work all my life.' On 22 September he tried out the new work at home, probably with a quartet accompaniment, and fixed the date of 11 October for its first public performance. 'A week after the concert at the latest,' he wrote to Tytus, 'I shall have left Warsaw... My music in my bundle, the string on my knapsack, the knapsack on my shoulder, and to the stage-coach.' What is more, he invited Konstancja and her fellow-pupils to participate in the concert. As conductor, Kurpiński had to give way for political reasons to Evasio Soliva, the singing instructor at the Conservatoire. Chopin played the E minor Concerto and ended with the Fantasy on Polish Airs. In his letter to Tytus of 12 October 1830 we read:

> *My dearest life! Yesterday's concert was a success; I haste to let you know. I inform your Lordship that I was not a bit, not a bit nervous, and played the way when I'm alone, and it went well. Full hall. [In fact, only 700 people were in the audience.] First Goerner's Symphony. Then my noble self's Allegro in E minor, which I just reeled off; one can do that on the Streycher piano. Furious applause.*

After an aria Chopin played the two remaining movements of the Concerto and, following the interval, the Overture to *William Tell*. Then came Konstancja in the Cavatina from Rossini's *La donna del largo* which 'she sang as she has sung nothing yet.' Then the Fantasy on Polish Airs:

> *This time I understood what I was doing, the orchestra understood what they were doing, and the pit understood as*

*well. This time the final mazurka elicited huge applause, after which – the usual farce – I was called up. No one hissed and I had to bow four times – but properly now because Brandt has taught me how to do it... I never succeeded in playing so comfortably with the orchestra... I am thinking of nothing now but packing; either on Saturday or on Wednesday I start, going via Cracow.*

The concert, it seems, had also finally broken the ice with Konstancja, for on 25 October Chopin called on her to take his leave. Then, on the morning of 2 November 1830, he bade farewell to his family and friends, and boarded the coach. Elsner and a number of friends accompanied him to Wola, the first village beyond Warsaw. There the pupils of the Conservatoire had gathered to sing a cantata especially composed by Elsner for the occasion. Chopin was exhorted never to forget Poland and to keep its harmonies in his soul wherever he might be. A silver goblet filled with Polish earth was presented to him. One can speculate that a few tears might have been shed – and many more, had anyone known then that, short of two weeks, he had exactly nineteen years left to live. Though he had no reason to think it at the time, Chopin would never again set foot on his native soil.

# Chapter 4

## Vienna, 1830–1831

# Vienna,1830–1831

Chopin's intention was to tour Europe, making the Hapsburg capital merely his first stop. However, not only did he alter his plan of making straight for Vienna but, once he had arrived there, he ended up staying for eight months – and this despite the fact that the welcome return he had expected did not materialize. Chopin was nothing if not indecisive.

Instead of travelling alone he was joined by Tytus in Kalisz, and the two travelled on to Breslau. Here they happened to wander into a rehearsal for a concert later that day which included a Moscheles concerto with a local pianist as soloist. During the break, Chopin sat down at the piano and began to play. On hearing him, the soloist backed out of the engagement. Instead of Moscheles, the audience that night enjoyed Chopin in two movements of his E minor Concerto.

From Breslau, the two friends continued to Dresden, Chopin in high spirits, turning down the offer of a paid concert. 'I have no time to lose,' he wrote to his family on 14 November, 'and Dresden will give me neither fame nor money.' Passing through Prague, he arrived in Vienna on 22 November full of self-confidence and optimism. The visit started well, with no less a figure than Hummel paying his respects the following morning. But the tone of his sojourn was set later that same morning when the publisher Haslinger, to whom Chopin had offered his 'Là ci darem la mano' Variations and C minor Sonata on his previous visit, refused to publish the two Piano Concertos unless Chopin gave him the copyright for nothing. Chopin always had a secure notion of his worth in monetary terms and was determined not to be exploited. This was the first brush of many with publishers. 'Perhaps [Haslinger] thinks that if he appears to have slight regard for my things I shall take him seriously, and give them to him for nothing?' he wrote to his friend Jan Matuszyński on 22 November. '"For nothing" is finished; now pay up, you animal!' 'Animal' was mild; later it would be 'crooks and Jews'.

Tytus and Fryderyk found an ideal apartment to rent on the third floor of a house in Kohlmarkt Street: three spacious rooms that were 'beautifully, luxuriously and elegantly furnished' with a low rent and a pretty young widow as landlady who expressed her love of Poles and contempt for Austrians and Germans. Chopin looked up some of those he had befriended the previous year, Czerny and Wilhelm Würfel among them, and also made the acquaintance of Dr. Malfatti, the Imperial physician and Beethoven's erstwhile friend. The piano manufacturer Graf promised the loan of an instrument. All seemed set fair.

Exactly a week after Chopin's arrival in Vienna, revolution broke out in Warsaw. There had been an attempt on the life of the hated Grand Duke Constantin in his Belvedere Palace followed by a failed attack on the Russian garrison. The news arrived in Vienna on 5 December. Because Austria was a close ally of the Russian Tsar and Vienna was the seat of the Hapsburg Empire, suddenly any Pole in the capital became persona non grata. Doors that had previously been open to

> Chopin always had a secure notion of his worth in monetary terms and was determined not to be exploited.

Chopin were now closed. 'Jasio,' he wrote to Matuszyński, 'today, at dinner in the Italian restaurant I heard: – "Dear God made a mistake when he created the Poles"... and another man answer "Nothing worthwhile ever came out of Poland". The dogs!'

There was no prospect of any concert, not even for charity. Chopin's dream of meeting the elite of Viennese society never materialized and invitations went unanswered. Tytus decided to return home to join the insurrectionists; Chopin dithered but was finally persuaded by Tytus to stay in Vienna. Poland and its art, it seemed, could be served more effectively at a distance. Malfatti, too, tried to persuade Chopin that every artist is a cosmopolitan. 'Even if that were so,' Chopin wrote to Elsner in Warsaw, 'as an artist I am still in the cradle, but as a Pole I have begun my third decade.' His older feelings predominated.

It was also a pragmatic decision to remain where he was: Chopin did not have the physique or the constitution of a fighter. Instead, he instructed his parents to sell the diamond ring which he had been given by Tsar Alexander; he bought shirt studs and handkerchiefs with Polish emblems and sought the company of his fellow countrymen now unable to enter Poland after the authorities had closed the border.

On Christmas Day 1830 he wrote to Matuszyński:

*This time last year I was with the Bernadines. Today I am sitting alone, in a dressing-gown, gnawing my ring and writing. If it were not that I should be a burden on my father, I would come back. I curse the day I left. I am up to my neck in evening parties, concerts and dances, but they bore me to death; everything is so terribly gloomy and depressing for me here.*

A few paragraphs later he asks: 'Shall I go to Paris? Here they advise me to wait. Shall I return home? Stay here? Kill myself? Stop writing to you? Give me some advice what to do.' Christmas Day on your own in a foreign city can be a depressing experience for anyone. For the twenty-year-old composer it was a crucial period: the break from the love and security of his family and the leap into a new life as an independent adult.

Chopin's fondness for the cello is evident in that it was the only solo instrument other than the piano for which he wrote anything of importance.

If he sometimes felt at a low ebb, Chopin enjoyed his time with the many musicians he encountered. Hummel was 'kindness itself'. His son, a talented artist, made a portrait in chalk of Fryderyk. Czerny introduced him to Diabelli. Through Würfel he met Josef Slavik, 'a fine violinist, still quite young, 26 at the most... Since Paganini I have heard nothing like him; he can play 96 staccato notes with one stroke of the bow, and so on; incredible.' The Bohemian Slavik (1805–1833) had come to Vienna in 1825 and had been the first to play Schubert's violin pieces. Had he lived longer, he would undoubtedly have made his mark on violin playing. Chopin worked with him on a set of Variations on an Adagio theme of Beethoven but this seems to have been lost. Another rewarding friendship came with Joseph Merk, lead cellist in the Imperial Orchestra. Chopin's fondness for the cello is evident in that it was the only solo instrument other than the piano for which he wrote anything of importance. To the Polonaise brillante for cello and piano written the previous year he added an Introduction. The work was dedicated to Merk and published in 1830 as Chopin's Op. 3.

The political situation aside, there were further reasons for Chopin's lack of progress in Vienna. There were simply too many other pianists vying for attention and among them the star was undoubtedly Sigismund Thalberg. The fact that he was the illegitimate son of Count Moritz von Dietrichstein – the Emperor's director of music – and Baroness von Wetzlar did not do him any harm but, that aside, Thalberg was a genuinely extraordinary pianist. A student of Hummel and Moscheles, he had made his Viennese debut in 1829. He not only looked the part, he really could deliver: flawless technique, incredibly even scales and great precision, all accomplished with a remarkable stillness at the keyboard. According to Moscheles, Thalberg acquired this self-control 'by smoking a Turkish pipe while practicing his exercises; the length of the tube was so calculated as to keep him erect and motionless'. 'Thalberg', remarked Liszt, 'is the only man who can play the violin on the piano.' Chopin was, perhaps unsurprisingly in the circumstances, less generous, writing to Matuszyński:

> He plays excellently, but he's not my man... Younger than I, he pleases the ladies, makes pot-pourris from The Dumb Girl [Auber's opera La Muette di Portici], gets his piano by pedal, not the hand, takes tenths as easily as I take octaves, wears diamond shirt studs, does not admire Moscheles; so don't be surprised that only the tutti of my Concerto pleased him.

He added acidly, 'He also writes a concerto' (Thalberg's Concerto in F minor, Op. 5 appeared the same year). Although there was obvious rivalry between them, their relationship was cordial enough for them to attend concerts together. Among these was one by a certain Aloys Schmidt, a pianist from Frankfurt, 'who', Chopin was pleased to report, 'has just fallen flat on his face here – though he's a man of forty, he composes as if he were eighty.'

Without the prospect of concerts, and

**Chopin was clearly capable of writing for orchestra but it was becoming evident that he was more comfortable expressing himself purely through the keyboard.**

burdened with emotional stress, it is understandable that Chopin was only composing fitfully around this time, with erratic results. He drafted what would be his final work for piano and orchestra, the Grande Polonaise, Op. 22. Here the orchestral contribution is even more perfunctory than in the earlier works, though the music itself is strikingly confident and attractive (today, it is seldom heard in this form, though the solo version has remained popular). Chopin was clearly capable of writing for orchestra but it was becoming evident that he was more comfortable expressing himself purely through the keyboard.

The Grande Valse Brillante, Op. 18 is his best-known work from this period though it consciously, even cynically, apes the fashionable Viennese waltzes that he so despised. 'Here, **waltzes** are called works!' he wrote to Elsner in January 1831. 'And Strauss and Lanner, who play them for dancing, are called Kapellmeistern. This does not mean that everyone thinks like that; indeed, nearly everyone laughs about it; but only waltzes get printed.' Haslinger 'lives only on Hummel' and is 'printing only Strauss,' he complained. Strauss or Lanner 'are frantically applauded after each waltz, and if they play a pot-pourri of airs from opera, dances and songs, the audience gets completely carried away. Which all goes to show how the taste of the Viennese public has declined.' Reading this, it is hard to believe that Beethoven had died only four years earlier.

Chopin's thoughts went constantly to his homeland, his family, absent friends and 'her' – Konstancja: 'Her image stands before my eyes,' he wrote in his diary in the spring of 1831. 'I think I don't love her any more, and yet I can't get her out of my head.' Such feelings stimulated him to set to music a number of poems by Polish nationalist poets. Chief among these was Stefan Witwicki (1800–1847). Expressing his gratitude to the composer, Witwicki suggested that Chopin might write an opera on nationalist lines. With a theme taken from Polish history, such a work might have proved to be a valuable propaganda tool if it had been staged in European capitals. Chopin toyed with the idea but his devotion to the piano proved too strong. The idea never bore fruit and he confined his sung love for Poland to pieces for voice and piano.

Chopin was marking time and he knew it. He pulled himself together sufficiently to give a concert at the famous Redoutensaal on 4 April. Billed simply as 'Herr Chopin (piano player)' he played the E minor Concerto as a solo on a programme with ten other artists. It made little impact: time to move on. When he finally decided to make for Paris, he found his route blocked. The Vienna police had mislaid his passport. Now legally a Russian subject, Chopin was told to apply to the Russian Embassy for a new one; his old passport was discovered but the Russians refused to endorse a journey to Paris, a center for Polish revolutionaries and exiles. He was advised by friends to pretend that his journey was to London via Paris, which did the trick.

> Arriving in Stuttgart a week later, he heard the news of Warsaw's downfall. The city fell, amid riots and a cholera epidemic, to the guns of the merciless General Paskiewicz.

In the company of a young man named Norbert Kumelski, Chopin finally left Vienna on 20 July 1831. They travelled along the Danube valley through Linz to Salzburg, Mozart's birthplace, and thence to Munich. Here, he was persuaded to give a concert and on 28 August in the Philharmonic Society Hall, Chopin played his E minor Concerto and Fantasy on Polish Airs. It was his first success since leaving Poland. But his elation was short lived.

Arriving in Stuttgart a week later, he heard the news of Warsaw's downfall. In January, the Poles had declared themselves a free state with no ties to the Tsar. In reply,

Nicholas I sent a fresh army of 200,000 men to stamp his authority on the 40,000 Polish nationalists in the capital. The result was inevitable. The city fell, amid riots and a cholera epidemic, to the guns of the merciless General Paskiewicz. Even the partial independence the Poles had retained since the Fourth Partition of 1815 disappeared when, six months later in February 1832, Poland became a province of the Russian Empire. The country did not regain its independence until 1919, and then for just twenty years. It was only in 1990, when Lech Walesa became the first popularly elected President of Poland, that Chopin's homeland finally achieved true independence.

In a memorable passage from his journal, Chopin reveals his complete devastation at the news of Warsaw's fate:

> Moscow rules the world! Oh God, do you exist? You are there and yet you don't avenge it.

*The suburbs area destroyed, burned. Jas, Wilus probably dead in the trenches. I see Marcel a prisoner! That good fellow Sowinski in the hands of those brutes! Paskiewicz! Moscow rules the world! Oh God, do you exist? You are there and yet you don't avenge it. How many more Russian crimes do You want? Or perhaps – maybe – you are Russian too!!? My poor father! The dear old man may be starving, and my mother not able to buy bread! Perhaps my sisters have succumbed to the ferocity of the Russian rabble. Oh father – so this is your reward in old age! Mother, poor suffering mother, you watched your own daughter die and now the Russians march over her very bones to come and oppress you! Did they spare her grave? They trampled it and covered it with a thousand fresh corpses. What has happened to her [Konstancja]? Where is she? Poor girl, perhaps in some Russian's hands – a Russian strangling her, killing, murdering! Ah my Life, I am alone here; come to me, I'll wipe away your tears, I'll heal the wounds of the present, remind you of the past – the days when there were no Russians... Perhaps I have no mother, perhaps some Russian has killed her, murdered her – My sisters, raving, resist – father in despair, nothing he can do – and I here, useless! And I here with empty hands! Sometimes I can only groan, and suffer, and pour out my despair at the piano! God, shake the earth, let it swallow up the men of this age, let the heaviest chastisement fall on France for not coming to our aid...*

*...The bed I go to – perhaps corpses have lain on it, lain long – yet today that does not sicken me. Is a corpse any worse than I? A corpse knows nothing of father, of mother, or sisters or Tytus; a corpse has no beloved, its tongue can hold no conversation with those who surround it – a corpse is as colorless as I, as cold, as I am cold to everything now...*

*...The clocks in the towers of Stuttgart strike the hours of the night. How many new corpses is this minute making in the world? Mothers losing children, children losing mothers – So much grief over the dead, and so much delight! ...Father! Mother! Where are you? Corpses? Perhaps some Russian has played tricks – oh wait – oh wait – But tears – they have not flowed for so long I could not weep – how glad – how wretched... Alone! Alone! – There are no words for my misery; how can I bear this feeling...*

**Though there is no direct evidence for it, the C minor 'Revolutionary' Étude is said to have been inspired by the fall of Warsaw. Whether or not this is in fact the case, the Poles believed (and still believe) it to be so.**

The anger and despair of this entry is mirrored in the most famous of the twelve Études, Op. 10 which Chopin was writing at the same time. Though there is no direct evidence for it, the C minor 'Revolutionary' Étude is said to have been inspired by the fall of Warsaw. Whether or not this is in fact the case, the Poles believed (and still believe) it to be so. The tormented torrents of the left hand set against the proud, defiant right hand is Chopin at the Warsaw barricades. Its brief two-and-a-half-minute duration was but one outpouring that would make its composer the very personification of his country's plight.

Despite all this – and his temporary contempt for the French – Chopin set off for Paris a few days later, arriving in mid-September 1831. The French capital was to remain his home for the rest of his life. Paris, not Warsaw, would see his most important years and witness all his greatest triumphs. Ironically, Chopin was still unaware of his father's ancestry or the French blood coursing through his own veins, though he did quickly become known as Frédéric Chopin. From France would flow an immortal string of compositions embodying the soul, mood and nationalism of Poland. Fate had decreed that the two halves of the young exile's genetic make-up should be reconciled in his music.

> France would flow an immortal string of compositions embodying the soul, mood and nationalism of Poland.

# Chapter 5

## Paris, 1831–1833

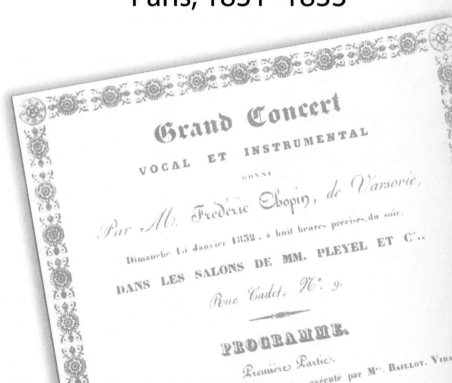

Grand Concert
VOCAL ET INSTRUMENTAL
DONNÉ
Par M. Frédéric Chopin, de Varsovie,
Dimanche 15 Janvier 1832, à huit heures précises du soir,
DANS LES SALONS DE MM. PLEYEL ET C.ⁱᵉ,
Rue Cadet, N.° 9.

PROGRAMME.

Première Partie.

1°. Quintetto composé par Beethowen, exécuté par M.ʳˢ BAILLOT, VIDAL
    URHAN, TILMANT et NORBLIN.
2°. Duo chanté par M.ˡˡᵉˢ TOMÉONI et ISAMBERT.
3°. Concerto pour le Piano, composé et exécuté par M. F. CHOPIN.
4°. Air chanté par M.ˡˡᵉ TOMÉONI.

Deuxième Partie.

1°. Grande Polonaise, précédée d'une Introduction et d'une Marche, comp
    pour six Pianos, par M. KALKBRENNER, et exécutée par Mess
    RENNER, MENDELSOHN-BARTHOLDY, HILLER, OSBORNE, SOW

# Paris, 1831–1833

With perfect timing, events had transpired to deliver the twenty-one-year-old Chopin into the ideal environment for his art to flourish and be recognized. Rarely has there been such a concentration of creative spirits as there was at this time living in Paris: Hugo, Heine, Lamartine, Chateaubriand, Baudelaire, Balzac, De Vigny, De Musset, Dumas, George Sand, Ingres, Delacroix, and pianist-composers such as Liszt, Kalkbrenner, Pixis, Hiller, Herz and Alkan. The musical establishment of Paris was headed by the aging figures of Cherubini, Paër and Lesueur; to the home-grown works of Auber and Hérold were added those of the new lions of the French opera houses: Bellini, Rossini and Meyerbeer. The generation of composers who were to dominate the next half-century after the deaths of Beethoven, Schubert and Weber had yet to make their significant marks: Verdi and Wagner were still in their teens, Liszt was just twenty, Schumann and Chopin were twenty-one, Mendelssohn twenty-two, Berlioz twenty-eight.

There is no doubt, then, that Paris – 'the capital of the nineteenth century' – was an invigorating place to be in 1831. Despite the fact that it was nearly half a century since the storming of the Bastille, the spirit of the 1789 Revolution had not subsided. The regime and defeat of Napoleon had been followed by the return of the monarchy in the form of Louis XVIII and his even more disastrous brother Charles X. Only fourteen months prior to Chopin's arrival, in a second revolution, Charles had been overthrown to be replaced by Louis Philippe, Duke of Orléans – 'The Citizen King'. The city was a hive of political and artistic activity comparable to no other. It was a period of momentous change, of challenges to the old order and of new forms of written, artistic and musical expression.

There had always been a strong link between Poland and France, but one consequence of the Polish situation was the arrival in Paris of a large number of refugees, most notably many of the monied aristocratic families with whom Chopin had been acquainted in Warsaw. Some had established themselves in Paris before the insurrection. A great number had left with their wealth intact, including the Czartoryskis, Radziwiłłs, Sapiehas, Platers and Potockis. Here, too, were several of Chopin's friends from his student days, such as Kazimierz Wodziński and Julian Fontana, the latter later becoming one of Chopin's closest friends. Poles found themselves made as welcome in Paris as they had been unwelcome in Vienna.

> The city was a hive of political and artistic activity comparable to no other. It was a period of momentous change, of challenges to the old order and of new forms of written, artistic and musical expression.

Paris was the most fashionable of cities and the piano was the most fashionable of instruments. By 1830, it was substantially the instrument that we know today (though cross-stringing and iron frames would not become standard until the 1850s). Hammer construction, keyboard action, frames and strings had radically improved in the previous ten years, resulting in instruments that produced a richer and more sonorous tone. A multitude of piano manufacturers had sprung up, each offering their own designs and patents, in much the same way that computers today are constantly updated. By 1845 there were said to have been 60,000 pianos in Paris (its population was one million). It was not only the favorite instrument of the Romantic musicians but a social phenomenon. Just as we now listen to a CD or an iPod to enjoy new music, the piano in the nineteenth century was the means by which most music was disseminated. A new symphony, opera or piece of chamber music would immediately be made available in a reduction for solo piano or piano duet. During the entire 1838 season of the Concerts du Conservatoire in Paris, for example, only a handful of symphonies were performed. If you wanted to hear a symphony by Beethoven or Haydn you generally heard it – or played it – on the piano. Naturally, pianists thronged to the capital. Chopin was certainly in the right place at the right time.

During the remaining eighteen years of his life, he lived at a number of addresses in Paris – 5 and 38 Chaussée d'Antin, 5 Rue Tronchet, 16 Rue Pigalle, 5 Square d'Orléans, 74 Rue Chaillot and 12 Place Vendôme – before his final resting place in the cemetery of Père Lachaise. His first apartment, though, was on the fifth floor of No. 27 Boulevard Poisonnière. He wrote to Kumelski on 18 September:

> You wouldn't believe what a delightful lodging... I have a little room furnished with mahogany, and a balcony over the boulevard from which I can see from Montmartre to the Panthéon and the whole length of the fashionable quarter; many persons envy me my view, but none my stairs.

He also confided to his friend that there was no lack of interest in him from 'charitable ladies' but that he was unable to take advantage of their kind offers. This was probably due to the venereal disease he had picked up as a result of an encounter in Vienna. Her name, we gather from a single mention in his correspondence, was Teressa [sic].

This first letter from Paris is as exuberant and optimistic as his diary entry from just ten days earlier had been depressed and anguished. It continues:

> *[I] am glad that I am remaining here; I have the first musicians in the world, and the first opera in the world. [...] There is the utmost luxury, the utmost ostentation; at every step there are warnings about venereal disease; shouting, racket, bustle, and more mud than it is possible to imagine.*

Paris is whatever you choose: you can amuse yourself, be bored, laugh, cry, do anything you like, and nobody looks at you, and everyone goes his own road.

Dr Malfatti had given Chopin a letter of introduction to Ferdinand Paër, conductor of the Court Theatre in Paris, and one of the most influential musicians of the day. By December Chopin had tracked down Tytus Woyciechowski in Poturzyń and excitedly unburdened himself in a letter:

> *Paris is whatever you choose: you can amuse yourself, be bored, laugh, cry, do anything you like, and nobody looks at you, and everyone goes his own road. Through Paër I have met Rossini, Cherubini, Baillot, etc. – also Kalkbrenner. You would not believe how curious I was about Herz, Liszt, Hiller, etc. – they are all zero beside Kalkbrenner. I confess that I have played like Herz, but would wish to play like Kalkbrenner. If Paganini is perfection, Kalkbrenner is his equal, but in quite another style. It is hard to describe to you his calm, his enchanting touch, his incomparable evenness, and the mastery that is displayed in every note; he is a giant walking over Herz and Czerny and all – and over me. What can I do about it? When I was introduced, he asked me to play*

*something. I should have liked to hear him first. I played my E minor [Concerto] which the Rhinelanders... and all Bavaria had so raved about. I astonished Kalkbrenner, who at once asked me if I was not a pupil of Field, because I have Cramer's method and Field's touch – that delighted me. I was still more pleased when Kalkbrenner, sitting down at the piano and wanting to do his best before me, made a mistake and had to break off! But you should have heard it when he started again; I had not dreamed of anything like it. Since then we meet daily; either he comes to me or I to him.*

Friedrich [Wilhelm Michael] Kalkbrenner (1785–1849) was a German pianist and composer of colossal vanity. 'After my death,' he told Chopin, 'or when I stop playing, there will be no representative of the great pianoforte school.' His pomposity had made him a laughing stock among his peers. Heine lampooned him as 'a bonbon fallen in the mud'. Many of his piano compositions are effective despite being in the superficial salon style of the day. Among the most interesting of them are the Études included in his Piano Method (Op. 108, published in about 1830) which include several for the left hand alone. Technically, Kalkbrenner's playing was fluent, accurate and supple with the fingers kept in very close contact with the keys. This was supplemented, according to Oscar Bie, with 'that special kind of sensuously charming touch which differentiated the Parisian school from the brilliant playing of the Viennese and the emotional style of the English'.

Chopin was seduced by Kalkbrenner's skill and celebrity and even considered taking up his offer of studying with him for three years. Chopin's parents were puzzled, Elsner was aghast, while Mendelssohn – to whom Chopin was introduced in December – told him he already played better than Kalkbrenner. Fortunately, the idea was dropped. In the words of Harold Schonberg, '[Kalkbrenner] would have destroyed the most original piano talent of the century.' Chopin, however, dedicated his E minor Piano Concerto to him. 'It was when I had just arrived in Paris,' Chopin explained years later somewhat disingenuously to his pupil Lenz. 'Kalkbrenner reigned supreme; it was necessary to pay court to him a little.'

Kalkbrenner, meanwhile, far from being put out by Chopin's decision not to take advantage of his teaching, volunteered to help his young friend make a mark in Paris. Chopin's natural reticence and insecurity had increased now that he was a small fish in a big pond. Should he be a pianist? The number of established rivals made him hesitate. Should he be a composer? His lack of experience and knowledge, and his few successes to date, made him pause. He began work on a third Piano Concerto but abandoned it (its single movement would become the rarely heard Allegro de concert); instead he stuck to the forms with which he was comfortable and continued work on a series of Études for solo piano.

Over the course of a few months, three key events combined to change Chopin's fortunes utterly. In July 1831 Robert Schumann picked up a copy of Chopin's Variations on 'Là ci darem la mano' in a Leipzig music shop. He had never heard of its composer but was sufficiently impressed by the work to write a review of it for the influential *Allgemeine Musikalische Zeitung*. Schumann was convinced that here was an example of what modern piano music should be aiming at. 'Hut ab, ihr Herren, ein Genie!' ('Hats off, gentlemen – a genius!') was his now-famous invocation, cited by all biographers of Schumann and Chopin as the moment when Schumann discovered Chopin's talent. The

> Chopin's natural reticence and insecurity had increased now that he was a small fish in a big pond. Should he be a pianist? The number of established rivals made him hesitate.

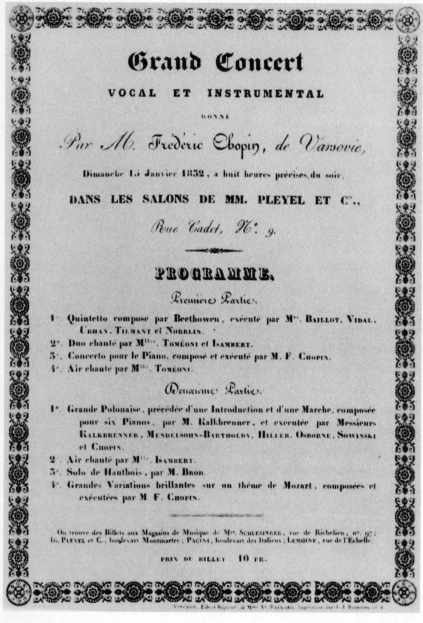

*Programme of Chopin's debut performance in Paris at the Salon Pleyel (The concert was advertised for 15 January 1832 but postponed until 26 February because Kalkbrenner was unwell.)*

piece was signed only by Schumann's initials. In fact, in an editorial note, he was identified merely as a young student of Professor Wieck. Unlike Chopin, Schumann, though just a few months younger, was a complete unknown. In his review, Schumann constructed a picturesque dramatic scenario for each of Chopin's Variations without realizing that explicit programme music was utterly foreign to Chopin's aesthetic ideal. No wonder, then, that despite the compliment paid to him Chopin's response was characteristically mocking. His letter to Tytus concluded: 'I could die laughing at this German's imagination'. Nevertheless, the review reached a wide audience.

Then, after several delays, came his Paris debut, backed by Kalkbrenner. The German, conveniently, was a partner in the firm of Camille Pleyel, a man 'famous for his pianos and his wife's adventures', as one contemporary wag characterized him. The Salon Pleyel was to be the venue, the date 26 February 1832. The programme consisted of Beethoven's Quintet, Op. 29, a group of operatic arias, Chopin's E minor Concerto (accompanied by a string quartet) and the 'Là ci darem' Variations, concluding with Kalkbrenner's Grande Polonaise with Introduction and March for six pianos. In this, Chopin was joined by Kalkbrenner himself, George Onslow (the Anglo-French pianist), Adalbert Sowinski (a second-rate Polish player), Camille-Marie Stamaty (an Italian) and Ferdinand Hiller, a pupil of Hummel who had become a close friend of Chopin and given the Parisian premiere of Beethoven's Fifth Piano Concerto.

The audience, which included Liszt, Mendelssohn, Herz and Pixis, applauded frantically. Chopin's friend Antoni Orlowski wrote home: 'Our dear Fryc has given a concert

Chopin's friend Antoni Orlowski wrote home: 'Our dear Fryc has given a concert which brought him some money. He has wiped the floor with all pianists here; all Paris is stupefied.'

which brought him some money. He has wiped the floor with all pianists here; all Paris is stupefied.' Liszt remembered the occasion years later, recalling that 'Chopin was not confused for a moment by the dazzlement or intoxication of the triumph. He accepted it without pride and without false modesty.' More importantly, François-Joseph Fétis, the most feared and respected critic of the day, wrote presciently in the *Revue Musicale*:

> *Here is a young man who, surrendering himself to his natural impressions and taking no model, has found if not a complete renewal of piano music, at least a part of that which we have long sought in vain, namely an abundance of original ideas of a kind to be found nowhere else... I find in M. Chopin's inspirations the signs of a renewal of forms which may henceforth exercise a considerable influence upon this branch of the art.*

A follow-up concert was in order and in May Chopin played the first movement of the F minor Concerto for a charity concert in the Conservatoire Hall. This time he had one of the best orchestras in Europe to accompany him but – shades of Warsaw – his soft playing could not be heard above the orchestra and the *Revue Musicale* thought the orchestration poor. Chopin was once again cast into the depths of despair. He thought of going to England or even America. Should he continue with a concert career?

Perhaps it was this occasion that confirmed once and for all that the conventional path of the public pianist-composer was not for him. He found the publicity surrounding these concerts distasteful, his playing was unsuitable for big halls, his intimate style better suited to the exclusive salons of the rich and famous. He admitted to Liszt:

*I am not fit to give concerts; the crowd intimidates me and I feel asphyxiated by its eager breath, paralyzed by its inquisitive stare, silenced by its alien faces; but you, you are made for it, for when you cannot captivate your audience, you at least have the power to stun it.*

One triumphant concert as a pianist and one critic hailing him as a composer of genius were not enough. His father was still supporting him, though Mikołaj Chopin's income had been greatly reduced since the Russians had shut down the Lycée and Conservatoire in Warsaw. With Paris in the grip of a cholera epidemic, Chopin, frustrated in his ambitions and running out of funds, might well have moved on had it not been for a chance introduction. Prince Valentin Radziwiłł took him to the home of Baron Jacob Rothschild, youngest son of the most important banking family in nineteenth-century Europe. Fabulously wealthy and influential, Rothschild welcomed Chopin into the family and, suddenly, the doors to all the principal families of Paris were opened to him.

Within a matter of months, Chopin had moved into a luxury apartment, boasted a manservant and his own carriage, and was clothed by some of Paris's finest shops. 'I am in the highest society,' he wrote to Dominik Dziewanowski in an undated letter of 1832:

*I sit with ambassadors, princes, ministers and even don't know how it came about, because I did not try for it... Though this is my first year among the artists here, I have their friendship and respect. One proof of respect is that even people*

61

*with huge reputations [Pixis and Kalkbrenner] dedicate their compositions to me before I do so to them... pupils of Moscheles, Herz and Kalkbrenner – in a word, finished artists – take lessons from me and couple my name with Field's. In short, if I were stupider than I am, I should think myself at the apex of my career, yet I know how much I still lack to reach perfection; I see it the more clearly now that I live only among first-rank artists and know what each one of them lacks.*

Chopin was to give five lessons on the day he wrote that letter, as he would on most other days. 'You think I am making a fortune? Carriages and white gloves cost more, and without them I should not be in "the best of taste".' His rates were exceptionally high – but when your teacher has been acclaimed a genius, has the most refined manners and background, and is utterly reliable as to his morals (and thus safe to be entrusted with wives and daughters), he could charge twenty francs a lesson, more if the lessons were in the homes of his pupils. By comparison, the average daily wage of an unskilled Parisian worker was one franc. The best seats at the opera cost about ten francs and the most expensive frock-coat would set you back 150. Chopin, compared with most of his musical contemporaries, rapidly became comfortably off.

The morning after Chopin's Paris debut, a minor publisher named Farrenc offered to buy the rights to everything that Chopin had in his portfolio: the two Concertos, the 'Krakowiak' Rondo, the Fantasy on Polish Airs and the Piano Trio were all paid for in cash. Chopin knew perfectly well that there were better publishers, but at that moment he desperately needed the money. By November, he had still not provided Farrenc with corrected copies of any of the scores. In the meantime, he craftily negotiated a long-term agreement with the foremost French publisher, Maurice Schlesinger, to put out all his works, including those he had already sold to Farrenc. Schlesinger also acquired three Nocturnes, eight Mazurkas and the twelve completed Études, shrewdly farming out the German rights to Probst of Leipzig in the knowledge that these shorter works would bring him a quick return. Other works would appear simultaneously in France, England (Wessel & Co.) and Germany (Kistner, and later Breitkopf & Härtel). Mikołaj Chopin wrote to his son in March 1833, telling him that the German edition of the Mazurkas and Nocturnes had reached Warsaw. They had sold out within three days. Whether or not Farrenc ever got his advance returned is unknown. Probably not: Chopin had a talent for spending money.

Within a year of arriving in Paris, Chopin's income had separated him from his fellow artists-in-exile. He rarely set foot in any of the churches where prayers for Polish deliverance were said at every Mass (Chopin is one of the very few great composers to have written no religious music); he was not drawn to writing a great national opera or using his position to highlight his country's woes – the art songs he fashioned from his compatriots' poetry sound perfunctory, written in a form that was uncongenial to him; he remained disengaged from direct political involvement, though he kept abreast of developments through his membership of the Polish Literary Society in Paris. In 1833 the Tsar granted a general amnesty to exiles that would have allowed Chopin to return home and visit his family. But he never took up the offer and, as time passed, thoughts of returning to Poland gradually receded.

Chopin is one of the very few great composers to have written no religious music

His friend Orlowski noted somewhat skeptically: 'Chopin is well and strong. He is turning all the heads of the ladies and making all the husbands jealous. He is in fashion. Soon we shall all be wearing gloves à la Chopin. Only sometimes he suffers from homesickness.'

# Chapter 6

## An Original Genius

# 'An Original Genius'

Let us pause temporarily and return to the start of 1833. Chopin saw in the New Year at a party in the Austrian Embassy with Rossini, Kalkbrenner – and Liszt. Even at twenty years of age, Liszt was a celebrity, though his myriad major works had yet to be written and his career as the greatest virtuoso of the nineteenth century was still in its infancy. The first pianist ever to give a complete recital without the aid of other musicians, the first to play an entire programme from memory – these advances were some years into the future. When he first encountered Chopin, his head was full of newly absorbed European literature, art and philosophy, and the music of Paganini, Berlioz and Schumann.

Chopin's love-hate relationship with Liszt dates from his earliest days in Paris. Its ambivalence throws into clear focus distinct elements of Chopin's personality and character. It is time to look at these in detail, along with the aspects of his playing and compositions that so fascinated his contemporaries.

Chopin was five feet seven inches tall with grey-blue eyes, dark blond, silky hair and a pronounced Bourbon nose. In 1840, he weighed just under 91 pounds. Liszt felt that:

*The fineness and transparency of his complexion bewitched*

*Profile portrait of Chopin by Albert Graefle*

> *the eye... his carriage distinguished, his manners so instinctively aristocratic that everyone treated him as though he were a prince. His gestures were full of grace and freedom, the tone of his voice was muffled to the point of being stifled.*

Liszt's rapid rise to fame, extraordinary keyboard athleticism, charismatic personality and stunning good looks would have made any rival envious. Chopin quickly realized he could never compete with this, let alone the Hungarian's physical strength and extrovert style of playing.

On first meeting Chopin, the writer, poet and playwright Ernest Legouvé (1807–1903) thought that he looked like 'the natural son Weber might have fathered had the mother been a duchess'.

The two pianist-composers lived close by and saw a great deal of one another. Superficially, they had much in common. Apart from both being supreme pianists they shared a love of opera and an admiration for their native folk music (though Liszt would take some time to investigate his), they were both immigrants, and they had a natural affinity with the salons of rich aristocrats. Their shared humble origins notwithstanding, both had adopted the airs and graces of the aristocracy: the greatest snobs are generally those whose background gives them least cause to be so.

Liszt's rapid rise to fame, extraordinary keyboard athleticism, charismatic personality and stunning good looks would have made any rival envious. Chopin quickly realized he could never compete with this, let alone the Hungarian's physical strength and extrovert style of playing. Liszt's ardent admiration of him made him feel awkward. Despite his apparent ease in society, in his private life there was a holding back, a mistrust of intimacy, and a reserve that Liszt captured well when he noted: '[Chopin] was prepared to give anything, but never gave himself... good-natured, affable, easy in all his relationships, even- and pleasant-tempered, he hardly allowed one to suspect the secret convulsions which agitated him.'

Liszt was fascinated by Chopin, whose refinement and individuality he at this point lacked. Chopin's musical characteristics were by now fully formed. They might have improved but they never fundamentally changed. Liszt was in genuine awe of his music and the influence on his own compositions was profound. Some forty years later, in 1872, Liszt wrote in a letter to Wilhelm Lenz:

> *You exaggerate, I think, the influence which the Parisian salons had on Chopin. His soul was not the least affected by them, and his work as an artist remains transparent, marvellous, ethereal, and of an incomparable genius – quite outside the errors of a school and the silly trifling of a salon. He is akin to the angel and the fairy; more than this, he sets in motion the heroic string, which has nowhere else vibrated with so much grandeur, passion and fresh energy as in his Polonaises.*

Chopin in turn was drawn to the glamorous Hungarian's unsurpassed, all-encompassing virtuosity and his uncanny ability as a sight-reader. 'I write to you without knowing what my pen is scribbling,' Chopin wrote to Ferdinand Hiller in June 1833, 'because at this moment Liszt is playing my Études, and transporting me outside of my respectable thoughts. I should like to steal from him the way to play my own Études.' Chopin found it hard to be this generous to Liszt (or anyone else for that matter). 'Liszt knew everything better than anyone,' Chopin wrote some years later when their friendship

He is akin to the angel and the fairy; more than this, he sets in motion the heroic string, which has nowhere else vibrated with so much grandeur, passion and fresh energy had cooled. '[...] he is an excellent binder who puts other people's works between his own covers... he is a clever craftsman without a vestige of talent.' Chopin's music was touched hardly at all by Liszt's. 'Liszt will live to be a deputy or perhaps even a king, in Abyssinia or the Congo,' said Chopin in a letter to Julian Fontana, 'but as for the themes of his compositions, they will repose in the newspapers.' Once, Liszt decided to write a review of a Chopin concert for the *Gazette musicale*. Ernest Legouvé told Chopin that for an artist to have a review from Liszt was very important, that 'Liszt will create a fine kingdom for you.' 'Yes,' replied Chopin sourly, 'within his own empire.'

One anecdote, perhaps apocryphal, illustrates better than any the difference between these two figures. They were both present at a soirée in 1843 where Liszt played one of Chopin's Nocturnes, adding his own string of fancy embellishments. 'Play the music as it is written,' Chopin demanded, 'or don't play it at all.' 'Play it yourself,' returned Liszt in a pique. Chopin did so. At the end, Liszt embraced Chopin and apologised for what he had done. 'Works like yours,' he said, 'should not be meddled with.' Let's hope the story is true.

The great Polish pianist Arthur Rubinstein, renowned for his interpretations of Romantic music, once compared the technical demands made by the music of both Chopin and Liszt.

*Even the most difficult figurations of Chopin belong to creative music. Liszt cultivated technical preciosity; the difficulties he contrived were a camouflage, and he exploited them for greater effect. Chopin was interested only in the musical idea, and the difficulties of his works are logically inherent in his thought... I can play a pyrotechnical Liszt Sonata, requiring*

*forty minutes for its performance, and get up from the piano*
*without feeling tired, while even the shortest Étude of Chopin*
*compels me to intense expenditure and effort.*

In several letters, Chopin's father rebukes his son for referring to various musical eminences as 'cowshit'. Though he enjoyed friendships with many major figures – among them Mendelssohn, Berlioz and Schumann as well as Liszt – he found it difficult to reciprocate their admiration. His musical goals were different. He found pieces inspired by literature or with autobiographical and programmatic references repugnant. Sensuality for its own sake was against his nature. Chopin was a Classicist: form, taste and style were everything. No wonder he disliked being called a Romantic composer.

> Chopin had little praise for the music of any other composers except his adored Bach and Mozart, and, later, the operas of his friend Bellini.

In fact Chopin had little praise for the music of any other composers except his adored Bach and Mozart, and, later, the operas of his friend Bellini. As far as his own repertoire was concerned, he preferred Hummel to Beethoven, whose 'passion too often approaches cataclysm'. He found the E flat Sonata, Op. 31 No. 3 'very vulgar' and was quite uninterested in any of the late works (he did, however, occasionally play the A flat Sonata, Op. 26). 'Where [Beethoven] is obscure and seems lacking in unity... the reason is that he turns his back on eternal principles; Mozart never,' was Chopin's pronouncement. One of the few 'modern' composers whom he liked was Weber: he made his pupils study the Konzertstück, Op. 79 and the Invitation to the Dance, Op. 65, a piece he himself played on several occasions, as well as the E minor and A flat Sonatas. He was also fond of Field's A flat Concerto and his Nocturnes.

Schubert, surprisingly, made little impression on him,

other than occasionally playing a few Marches and Polonaises
as duets with his pupils. He did not care for Mendelssohn's
music overmuch, though admired the first of the Songs
without Words, Op. 19 No. 1 as 'a song of the purest virginal
beauty', and coached at least one pupil (Mme. Camille
Dubois) in the G minor Concerto. Schumann appealed even
less: 'Carnaval is not music at all', he told his friend Stephen
Heller (this of a work that includes an evocative portrait of
him!). Although Chopin dedicated his Second Ballade to
Schumann, the inscription 'À Monsieur Robert Schumann'
seems a mere courteous formality in return for Schumann's
dedication to Chopin of his Kreisleriana. Berlioz left him
bemused. He is quoted as saying, '[Berlioz] composes
by splashing his pen over the manuscript and leaving the
issue to chance'. Berlioz, for his part, thought that Chopin's
melodies charmed and captivated by their very strangeness.
But, writing in Le Rénovateur of 15 December 1833, he
added:

> Unfortunately virtually nobody but Chopin himself can
> play his music and give it this unusual turn, this sense of
> the unexpected which is one of its principal beauties [...] As
> interpreter and composer, Chopin is an artist apart, bearing
> no point of resemblance to any other musician I know.

There are dozens of contemporary reports of Chopin's
own playing, almost without exception couched in the
most rapturous terms. One such was from the young Karl
Halle (1819–1895), the German pianist and conductor who
would later become famous as Sir Charles Hallé, founder of
Manchester's Hallé Orchestra. Here is the seventeen-year-
old, in a letter to his parents written on 2 December 1836:

*...I heard – <u>Chopin</u>. That was beyond all words. The few senses*
*I had have quite left me. I could have jumped into the Seine.*
*Everything I hear now seems so insignificant that I would*
*rather not hear it at all. Chopin! He is no man, he is an angel,*
*a god (or what can I say more?). Chopin's compositions played*
*by Chopin! That is a joy never to be surpassed... Kalkbrenner*
*compared to Chopin is a child. I say this with*
*the completest conviction. During Chopin's*
*playing I could think of nothing but elves and*
*fairy dances, such a wonderful impression*
*do his compositions make. There is nothing*
*to remind one that it is a human being who*
*produces this music. It seems to descend from*
*heaven – so pure, so clear, and spiritual. I feel*
*a thrill each time I think of it.*

> Chopin's youthful gift for mimicry and clowning never left him, even though his ebullient sense of humour is almost invariably overlooked by scholars who see nothing but the wrinkled forehead of a Great Composer.

Nearly sixty years later, the elderly Hallé recalled that same evening:

*I can confidently assert that nobody has ever been able to*
*reproduce [his works] as they sounded under his magical*
*fingers. In listening to him you lost all power of analysis; you*
*did not think for a moment how perfect was his execution*
*of this or that difficulty; you listened, as it were, to the*
*improvisation of a poem, and were under the charm as long*
*as it lasted.*

Not that all Chopin's appearances in the salons of Paris were confined to serious music-making and murmured oohs and aahs. Chopin's youthful gift for mimicry and clowning never left him, even though his ebullient sense of humour is almost invariably overlooked by scholars who see nothing but the wrinkled forehead of a Great Composer. (Chopin's letters await an English translation that does full justice to the charm and jokiness of the original Polish.) Count Tarnowski recalled how Chopin liked to express individual characteristics on the piano and often amused himself by playing such musical portraits:

> *Without saying whom he had in his thoughts, he illustrated the characters of a few or of several people present in the room, and illustrated them so clearly and so delicately that the listeners could always guess correctly who was intended, and admired the resemblance of the portrait.*

(Elgar was to use the same trick three-quarters of a century later when assembling the series of musical portraits of his friends in the 'Enigma' Variations.) Liszt was an easy target and Chopin delighted in sending up his friend in this manner, especially when he was present. Liszt, of course, was clever enough to get his own back and mimic Chopin.

When the conditions were right for Chopin to play, even the most seasoned professionals sensed they were experiencing something unique. In May 1834, Mendelssohn spent a morning at the piano with Chopin and Hiller. 'As a pianist Chopin is now one of the greatest of all,' he wrote to his mother, 'doing things as original as Paganini does on the violin, and bringing about miracles that one would never have believed possible.' Although Mendelssohn felt that both Chopin and Hiller suffered from the 'Parisian tendency of overdoing passion and despair, and too often lose sight of calm, discretion and the purely musical', he had the grace to admit that 'I on the other hand perhaps do this too little'.

In a second letter written fifteen months later, Mendelssohn described another day he had just spent in Chopin's company.

That his sister Fanny did not share his enthusiasm is clear from one of his letters to her:

> I cannot deny, dear Fanny, that I have lately found that you are not doing him sufficient justice in your judgement; perhaps he was not in the right humor for playing when you heard him, which can often be the case with him. But, as for myself, his playing has enchanted me afresh, and I am persuaded that if you, and Father also, had heard him play some of his better pieces as he played them to me, you would say the same. There is something entirely original in his piano playing, and it is at the same time so masterly, that he may be called a perfect virtuoso; and as, in music, I like and rejoice in every style of perfection, that day was most agreeable to me. It was so pleasant to be once more with a thorough musician, and not with those semi-virtuosi and semi-classicists...

What so attracted the fastidious, cultured Mendelssohn was the marriage of style and technique to original and genuine musical ideals. In Chopin's music and playing there was not a trace of technique for technique's sake, which was a refreshing change from the superficialities of such figures as Pixis, Herz, Kalkbrenner and Thalberg. To put this in context, it must be remembered that the now-forgotten Henri Herz was, purely in commercial terms, the most successful composer of the day. For twelve years, until the late 1830s, he outsold everyone.

What Chopin was offering was, rather, a new musical and technical keyboard aesthetic that would influence generations to come. Other pianists may have competed with him in dexterity, evenness of touch and clarity of

75

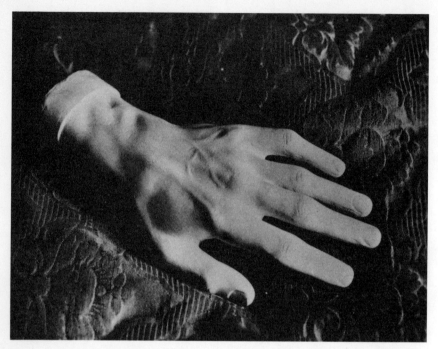

*Cast of Chopin's*
*left hand*

articulation. This was the refined elegance of the Clementi-Hummel school of playing. What set Chopin apart, however, was the wide range of expression he could conjure from the keyboard, tinged with that innate melancholy which has touched the hearts of audiences from that day to this. Because of his slight build and lack of physical strength, he had of necessity to exploit the softer tones of the instrument. It has been said that no one in history has ever had such control over the subtle shadings of dynamics. Moscheles said that 'his pianissimos required only a mere breath'.

Chopin's slim hands, would 'suddenly expand and cover a third of the keyboard. It looked like the mouth of a serpent about to swallow a rabbit whole.'

'He has found how to render [his Mazurkas] doubly interesting by playing them with the utmost degree of softness, piano to the extreme,' reported Berlioz, 'the hammers merely brushing the strings, so much so that one is tempted to go close to the instrument and put one's ear to it as if to a concert of sylphs or elves.' A whole evening of this was evidently too much for some. Thalberg once left after a Chopin recital and shouted all the way home: 'I need some noise because I've heard nothing but pianissimo all evening.'

Combined with this extraordinary tonal control was the feeling of improvisation and spontaneity achieved from a very supple body and the creative use of rubato. According to his pupil and friend Adolf Gutmann, 'he could throw his legs over his shoulders, like a clown' and several pupils remarked how his fingers seemed to have no bones and that 'they appeared to be made entirely of rubber'. Others have remarked on the startling elasticity of Chopin's slim hands, which were not especially large. Stephen Heller described how they would 'suddenly expand and cover a third of the keyboard. It looked like the mouth of a serpent about to swallow a rabbit whole.'

A vital part of Chopin's armory was this use of rubato. The term derives from the Italian for 'robbed' and it indicates a certain rhythmic freedom. Liszt explained it to one of his pupils thus: 'Look at these trees! The wind plays in the leaves, stirs up life among them, the tree remains the same. That is Chopinesque rubato.' A pupil of Chopin's, Karol Mikuli (1821–1897), recalled:

> *In keeping tempo, Chopin was inflexible, and it will surprise many to learn that the metronome never left his piano... One hand, the accompanying hand, always played in strict tempo, while the other – singing, either indecisively hesitating or entering ahead of the beat and moving more quickly with a certain impatient vehemence, as in impassioned speech – freed the truth of the musical expression from all rhythmic bonds.*

The rule seems to have been that, while the rhythm might fluctuate, the underlying metrical pulse remained constant.

So rhythmically free could his playing be that some took his rubato to be erratic timing. Chopin, who rarely raised his voice or lost his temper, screamed at Meyerbeer when the latter insisted that Chopin was playing one of his own Mazurkas in 2/4 instead of 3/4. Charles Hallé noticed the same thing years later, though he obviously caught Chopin in a better mood. At first the composer denied he was playing in 4/4 rather than 3/4. When Hallé counted as Chopin played, Chopin had to confess that Hallé was right, laughing that it was 'a nationalistic trait', but he would never otherwise admit to playing anything out of strict time. Madame Elise Peruzzi, daughter of the Russian consul-general to the United States, frequently heard Chopin play at private gatherings in Paris about 1838:

> When I knew him he was a sufferer and would only play occasionally in public, and then place his piano in the middle of Pleyel's room whilst his admirers were around the piano. His speciality was extreme delicacy, and his pianissimo was extraordinary. Every little note was like a bell, so clear. His fingers seemed to be without any bones, but he would bring out certain effects by great elasticity. He got very angry at being accused of not keeping time, calling his left hand his maître de chapelle and allowing his right hand to wander about ad libitum.

The Études and many of Chopin's more lyrical pieces demanded new thoughts on fingering and pedalling. Numerous of the Études have interval stretches of at least a tenth; frequent use of the thumb on the black keys and passing certain fingers over others were radical departures in Chopin's day. Mikuli, a reliable source, left a detailed observation of his teacher's technical advances:

> *In the notation of fingering, especially of that peculiar to himself, Chopin was not sparing. Here pianoforte-playing owes him great innovations which, on account of their expedience, were soon adopted, notwithstanding the horror with which authorities like Kalkbrenner at first regarded them. Thus, for instance, Chopin used without hesitation the thumb on the black keys, passed it even under the little finger (it is true, with a distinct inward bend of the wrist), if this could facilitate the execution and give it more repose and evenness. With one and the same finger he took often two consecutive keys... without the least interruption of the sequence being noticeable. He frequently crossed the longer fingers over each other, without the help of the thumb (see Étude, Op. 10 No. 2)... The fingering of chromatic thirds based on this principle (as he indicates in Étude, Op. 25 No. 5) offers, to a much higher degree than the then-usual method, the possibility of the most beautiful* legato *in the quickest tempo and with a perfectly quiet hand.*

Chopin's preferred instruments were those by Pleyel, particularly, Liszt tells us, 'on account of their silvery touch which permitted him to draw from them sounds that... [married] crystal to water'. If he was engaged for a soirée at the house of one of his Polish or French friends, he would often send his own instrument if there did not happen to be a Pleyel in the house. 'When I am indisposed,' Chopin stated, 'I play on one of Érard's pianos and there I easily find a ready-made tone. But when I feel in the right mood and strong enough to find my own tone for myself, I must have one of Pleyel's pianos.'

The question of Chopin's strength and health will concern us increasingly, as it affected not only his lifestyle but the music he wrote and the way in which he performed it. The eminent pianist and composer Ignaz Moscheles put it in a nutshell. 'What is Chopin like to look at?' he asked; answer: 'His music.'

# Chapter 7

## Friends, Lovers and Pupils

# Friends, Lovers and Pupils

By the age of twenty-three, Chopin was an established star in the musical capital of the world. Yet for the whole of the 1833–4 season he did not give a single public concert, appearing only once for a charity event on 15 December at which he, Liszt and Hiller gave a performance of Bach's Concerto for three pianos. It was Hiller who introduced Chopin to the Sicilian opera composer Vincenzo Bellini, who had arrived in Paris in the autumn of 1833. The discovery of Bellini's 'never-ending melody' was of immense importance to Chopin. He had already begun incorporating elements of bel canto into his writing, most notably in the dream-like Nocturnes that he had begun to compose. Chopin was by no means the first composer to write in this genre. The form, at least as far as the piano was concerned, had been invented and popularized by the Anglo-Irish pianist-composer John Field.

Chopin had always admired Field and finally got to hear him when he gave a concert in Paris in 1832. Alcohol and lack of practice had by then taken their toll and his playing dreadfully disappointed Chopin; but Field's concept of spinning a long-breathed cantilena on the keyboard had caught his imagination. The notion of transforming the sound of a percussive instrument into a human voice was at the very heart of Chopin's outlook. This was now reinforced by his friendship with Bellini. It was appropriate that Chopin should dedicate his second set of **Nocturnes**, Op. 15 to Hiller, who was the musician closest to Chopin at this time. 'I think I can say that Chopin loved me,' Hiller later recalled, 'but I was in love with him.'

Another friend who had become an important part of Chopin's life was the young cellist August Franchomme. They hit it off immediately and soon hardly a day passed when the unassuming cellist did not call on Chopin, invariably accompanied by Liszt (who had introduced the two). The publisher Schlesinger had commissioned Chopin to write a work based on themes from Meyerbeer's opera *Robert le diable*, then all the rage. The resulting Grand Duo concertante for piano and cello is a collaborative effort between Franchomme and Chopin, and was published in 1833.

*Vincenzo Bellini*

CD 1
tracks 4, 5
www.naxosbooks.com

Friends and acquaintances he certainly had in abundance by this time. '[Chopin] disliked being without company,' Hiller noted:

>...something that seldom occurred. In the morning he liked to spend an hour by himself at his grand piano; but even when he practised – or how should I describe it? – when he stayed at home to play in the evenings, he needed to have at least one of his friends close at hand.

One element of Chopin's life was glaringly absent: any relationship with the opposite sex. The news of Konstancja Gladkowska's marriage did not seem to distress him unduly. 'It doesn't preclude a platonic love,' he suggested in a letter to Tytus. The focus for his romantic ideal of love had faded with all the excitement of the past year. There had been at least one sexual encounter before he arrived in Paris, but Chopin, though he might have turned the ladies' heads, remained aloof from the messy business of an intimate physical relationship. This was subsumed in his music. As Hiller observed, 'he rarely opened his heart out, but at the piano he abandoned himself more completely than any other musician I have ever heard.'

How far he was from replicating Liszt's infamous amorous exploits, of which more later, is revealed in a letter to Tytus (December 1831). He had been invited by the pianist Pixis to call on him. Pixis, then in his mid-forties, was living with a pretty fifteen-year-old girl whom he kept from public view and hoped to marry. Pixis was not at home when Chopin called. Chopin was just explaining the object of his visit to the 'young pupil' when her beau came puffing up the stairs. Chopin and Pixis had already met, albeit briefly, in Stuttgart but Pixis did not recognize him and immediately flew into a jealous rage, demanding to know what was going on between the two:

*At last the old man realized: – swallowed, took my arm, conducted me into the salon, didn't know where to put me to sit, he was so afraid I should take offence... Afterwards he accompanied me downstairs and seeing that I was still*

*laughing – (I could not hide my amusement at the joke of*
*anybody supposing me* capable de *that sort of thing) – he then*
*went to the concierge to find out when and how I got on the*
*stairs, and so on. From that day, Pixis can't say enough in*
*praise of my talent to all the publishers… How do you like it?*
*I, as a* séducteur!

There are stories of a relationship with the Countess
Delfina Potocka (?1807–1877) whose immense appetite for
sex and numerous affairs earned her the nickname 'The Great
Sinner'. She was a striking beauty who was said to possess
one of the finest singing voices of the day; she certainly
cast a spell under which Chopin, like many others, fell. But
there is no shred of evidence to suggest that he became
another notch on her bedpost. In 1945 a bundle of letters
purporting to be from Chopin to Delfina surfaced under
suspicious circumstances. If the letters had been genuine
then they would have been more revealing and frankly erotic
than anything else ever penned by the composer. They are
completely at odds with the restrained, refined, emotionally
reticent Chopin and have since been dismissed as sordid
frauds.

On the other hand, Chopin made the significant gesture
of dedicating to Delfina his F minor Piano Concerto, a
work originally inspired by Konstancja. The Countess was
also to receive the dedication of his famous 'Minute' Waltz,
thus making her one of very few people to whom Chopin
dedicated more than one work. She repaid his devotion,
remaining a loving friend for the rest of the composer's life.
She rushed from Nice to be with him during the final days of
his life, singing to him as he lay on his deathbed.

For the first six years that he was in Paris, Chopin's sex life
is a blank. Anything more is supposition. He enjoyed flirting,

he loved the company of women, but that, it seems, is as far as it went. The risk of repeating his experience with 'Teressa' in Vienna would have inhibited any casual sexual encounter, even if such behavior had been in his nature. When Liszt's mistress, the Comtesse d'Agoult, invited Chopin to spend the summer of 1833 on her estate, he declined. He preferred the company of Franchomme and his humble family at their home near Tours.

In the whole of his career, Chopin gave no more than about thirty public concerts, yet the impression left by those few appearances was enough to make his playing the stuff of legend. With ambitions far removed from those of the myriad other itinerant virtuosi, his income derived almost exclusively from teaching and the sale of his music. It is hard to see how Chopin found time to write anything. He found composing – physically notating the music – a laborious process. Glance at any Chopin manuscript and you would find a mass of corrections, amendments and second thoughts. Innately lazy, with his hectic schedule of teaching and socializing combined, it is no wonder that he found it a challenge to produce a second batch of works to sell to Schlesinger. Nevertheless, over the next year or so, two works that he had begun in Vienna were to appear (the Grande Polonaise Brillante, to which he added a nocturne-like introduction entitled Andante spianato, and the **G minor Ballade**) as well as the first set of Études ('composed and dedicated to his friend F. Liszt by Fréd. Chopin' ran the title page), the first Scherzo, Op. 20, the four Mazurkas, Op. 24, two Polonaises, Op. 26, and the two Nocturnes, Op. 27.

> The more far-sighted critics saw in these pieces one of the most original and radical musical minds since Beethoven.

CD 1
track 12
www.naxosbooks.com

The more far-sighted critics saw in these pieces one of the most original and radical musical minds since Beethoven. The harmonic structure, the unusual harmonies and striking modulations, the manner in which the piano was treated, the use of folk elements, the way in which ornamentation was integrated rather than applied, the piquant deployment of rubato, the sheer individuality of the music allied to an extraordinary melodic gift – all these elements and more pointed to the fact that the Parisians had in their midst a composer of genius.

But he was also a born teacher, according to one of his pupils, Maria von Harder. Perhaps it was a gift inherited from his father:

*Expression and conception, position of the hand, touch, pedalling, nothing escaped the sharpness of his hearing and his vision; he gave every detail the keenest attention. Entirely absorbed in his task, during the lesson he would be solely a teacher, and nothing but a teacher.*

In the years to come, his fame as a pedagogue spread far and wide, with pupils coming not only from France and Poland but also from Lithuania, Russia, Bohemia, Austria, Germany, Switzerland, Great Britain, Sweden and Norway.

Generally, Chopin would devote the summer months to composition and teach for six months of the year from October or November to May. Everything was conducted in a strictly businesslike manner. Lessons began punctually at 8.00 am with Chopin dressed impeccably. Generally they would last an hour (though longer if the student was particularly gifted), the student playing the Pleyel grand, Chopin accompanying or demonstrating on an adjacent Pleyel upright. Twenty francs were left on the mantelpiece. Depending on Chopin's availability, and the individual talents, needs and finances of each pupil, there could be anything between one and three lessons a week.

'Liszt cannot equal Chopin as a teacher,' wrote the teenage Carl Filtsch, who studied with Chopin from 1841 to 1843. 'I do not mean that Liszt is not an excellent teacher; he is the best possible until one has the good fortune of knowing Chopin, who is, in terms of method, far ahead of all other artists.' Filtsch (1830–1845) was a musical prodigy, a Transylvanian-born pianist and composer who died prematurely in Venice after a series of brilliant concerts in Paris, London and Vienna. 'Mon Dieu, quel enfant!' exclaimed Chopin:

> *Never has anybody understood me like this child, the most extraordinary I have ever encountered... He plays me almost all my own compositions without having heard me, without me showing him the least thing – not completely like me (for he has his own style) but certainly no less well.*

Chopin's teaching method was far removed from that of Kalkbrenner, who advised his pupils to read a newspaper while practicing technical exercises. Kalkbrenner emphasized the importance of purely mechanical study, with an almost exclusive emphasis on finger action. To help this, Kalkbrenner used a guide-mains (hand guide), a rod fixed to the front of the keyboard at a slightly raised level. The forearm rested on this, thereby supposedly alleviating all tension in the wrist and freeing the fingers of all weight in order to encourage their independence. Fingers and wrists only – that was Kalbrenner's precept – and no use of the forearm or upper arm. Chopin mocked, 'It's like learning to walk on one's hands in order to go for a stroll... One cannot try to play everything from the wrist, as Kalkbrenner claims.' Chopin's own music rather proves the point.

Pupils of Chopin would first study the scales with many black keys. B major was the easiest, Chopin asserted, C major the most difficult. For studies he recommended Cramer's Études, Clementi's Gradus ad Parnassum, some of Moscheles's Studies in Style, Bach Keyboard Suites and, in pride of place, selections from The Well-Tempered Clavier. Concertos and sonatas by Clementi, Mozart, Bach, Handel, Scarlatti, Dussek, Field, Hummel, Ries and Beethoven as well as works by Weber, Moscheles, Mendelssohn, Hiller, Schumann, and his own pieces, were arranged on the music stand, carefully ordered by difficulty. Touch and phrasing were all. Chopin discouraged pupils from using the sustaining pedal (often wrongly called the 'loud pedal') until their touch had been perfected. This enforced his belief that the tone must be created by the fingers, not by the artificial means of the pedal. Phrasing, he avowed, should be as natural and effective as speech. If they did not get the point – and even when they did – he urged them to go the opera and listen to the great stars of the day in order to understand his aims. 'You have to sing if you wish to play.' That was his mantra.

Chopin treated his pupils with exemplary courtesy, patience and perseverance. But lessons could become stormy. According to George Sand, 'when roused, Chopin was terrifying'.

Chopin treated his pupils with exemplary courtesy, patience and perseverance. But lessons could become stormy. Rarely in the early years, but increasingly as he grew weaker, he would fly off into a rage – and, according to George Sand, 'when roused, Chopin was terrifying'. When he was ill or irritable, male pupils in particular were prone to these 'leçons orageuses'. One of his pupils, Georges-Amédée-Saint-Clair Mathias (1826–1910), recalled that he saw him break a chair when an inattentive pupil bungled a passage. Hair would be torn out, pencils reduced to fragments and strewn over the floor as a result of bad playing or wrong notes. 'No doubt,' suggested the great pianist Alfred Cortot, '[these violent attacks] had their origin in Chopin's urgent need of rest. Rest he could never take because of the endless material cares of his daily existence.' This would seem to be confirmed by Chopin's remark to one of his most promising pupils, Frederike Streicher (née Müller, 1816–1895), who gave up her career after her marriage in 1849. 'I am furious,' he said. 'I have no time to be ill!'

Ironically, despite his reputation and financial success as a teacher, Chopin was unlucky with most of his pupils, the majority of whom were mediocre. Some who were genuinely talented were prevented by their social status from ever having a professional career. Three of his most gifted students, Filtsch, Caroline Hartmann and Paul Gunsberg, died young. From approximately 150 students, only two important names emerged as teachers in their own right: Mathias and Mikuli. The latter studied with Chopin from 1844 and made one of the first authentic editions of his music. Among Mikuli's students, the most famous were Moriz Rosenthal and Raoul Koczalski. The German-Pole Mathias began lessons with Chopin around 1838, eventually going to the Paris Conservatoire in 1862 where he taught for more than thirty years. Among the better-known pianists who studied with him were Teresa Carreño, Isidor Philipp, Raoul Pugno and Ernest Schelling, as well as the composers Erik Satie and Paul Dukas.

Sadly, none of Chopin's pupils made disc recordings, though three of them lived long enough to have done so: Camille Dubois died in 1907, Pauline Viardot in 1910, while the obscure Henry Peru – the last of the line – who may or may not have studied with the composer, survived until 1922.

The disc recordings of Chopin's music made by his 'grand-pupils', Rosenthal, Koczalski and Pugno, and the piano rolls made by Carreño, are no guarantees of authenticity, despite the benefit of these pianists having studied with pupils of Chopin. Alfred Cortot, Alexander Michałowski, Natalia Janotha, Francis Planté (the earliest-born pianist to record Chopin's music) and Vladimir de Pachmann all received advice from pupils or disciples of Chopin. All were great artists in their own right, quite able to make their own interpretative decisions; but their documents in sound are the closest we can get to Chopin's own way of playing and as such are invaluable. Hearing them, it is hard not to persuade oneself of their authority.

The truth is, though, that unlike Hummel, Czerny, Henselt or Liszt, Chopin did not create a new school of playing. 'Too much of an aristocrat and poet to become a leader,' suggested the musicologist Jean-Jacques Eigeldinger, 'Chopin was content to suggest and imply, winning devotion without any attempt to convince. Such an attitude could hardly be conducive to an analytic approach on the part of his disciples.'

# Chapter 8

## Maria, 1834–1837

# Maria, 1834–1837

In May 1834, Hiller persuaded Chopin to leave Paris and his students, and join him on a trip to the Lower Rhine Music Festival in Aachen organized by Mendelssohn. The three friends delighted in each other's company and, said Mendelssohn to his mother:

> *Of course we betook ourselves to the piano where I had the greatest enjoyment... After the festival we travelled together to Düsseldorf and passed a most agreeable day there, playing and discussing music; then I accompanied them yesterday to Cologne. Early this morning they went off to Coblenz per steamer, I in the other direction, and the pleasant episode was over.*

In the memorable epithet of Ernest Legouvé, 'Chopin was a good pianist until midnight, when he became sublime.' One anecdote related by Hiller explains precisely how such things were written about Chopin, how he operated, and what effect his playing had on complete strangers. He recalled a visit made around this time by the three pianist-composers to the house of Mendelssohn's friend, the distinguished painter Wilhelm Schadow (1788–1862). Several other young artists were also there and everyone launched themselves into an evening of chatter and conviviality – everyone, that is, except Chopin, 'whose reticence kept him in the corner, unnoticed,' recorded Hiller:

> *Both Mendelssohn and I knew that he would get his own back on us for this, and we waited in happy anticipation. Eventually, the piano was opened and I played for a while, followed by Mendelssohn. But when we asked Chopin to play something too, everyone looked around in surprise. He had only played a few bars when everyone, especially Schadow, began to look at him in a very different way – they had never heard anything like it before. In wild enthusiasm they begged him to play again and again.*

Back in Paris, Chopin moved into an expensive new apartment in Rue de la Chaussée d'Antin, a few doors down from his previous one. The rent was shared by his friend Jan Matuszyński, who had taken a teaching post at the École de Médicine. In December he played in public three times: in a private concert organized by Delfina Potocka; a movement of his E minor Concerto and the new Andante spianato as part of a Berlioz concert; and, on Christmas Day, some pieces for duet and for two pianos with Liszt in the Salle Pleyel.

He had only played a few bars when everyone, especially Schadow, began to look at him in a very different way – they had never heard anything like it before. In wild enthusiasm they begged him to play again and again.

The flu epidemic of March 1835 left Chopin with bronchitis and coughing up particles of blood. He had hardly recovered from this before three further concerts: 22 March with Hiller; 4 April for a Polish charity in which he gave a rare performance of his E minor Concerto accompanied by full orchestra; and 26 April at the Conservatoire, where he played his Andante spianato and Grande Polonaise Brillante.

Then came great news: a letter from his parents informed him that they had left Warsaw on a trip to Karlsbad. Chopin left Paris at once and arrived at the spa on 15 August. 'Our joy is indescribable!' wrote Chopin. 'We don't stop telling each other how many times we have been thinking of one another... we drink, eat together, hug each other, reproach each other; I am at the height of my happiness.' Among the other residents of Karlsbad was Count Thun-Hohenstein, whose sons and daughter had taken lessons from Chopin. The Count invited the Chopins to his castle at Tetschen on the Elbe, and they stayed there until 14 September when Mikołaj and Justyna returned to Warsaw. Although they were not to know it, they would never see their son again. Chopin himself left for Paris five days later, accompanied by one of Count Thun-Hohenstein's sons who was going to Dresden.

*Maria Wodzińska*

It was all most propitious for, in Dresden, Chopin bumped into Felix Wodziński, who had been one of his father's boarders. The Wodzińskis had left Poland during the 1831 revolt and settled in Geneva. Here they were now, the whole family, his old friends, passing the summer months in Dresden. The Wodzińskis also had a daughter, Maria, who had been eleven years old when Chopin last saw her. She was now an arresting beauty of sixteen. The two fell in love almost at once.

Maria had become a fine pianist (good enough to later play one of Chopin's Ballades at a concert in Warsaw) and even composed a little. For the first time since Konstancja, Chopin let his defences down. After spending two weeks in Dresden, and making vague plans to return in the spring, Chopin left for Leipzig where he had promised to meet Mendelssohn. Here, another historic meeting took place: in the home of the respected pianist and teacher, Friedrich Wieck, Chopin was introduced to his great champion Robert Schumann. There too was Wieck's daughter, Clara, who was later to marry Schumann and was one of the first pianists of either sex to have played Chopin's works in public – she had performed the 'Là ci darem' Variations in Leipzig as early as July 1832. To the delight of Robert and Clara, Chopin himself played, even managing to charm the irascible and highly suspicious Wieck. Then Clara took her turn, with Chopin declaring: 'she is the only woman in Germany who can play my compositions properly'.

> For the first time since Konstancja, Chopin let his defences down.

After this charming interlude, Chopin set off for Heidelberg, where the bronchitis he had suffered in the spring returned. He arrived back in Paris at the end of October and was immediately thrust into a social whirl as well as playing host to Maria Wodzińska's elder brother, Antoni, arranging a concert to help a violinist friend, Karol Lipinski, and playing at various charity events.

As a result of his serious illness in Heidelberg, rumors of Chopin's death began to circulate, reaching Warsaw ears in December 1835. Even those who knew them to be false were disturbed: the Wodzińskis were worried, knowing their daughter's feelings towards Chopin. The Chopins were equally concerned, and Mikołaj wrote to his son urging him to take care of his health for fear of harming his plans over 'a certain person'. Matuszyński, too, advised his friend to exert himself less, to wear thick boots during the winter, and to look after himself better. Chopin heeded none of these warnings and by March was ill again.

Instead of returning to Germany in the spring of 1836, as he had planned, Chopin remained around Paris. The reason for this decision is intriguing. Why not visit the Wodzińskis to see his beloved? Had he been in unusually poor health, his reluctance to travel would have been understandable: he would have had no wish to let Maria's family see an invalid. But that was not the case. Instead he went to the lake of Enghien, no more than two hours north of Paris, almost certainly in order to stay at the lakeside villa of Delfina Potocka. A year later, Chopin and his friend Józef Brzowski were driving past the place. Brzowski wrote in his diary: 'He turned my attention to the wide lake, and, on its edge, the little villa in which he had spent the previous summer. His face became suffused with the pleasantness of the memory; it must have been a very happy period in his life.'

What on earth was going on there in the summer of 1836? If it was indeed Delfina's villa at which he stayed, was she there at the same time? If so, was she nursing him back to health? Or had Chopin merely accepted his doctor friend Matuszyński's advice and gone there to benefit from the healing waters and baths of Enghien? On the opposite side of the lake was another attraction: the beautiful Florentine villa of the homosexual Marquis de Custine. He held open house there for an intimate circle that included Chateaubriand, Stendhal, Heine, Hugo, Meyerbeer, Berlioz and now Chopin. We know that Chopin was made especially welcome by the avuncular Marquis but such enjoyable company and lavish hospitality could surely not have been the sole reason for his pleasant feelings about Enghien.

At the beginning of July, however, the Wodzińskis beckoned and at the end of the month Chopin found himself with Mrs Wodzińska and her two daughters in Marienbad, another Bohemian spa close to Karlsbad. The relationship with Maria intensified throughout August – long country walks, making music together, she painting a watercolor of him, he composing for her. The exquisite A flat Study that would open the second set of **Études**, and a song called

*Portrait of Chopin by Maria Wodzińska*

CD 1
tracks 13, 14
www.naxosbooks.com

99

The Ring were composed here. When the Wodzińskis left for Dresden, Chopin went with them. Two weeks later, on 9 September, at the 'grey hour' (twilight), Chopin proposed to Maria. She accepted, but her family were cautious. The matter of the 'grey hour', a phrase which immediately became the family's code-word for the proposal, was put on probation. Chopin was enjoined by Mrs Wodzińska to avoid late nights and look after his health. 'Keep well. Everything depends on that,' she wrote to her prospective son-in-law. 'You must realise that this is a trial period.'

On the way home, he dropped off in Leipzig to visit Schumann again. Despite his misgivings over the German's earnest, wordy enthusiasm for his music, Chopin felt that he owed his champion some attention and presented him with a copy of his new Ballade in G minor. Schumann, under his pen-name Florestan, had recently written a lengthy essay in praise of Chopin, declaring that if the Tsar knew 'what a dangerous enemy threatens him in [his] works, in the simple melodies of his **Mazurkas**, he would forbid his music. Chopin's works,' Schumann pronounced in a memorable phrase, 'are cannons buried in flowers.' He concluded: 'In every piece we find, in his own refined hand, written in pearls, "This is by Frédéric Chopin"; we recognize him even in his pauses, and by his impetuous respiration. He is the boldest, the proudest poet-soul of today.'

> Chopin's works,' Schumann pronounced in a memorable phrase, 'are cannons buried in flowers.' He is the boldest, the proudest poet-soul of today.'

CD 1
track 16
www.naxosbooks.com

Returning to Paris, Chopin flung himself once more into the social round. Liszt, who had spent the previous sixteen months in Switzerland with his mistress, had returned. The Comtesse d'Agoult, born Marie de Flavigny in Germany of French parentage in 1805, was noted as one of the most beautiful women of her day and had married the Comte d'Agoult in 1827. Her elopement with Liszt in June 1835 had caused a scandal: only six months after the premature death of her elder daughter, she had abandoned her husband, palatial home and younger daughter, run away with Liszt, and in December that year given birth to their daughter Blandine. Their second daughter, Cosima, born on Christmas Day 1837, was later to marry the pianist-conductor Hans von Bülow before eloping with, and eventually marrying, Richard Wagner.

> On the few occasions when he and George Sand met, he made little impression on her and vice-versa.

Now the Comtesse ensconced herself in the Hôtel de France and proceeded to establish, with a certain degree of defiance, one of the most famous salons of the day. Anybody in the world of music, literature, arts or science might be seen at her soirées: Balzac, Delacroix, Lamartine, Meyerbeer, Heine, Berlioz, the tenor Adolphe Nourrit, the Polish poet Adam Mickiewicz, Liszt (of course), Chopin and – moving into a small room in the same hotel on 24 October – the writer George Sand. Following the lead of her friend, Marie d'Agoult would also write novels under a male pseudonym, Daniel Stern.

Chopin did not particularly enjoy these evenings at the Hôtel. He disliked it when the conversation turned to politics, philosophy and intellectual chit-chat, or when the music was not to his taste. His reticence was not conducive to the ambience of this non-stop party. Only at the piano could he shine. On the few occasions when he and George Sand met, he made little impression on her and vice-versa. He was no competition for the noisy glamor of Liszt, Berlioz, Meyerbeer and Mickiewicz (whom Sand thought 'the first cousin of Goethe and Byron'). Chopin, on the other hand, was not impressed by this short, plump writer who dressed in men's clothing, smoked cigars and wrote under a man's name. One evening, on leaving the Hôtel de France with Hiller, Chopin commented, 'What an unattractive person La Sand is. Is she really a woman?'

The relationship with Maria Wodzińska continued through letters to both daughter and mother; but, during the next few months, interest from the Wodzińskis waned noticeably. Chopin was certainly not heeding their advice to take better care of himself and, as winter gripped Paris, his health deteriorated. Nor did he help himself by admitting news in his letters to Maria's family such as 'the doctor has ordered me to Ems, but I don't know where or when I shall go'. By January 1837, any suggestions of a meeting in May or June had been quietly dropped. The Wodzińskis were stalling. Maria's letters to Chopin, once full of hope and embraces, soon dwindled to a pathetic 'Adieu. I hope you will not forget us.' Hope was the only thing that Chopin had left.

In the early months of 1837, Paris enjoyed a series of concerts in which the two arch-rivals, Franz Liszt and Sigismund Thalberg, sought to establish their supremacy at the keyboard. Thalberg would play one concert to huge acclaim, only to be capped by Liszt the following week – and so on. The remarkable Princess Belgiojoso, an Italian expatriate (legend has it that she kept the mummified body of one of her former lovers in her closet), managed to persuade the two pianists to appear together for charity in her salon. Her verdict on the two? 'Thalberg was the best pianist in the world, Liszt the only one.' One by-product of their rivalry was for the Princess to commission a piece from Liszt. At a charity gala to raise further money for Italian refugees, Liszt, Thalberg, Chopin, Czerny, Herz and Pixis would all play their own variation on a given theme (from Bellini's *I Puritani*). The concert never took place but the music was assembled by Liszt and published as Hexameron. Chopin's sensitive treatment of the theme forms the sixth variation.

As his feelings towards Liszt cooled, Chopin withdrew further from the Hôtel de France set. He disliked the way in which the Hungarian constantly drew attention to himself, was disgusted that he had used Chopin's apartment to make love to Marie Pleyel, and was quite horrified at the vicious way in which he had attacked Thalberg in the press. Although quietly delighted by the latter's humiliation in the concert hall, Chopin was aghast at seeing how Liszt enjoyed rubbing salt in the wounds.

With no word from the Wodzińskis, the next few months were spent teaching, composing, socializing, hopping between Paris and Enghien, and occasionally being confined to bed, 'coughing with infinite grace', as Marie d'Agoult put it. Invitations from Custine to join him in Wiesbaden and from Marie d'Agoult to stay at George Sand's estate at Nohant were turned down. Finally, he could bear the suspense of waiting for a summons from the Wodzińskis no longer and decided to go to London in the company of Pleyel with a Polish friend of Julian Fontana, Stanisław Koźmian, acting as guide.

> Chopin insisted on travelling incognito and being introduced everywhere as Monsieur Fritz.

They arrived there on 7 July 1837, little more than a fortnight after the coronation of Queen Victoria. Chopin insisted on travelling incognito and being introduced everywhere as Monsieur Fritz. He appeared to be in poor health and, for that reason, did not wish to see anybody. Ignaz Moscheles noted in his diary: 'Chopin, who passed a few days in London, was the only one of the foreign artists who visited nobody and also did not wish to be visited, as every conversation aggravates his chest complaint. He went to some concerts and disappeared.'

In fact, that was not the whole truth. As Koźmian revealed, Pleyel and Chopin put up at one of the best hotels, kept a carriage, and enjoyed three weeks of frenetic activity. '[They] are simply looking for ways of spending money. One day we go to Windsor, another to Blackwall, another to Richmond... I haven't seen [the opera] *Ildegonde* yet because Chopin does not want to listen to boring music.' One evening, however, 'Monsieur Fritz' relented and consented to spend an evening with Pleyel's English counterpart and friend James Broadwood, who invited them to dine at his house in Bryanston Square. The disguise, of course, could only be preserved as long as Chopin kept his hands off the piano. After dinner, he sat down to play: suspicion was aroused and the truth extracted.

In his biography of the composer, Niecks reproduces an astute appraisal of Chopin in the form of a review of the Nocturnes and Scherzos, probably written by J.W. Davidson, in the *Musical World* of 23 February 1838:

*Were he not the most retiring and unambitious of all living musicians, he would before this time have been celebrated as the inventor of a new style, or school, of pianoforte composition. During his short visit to the metropolis last season, but few had the high gratification of hearing his extemporaneous performance. Those who experienced this will not readily lose its remembrance. He is, perhaps, par eminence, the most delightful of pianists in the drawing-room. The animation of his style is so subdued, its tenderness so refined, its melancholy so gentle, its niceties so studied and systematic, the tout ensemble so perfect, and evidently the result of an accurate judgement and most finished taste, that when exhibited in the large concert-room, or the thronged saloon, it fails to impress itself on the mass.*

Maria, like Konstancja, would remain an untouched, unattainable romantic ideal.

Pleyel and Chopin arrived back in Paris in the last week of July. Chopin had hoped that after London he would travel to Holland and thence to Germany to meet up with Maria and her family; but a letter (which has not survived) had reached him in London. Clearly, the Wodzińskis had decided that their daughter could not marry a man with such a fragile constitution. Maria's life and affairs were controlled by her parents. There was to be no argument or discussion. Without doubt, Teresa Wodzińska, Maria's mother, genuinely liked Chopin – the feeling appears to have been mutual – but Chopin had failed his probationary period. Maria, like Konstancja, would remain an untouched, unattainable romantic ideal.

Chopin resigned himself to his fate. He bundled together all the letters and mementos of Maria, tied the packet with a ribbon and wrote on it 'Moja bieda', a phrase usually translated as 'My sorrows'. The inscription, though,

*Chopin's packet of Maria's letters, marked 'Moja bieda' ('My sorrows')*

has a more poetic inference that is difficult to translate (and illustrates that Chopin could be creative also in his use of language). The closest approximation in English might be 'A poor boy am I'. The packet remained among his possessions for the rest of his life.

Chopin's courtship of Maria Wodzińska can hardly be said to have been the most ardent. Indeed, given his age, looks and talent, his wooing of her (or any other woman for that matter) appears positively anaemic. But all that was about to change – and in the most unlikely way.

# Chapter 9

## Sand and Majorca, 1838–1839

# Sand and Majorca, 1838–1839

Chopin coped with his disappointment by burying himself in his work. The end of the year passed with the usual round of charity concerts and fundraising for Polish causes. In February he was commanded to play for Louis-Philippe and the rest of the Royal Family. His recital was followed a few days later on 3 March 1838 by a remarkable concert given by the young pianist Charles-Valentin Alkan, in which Chopin and his pupil Adolf Gutmann joined Alkan and his teacher Pierre Zimmerman in a performance of Alkan's arrangement for two pianos, eight hands, of Beethoven's Seventh Symphony. 'Chopin survived this alarming event,' writes Alkan's biographer Ronald Smith, 'but a few years later pleaded insufficient strength to take part in a repeat performance.'

Chopin had been friends with Alkan since the early 1830s. They shared the same artistic ideals, were similarly fastidious, and enjoyed the same entertainments. Alkan, just three years younger, was to remain close to Chopin for the rest of Chopin's life, one of a small coterie of faithful intimates. Liszt reckoned that Alkan had the greatest technique he had ever known. That from Liszt was quite some compliment, but it will come as less of a surprise to anyone familiar with such Alkan works as the Concerto for Solo Piano, 'Les Quatre

Âges' Sonata or the Trois Grandes Études, Op. 76, all of them mind-boggling in their virtuosity.

On the evening of 8 May 1838, Chopin was invited to dinner at the apartment of his friend the Marquis de Custine. Among his fellow guests were members of the aristocracy, Victor Hugo, the poet and statesman Adolphe Lamartine, George Sand, the tenor Louis Duprez, and Franchomme with his cello. At length, it was Chopin's turn to play for the assembled company. Listening to him improvise in the semi-darkness, George Sand fell in love.

A few weeks later she wrote to Albert Grzymała. A wealthy Polish patriot, Grzymała was a trusted friend and confidant of Chopin (he had known him since he was a boy in Warsaw) who had come to play the same role for George Sand. In her letter Sand admitted her feelings:

*I must say that I am confused and amazed at the effect this little creature wrought on me. I have still not recovered from my astonishment, and if I were a proud person I should be feeling humiliated at having been carried away by my emotions at a moment in my life when I had thought that I should be settled for good.*

So who was this woman who wore trousers, smoked cigars and wrote novels under a man's name? An habitué of the most fashionable salons, befriended by the great and the good of Paris, she had, until now, been simply part of the audience in Chopin's life. George Sand was born in 1804 and baptised Amandine Aurore Lucie Dupin. According to her four-volume autobiography *Histoire de ma vie*, published in 1855, it was the class conflicts within her immediate family that shaped her life and social consciousness. Her father, Maurice Dupin, a Napoleonic cavalry officer, was descended from an illegitimate daughter of the Marshal de Saxe, himself the natural son of Frederick Augustus II, King of Poland and Elector of Saxony (1696–1704), and of his mistress, Aurore de Koenigsmark. Aurore Dupin was therefore named after an eighteenth-century courtesan. Her mother, Sophie Delaborde, was the penniless daughter of a Parisian bird-seller. She had borne an illegitimate child prior to her marriage to Maurice Dupin, a fact that was never forgiven by his mother (née Marie-Aurore de Saxe, Comtesse de Horn).

In 1808, Aurore's younger brother Auguste died. Only a week later her father was killed by the injuries he sustained when he fell from his horse. The deep hostility between Sophie and her mother-in-law prompted the former to move to Paris, leaving Aurore to be brought up by her grandmother in the family home. This was a substantial eighteenth-century manor house at Nohant in the Berry region of France, some 180 miles south of Paris. Aurore spent most of her childhood there and saw her mother only rarely.

On her grandmother's death in 1821 she inherited Nohant, and the following year, aged eighteen, married Casimir, the son of Baron Dudevant. The couple had two children, Maurice (1823) and Solange (1828). Dull, unimaginative and not predisposed to music, Casimir was an unsuitable partner for an independent, life-affirming Bohemian spirit. Although she went to great lengths to please him, it was to no avail; after nine years she left him and moved to Paris with her children, determined to make her living as a writer. He went off to live in the family château at Guillery with his servant Jeanne Dalias.

The first of Aurore's long succession of lovers was the writer Jules Sandeau from whose name she took her pseudonym (they wrote a novel together in 1831 entitled *Rose et Blanche*). She then proceeded to have affairs in fairly quick succession with Prosper Mérimée, Alfred de Musset (who took to absinthe when the relationship broke up), Michel de Bourges, Pietro Pagello and, almost certainly, Liszt. In 1837, after his victory over Thalberg, the charismatic Hungarian took himself off to Nohant with George Sand for several months while his neurotic Countess was ill in Paris. 'It would be a libel on George Sand to infer that she did not make the best uses of this opportunity,' suggests Sacheverell Sitwell. 'Her custom was to write all through the night, from ten o'clock till five in the morning; and they worked from the same room and smoked the same box of cigars.'

Sand's first three novels, *Indiana* (1832), *Lélia* (1833) and *Jacques* (1834), were candidly erotic and created a succès de scandale, enjoying wide popularity and establishing her reputation. Some of them were even turned into stage works. In England she was regarded as an evil influence – anti-marriage and a disrupter of family unity. Physically, she was no conventional beauty – she was less than five feet tall, and stout – but her magnetism made up for all that. One Edouard Grénier was particularly struck by her face:

> Sand's first three novels, were candidly erotic and created a succès de scandale, enjoying wide popularity and establishing her reputation.

*[It] attracted all my attention, the eyes especially. They were wonderful eyes, a little too close together, it may be, large, with full eyelids, and black, very black, but by no means lustrous; they reminded me of unpolished marble, or rather of velvet, and this gave a strange, dull, even cold expression to her countenance. Her fine eyebrows and these great placid eyes gave her an air of strength and dignity which was not borne out by the lower part of her face. Her nose was rather thick and not over shapely. Her mouth was also rather coarse and her chin small. She spoke with great simplicity, and her manners were very quiet.*

When Chopin had first encountered Sand in the autumn of 1836 she was by far the more famous of the two, Chopin still being considered by many merely as a pianist. Liszt had brought her along to a soirée chez Chopin. The composer Józef Brzowski described the occasion:

> Madame G. Sand, dark, dignified and cold... her dress fantastic (obviously proclaiming her desire to be noticed), composed of a white frock with a crimson sash and a kind of white shepherdess's corsage with crimson buttons. Her dark hair parted in the middle, falling in curls on both sides of her face and secured with a ribbon around her brow. Nonchalantly she took her place on the sofa near the fireplace, and, lightly blowing out clouds of smoke from her cigar, answered briefly but seriously the questions of the men sitting beside her... After Liszt and he had played a sonata, Chopin offered his guests ices. George Sand, glued to her sofa, never quitted her cigar for a moment.

Chopin, having initially felt repelled by George Sand, was now irresistibly drawn to her. It seemed an implausible alliance between a sexually inexperienced, physically coy dandy of slight build and an infamous, outspoken, predatory mother of two. But here was a sophisticated and brilliant woman with whom he felt entirely comfortable and in whom he could confide his feelings, even admit to his continuing despair over the loss of Maria Wodzińska. In short, George Sand presented a mother figure who was physically attracted to him; and, as he now found to his alarm, he in turn was attracted to her. It has been said that Sand was the man in all her relationships, but with her determination to conquer and possess there also came an unmistakably tender concern. She was going to mother him.

Chopin, having initially felt repelled by George Sand, was now irresistibly drawn to her. Here was a sophisticated and brilliant woman with whom he felt entirely comfortable and in whom he could confide his feelings.

From early on in the relationship she referred to her new love as 'the little one'. Only with hindsight could it be said that she used Chopin 'as a toy for literary copy' (Huneker) to be thrown over 'after she had wrung out all the emotional possibilities of the problem'. Sand was to be Chopin's bedrock for the next nine years and by far the most important and influential person to come into his life.

Sand was by this point legally separated from her husband but still in the throes of an affair, this time with the playwright Félicien Mallefille. Chopin, as usual, was irresolute ('with him only his cough is dependable,' said Marie

*Portrait of George Sand in 1832 by Auguste Carpentier*

d'Agoult) and was anxious at the prospect of emotional entanglement with anyone, let alone someone of Sand's experience. There was also the messy business of a sexual union to be considered. He sought advice from Grzymała, in all likelihood unaware that Sand had already added Grzymała to her list of conquests. Grzymała in turn wrote to Sand, urging her not to trifle with Chopin's emotions. Sand replied, asking Grzymała's opinion as to whether she could make Chopin happy or not. By the beginning of June, after further shilly-shallying, Chopin and George Sand had consummated their relationship.

Mallefille arrived back in Paris ignorant of his lover's change of affections. At a soirée of Countess Charlotte

Marliani, Chopin played, prompting a eulogy from the playwright, 'as a proof of my affection for you and my sympathy for your heroic country... hidden in the darkest corner of the room, I wept while following in my mind the desolate images you conjured up.' As he wrote the note, Sand and Chopin were having their joint portraits painted in the studio of their friend Eugène Delacroix. It is a fascinating picture. Sand is looking down enraptured at Chopin's unseen hands, a handkerchief in her left hand, a cigar stub held between the thumb and forefinger of her right hand; the head and shoulders of Chopin, looking dashingly romantic, are in the bottom right corner of the canvas, quite out of proportion with the figure of Sand. Perhaps this was why the portrait was left unfinished. After Delacroix's death, it was sold on and the canvas cut into two unequal parts. Sand eventually found her way to Denmark, Chopin to the Louvre. It is perhaps the best-known portrait of the composer (see title page).

Sand sent Mallefille off to Normandy with her son Maurice. Now she could have Chopin to herself and wrote to Delacroix in September: 'I am still in the state of intoxication in which you last saw me. There has not been the slightest cloud in our clear sky, not a grain of sand in our lake. I am beginning to think that there are angels disguised as men.'

Two people were less than happy about this blissful attraction of opposites. The Marquis de Custine, himself probably infatuated with Chopin, wrote to a friend, 'The poor creature does not see that this woman has the love of a vampire.' And there was the jilted Mallefille, who took to stalking the two lovers. One evening he accosted Sand in the street, waving a gun. It was time to leave Paris. George Sand had, in any case, been planning to spend the autumn and winter in Italy to improve the delicate health of fifteen-year-old Maurice, who suffered from severe rheumatism. Italy was exchanged for

Majorca, and on 18 October Sand, with Maurice, Solange and a maid, left the city. Chopin, insisting on preserving the social proprieties, travelled separately, leaving on 25 October armed with some treasured volumes of Bach, a pile of manuscript paper, and various unfinished works, including seventeen of the 24 **Preludes**. He had begun these in 1828 and had already sold them to Pleyel, their dedicatee, for 2,000 francs, of which he had received 500 in advance. To further finance what was likely to be a protracted stay, Chopin had also borrowed 1,500 francs from his banker friend Auguste Léo and a further 1,000 from an unknown source.

The party met up at Perpignan with Chopin arriving, after four nights in a stage-coach, 'as fresh as a rose and as rosy as a turnip', according to Sand in a letter to Charlotte Marliani. This was the first time that Chopin had ever met Maurice and Solange (the latter 'a wilful little girl of nine'). Because communications by land had been interrupted by the civil war, the five of them sailed from Port Vendres to Barcelona where they boarded a little steamer, El Mallorquin, that took them to Palma. The passenger lists record the travellers as: First Class – Madame Dudevant (married); Mr. Maurice, her son, a minor; Mademoiselle Solange, her daughter, a minor; Mr. Frédéric Chopin, musician. Second Class – Mademoiselle Amélie, lady's maid. They left at 5 p.m. on 7 November and landed the following morning at 11.30 a.m.

Despite letters of introduction to some of the leading families on the island, the party was unable to find anywhere to stay. All accommodation was apparently taken by refugees from the mainland; but, as Señora Choussat de Canut, wife of the island's leading banker, pointed out, the lack of lodgings may have had something to do with the prospect of 'an unattached woman who smoked cigars, accompanied by two long-haired boys and a little girl who wore boys' clothes, none of whom went to church'. Most of the inhabitants were poor, deriving their living from wine-making, farming, or mining marble and copper. The Majorcans' quiet, pastoral way of life had not changed for centuries. Barbary pirates they were used to, but not visitors like these.

To start with, Chopin and Sand rented a noisy room above a barrel-maker's workshop. A week later, they found a small house to rent at Establiments, some five kilometers from the city, called 'Villa Son Vent' ('House of the Wind'). On 19 November, Chopin wrote elatedly to Julian Fontana in Paris:

> *I am in Palma among palms, cedars, cacti, olives, pomegranates, etc. Everything the Jardin des plantes has in its greenhouses. A sky like turquoise, a sea like lapis lazuli, mountains like emerald, air like heaven. Sun all day, and hot; everyone in summer clothing; at night guitars and singing for hours. Huge balconies with grape-vines overhead; Moorish walls. Everything looks towards Africa, as the town does. Go to Pleyel; the piano has not yet come. How was it sent? You will soon receive some Preludes. I shall probably lodge in a wonderful monastery, the most beautiful situation in the world; sea, mountains, palms, a cemetery, a crusaders' church, ruined mosques, aged trees, thousand-year-old olives. Ah, my dear, I am coming alive a little – I am near to what is most beautiful. I am better...*

The letter reached Fontana in Paris on 28 December. By then, everything in Majorca had changed. Initially the weather had proved a tonic for Chopin's health. With Sand and her children, he enjoyed long walks in the country and along the seashore. Then, with sudden vehemence, winter set in. On the way back home from one excursion, a violent wind blew in from the sea, buffeting Chopin so much that his lungs were affected. Gales and rain battered the villa, the plaster walls swelling with the rising damp and a chimneyless charcoal stove providing the only source of heating. Chopin began to cough. His next letter to Fontana (3 December 1838) tried to make light of his situation:

I have been as sick as a dog these last two weeks; I caught cold in spite of three of the most famous doctors on the island. One said I had died, the second that I am dying, the third that I shall die.

> *I have been as sick as a dog these last two weeks; I caught cold in spite of 18 degrees of heat, roses, oranges, palms, figs and three of the most famous doctors on the island. One sniffed at what I spat up, the second tapped where I spat from, the third poked about and listened to how I spat it. One said I had died, the second that I am dying, the third that I shall die.*

In fact, the doctors had diagnosed tuberculosis and, as was their duty, reported the case to the authorities. The landlord was informed and promptly demanded the departure of the party as well as an exorbitant sum of money to refurnish and decorate the entire house – by law anything touched by a tuberculotic had to be burnt. The visitors took refuge in the (now demolished) French consulate in the 'Illeta d'en Moragues'.

As it happened, Chopin and Sand had already earmarked alternative accommodation: an old, abandoned Carthusian monastery – the Cartuja, as it is known – at Valldemosa, which they had spotted during an early excursion. The sole inhabitants were an old serving woman, a sacristan who acted as general factotum, and a Spanish political refugee and his wife. Having arranged to take over the quarters of the latter two, on 15 December the visitors moved all their belongings, including Chopin's rented piano, up the mountainside. Despite the setbacks, Sand wrote optimistically:

*[Chopin] is recovering, and I hope he will soon be better than before. His goodness and patience are angelic. We are so different from most of the people and things around us... our family ties are only more strengthened by it and we cling to each other with more affection and intimate happiness.*

The views were spectacular ('Everything the poet and painter might have dreamt up has been created in this place by nature,' wrote Sand), though its location meant it enjoyed little sunshine and was exposed to high winds and heavy mists rolling in from the sea. The quarters were primitive, with rickety furniture, and a clay floor covered with rush matting. The cell in which Chopin worked was, as he described it to Fontana:

*The shape of a tall coffin, with a great dusty vault where... with doors larger than any pair of gates in Paris, you can imagine me, my hair uncurled, without white gloves, pale as ever... Next to my bed there is a hopeless square desk I can hardly write on, on it a leaden candlestick (a luxury here) with a candle in it, my Bach, my own scrawls and (not my) waste paper – silence – you could scream – there would still be silence. Indeed, I write to you from a strange place.*

It was strange, isolated – and hostile. George Sand found she had her work cut out in the roles of mother, lover, nurse, cook and writer (she was working on her new novel *Spiridion*), quite apart from bartering with the contemptuous locals for provisions. The peasants of Valldemosa had taken a decided dislike to their unconventional visitors who kept themselves to themselves, did not attend church, and flouted any number of social conventions. Chopin's health, though improving, dictated that he did not leave the monastery. He was now passionately in love with Sand and grew increasingly agitated whenever he was left alone for any length of time. Valldemosa, according to Sand, had become for Chopin 'a place full of hidden terrors and phantoms'.

This state of mind produced some of the most poignant and heart-rending music Chopin ever composed. On 22 January 1839 he completed his 24 Preludes, Op. 28. Many had been written before he left for Majorca, but at least four were composed on the island, including those in E minor and B minor (which were played on the organ at Chopin's funeral), and probably the one in D flat major now known as the 'Raindrop' Prelude. On the same piece of paper as the E minor Prelude is the melancholic A minor Prelude and the E minor Mazurka from the Op. 41 set. More minor key masterpieces saw the light of day – the C minor Polonaise, a striking contrast with the optimistic A major Polonaise, written just before the departure for Majorca, and the C sharp minor Scherzo, with its chorale-like second subject.

One reason for this rush of creativity was the arrival, at last, of a Pleyel piano, though it languished with the Palma customs authorities for three weeks while Chopin negotiated a reduction in the ridiculous duty demanded. Only with the Pleyel at hand could Chopin finalize his new compositions before sending some of the manuscripts to Fontana for fair copying. With a string of precise business instructions, he signed off with the news that he might not return to Paris until May.

Then, on 11 February, Chopin and Sand abruptly packed up and left. The reasons for their change of mind is uncertain. Although their joint funds were running low, the weather had turned mild and Chopin had at last got his hands on his beloved piano. It is probable that George Sand could simply stand it no more. The peasants had taken great exception to the behavior of this arrogant, impatient woman who was estranged from the Church and yet dared to establish herself in a monastic cell with a man who was not her husband. 'Goodness only knows,' said the parish priest, 'how many mortal sins she is amassing!' For her part, Sand recorded in her account of the Majorcan adventure, published in 1841 as *Un hiver à Majorque*:

> *On Sunday mornings, the great sea-shell which blared out down in the village and out on the roads to hasten the belated worshipper to church blared out to us in vain in the Cartuja. We were deaf, because we did not know what it meant; and when we knew, then we were deafer still. They found a way to satisfy the glory of God in a most un-Christian manner. They leagued themselves together so that none should sell us their fish, their eggs, or vegetables, save at outrageous prices.*

Their treatment by the locals, Chopin's delicate health, his abhorrence of Majorcan cooking, the lack of proper facilities to care for him, the burden of the whole journey, the stress of housekeeping in these conditions with two children, the attitudes of the servants...all these factors took their toll on Sand:

> *For the first time my life, I found myself being excessively put out by very minor catastrophes, losing my temper over too much pepper in my soup, or about its being made away with by the servants, worrying over a fresh loaf which wouldn't come... If I live to be a hundred I shall never forget my joy whenever the provisions bag arrived at the Cartuja [from Palma].*

The journey home was a nightmare. Unable to hire a sprung carriage (no one wanted to risk its infection and then destruction because of a tuberculotic), Chopin had to be transported in a farm cart down the nine miles of bumpy roads into Palma. By the time he arrived at their overnight accommodation, he had suffered a lung hemorrhage, coughing uncontrollably and spitting blood. The 'export duty' on the Pleyel was so astronomical that it was decided to sell the instrument there and then. Boarding the El Mallorquin once more (the log shows that they embarked on 13 February at 3 pm), they were aghast to discover that this time they were sharing the voyage with a cargo of live pigs. Unlike last time, this crossing was a rough one, and Chopin was left gasping for breath in the airless cabin filled with the stench of his seasick, defecating porcine shipmates. By the time the steamer reached Barcelona, Chopin was vomiting 'bowlfuls of blood'.

After resting for a week in a hotel, Chopin and Sand left for Marseilles, arriving back in France on 24 February. Here they remained until May while Chopin recovered. He may have been sick in body, but the string of letters written to Fontana reveal his mental energy, his business acumen – and how much he needed money and ever more money. Chopin was increasingly using his friend not only as a general factotum and copyist but as his agent in absentia. He shot off a welter of irritable instructions telling Fontana exactly how to play one publisher off against another, the amounts to negotiate for each work, and what his fallback positions should be.

It is abundantly clear how much Chopin despised his publishers – dismissing them behind their backs as 'pigs', 'a band of Jews', 'cheats', 'fools', 'rascals' and 'scoundrels'. Here he is reacting to the news that Pleyel had refused to pay 1,000 francs for the Second Ballade and a further 1,500 for the two Polonaises, Op. 40:

*I did not think that Pleyel would play the Jew with me but, if so, give him this letter. I think he won't cause you any trouble about the Ballade and the Polonaise[s]. But, in the opposite event, get 500 for the Ballade from Probst, and then take it to Schlesinger. If I have got to deal with Jews, let it at least be Orthodox ones... So, if Pleyel makes even the smallest difficulties, you will go to Schl., and tell him that I will give him the Ballade for France and England for 800 (he won't give a thousand), and the Polonaises for Germany, England and France for 1,500 (and if he won't give that, then for 1,400, or 1,300, or even 1,200).*

Chopin always knew his commercial value. Marseilles proved to be a happy time for the two lovers, with Sand writing to Charlotte Marliani in April:

*Chopin is an angel... his goodness, his tenderness and his patience sometimes make me feel anxious; I feel that he is too fine, too exquisite, too perfect to live long in this crude and heavy earthly world. In Majorca, when he was mortally ill, he made music which smelt of paradise. But I have grown so used to seeing him in heaven that I do not think life or death means anything to him. He does not really know himself which planet he is on. He has no idea of life as we think of it and as we feel it.*

Chopin, for his part, was sure that Grzymała 'would love her even more if you knew her as I now know her'.

The only blot on the horizon was news of the death of Chopin's friend, the tenor Adolphe Nourrit. In a fit of despair he had committed suicide in Naples. His body was brought back to Marseilles for burial. During the service Chopin played a gentle Schubert song on the organ.

After a brief visit to Genoa in May, Chopin and Sand began a slow journey back to the countryside of Berry. On 1 June 1839, Chopin caught his first glimpse of Nohant. It was a place that was to play a central role in his life for the next eight years.

# Chapter 10

## Concerts, Composing and Coughing, 1839–1841

# Concerts, Composing and Coughing, 1839–1841

Carved on the panelling of George Sand's bedroom at Nohant is the date '19 June 1839'. No one is certain of the meaning of the graffiti, carved within a fortnight of their return from the horrors of their Majorcan adventure; but the fact that it appears in Sand's bedroom and that there is no other graffiti at Nohant suggests it had great significance to Chopin and Sand. Was it to record the anniversary of the day that they first became lovers?

On the other hand, Sand confessed much later in a letter to Grzymała that she and Chopin stopped having a sexual relationship at this time on account of his health. By that point, however, she had many ulterior motives for asserting this; and in any case, the idea of George Sand living a chaste life for eight years is hardly convincing (neither, as we shall see, did it occur).

What is important is the nature of the relationship between the two of them. There is absolutely no doubt that both of them were deeply in love and totally committed to one another. Sand provided Chopin with a stable home life, the first time he had experienced this since leaving Warsaw. Increasingly, he came to rely on her for ministering to his every need, and so creating the ideal conditions in which to compose. George Sand, for her part, was happy to abandon the reckless life that she had led before meeting Chopin, and forgo her infamous reputation. She knew that she had taken on a genius along with all the shortcomings and frailties (mental as well as the obvious physical ones) that it implied. Her maternal instincts and the strong desire to simply make her amour happy – a trait which had shown itself during her marriage to Casimir Dudevant – were dominating factors. Sand's letters to her confidants are littered with references to 'the little one', 'Fric-Fric', 'my dear boy', 'little Chip-Chip', 'Chopinet' and the like. 'I look after him like a child,' she wrote, 'and he loves me like his mother.'

The manor house with its extensive gardens, an old tower that housed a flock of noisy doves, woods abounding with wild strawberries, the peace of the surrounding countryside and the nearby river Indre, combined to cast their spell on the newcomer. Within a short time he had written the Nocturne in G (Op. 37 No. 2), the F sharp Impromptu and, most notably, the Second Sonata in B flat minor, one of the greatest masterpieces in the Romantic piano literature. Three of its four movements were composed at Nohant, Chopin adding the earlier **Funeral March** (1837) as its celebrated third movement. George Sand wrote in *Histoire de ma vie*:

> *His creation was spontaneous and miraculous... he found it without seeking it, without foreseeing it. It came on his piano suddenly, complete, sublime, or it sang in his head during a walk, and he was impatient to play it himself. But then began the most heart-rending labor I ever saw. It was a series of efforts, of irresolutions and of frettings to seize again certain details of the theme he had heard; what he had conceived as a whole he analyzed too much when wishing to write it, and his regret at not finding it again, in his opinion, clearly*

*defined, threw him into a kind of despair. He shut himself up in his room for whole days, weeping, walking, breaking his pens, repeating a bar a hundred times, writing it and effacing it as many times, and recommencing the next day with a minute and desperate perseverance. He spent six weeks over a single page to write it at last as he had noted it down at the very first.*

*The manuscript of Chopin's Funeral March, in the composer's hand*

It speaks volumes for Chopin's restless, dissatisfied nature that by the end of the summer he was aching to return to Paris – to his friends, his exiled compatriots and the social whirl of the city. As early as July, Sand told Grzymała that she was afraid that Chopin was bored at Nohant, being unused to solitude and the simple life. 'I am prepared to make any sacrifice rather than see him devoured by melancholy. Come without fail,' she pleads, 'and observe Chopin's real state of mind.' (He arrived a few weeks later.) Yet Sand had her own reasons for decamping to Paris: her play *Cosima* was to be produced there; Solange had been despatched to boarding school; Maurice, who was developing into a talented artist, wanted a studio to further his studies. Julian Fontana was directed to find separate apartments for Chopin and Sand. To the outside world, the couple preferred to keep the illusion of being artistic colleagues rather than live-in lovers. Not even Chopin's parents were in on the secret.

During the next seven years (with one exception: 1840), Chopin and Sand divided their lives between Paris and Nohant. The winter season was spent teaching and entertaining. Summer in the country was more conducive to sustained composition (almost all Chopin's music over the next few years was completed at Nohant). His Paris base from October 1839 until May 1842 was at 5 Rue Tronchet, just behind the Madeleine; hers was much further out, at 16 Rue Pigalle.

Fontana leapt to obey Chopin's meticulous, if rambling, instructions to choose a wallpaper for the main rooms with a narrow dark green stripe for the border, something different for the hall ('I like a pearl color; it is neither glaring nor common-looking'), to choose furniture, to tell Wessel (Chopin's London publisher) that there were six new manuscripts to be sold at 300 francs each, that his spring mattress bed needed repairing, to have the chairs and everything well beaten – all in a letter ending with a cheery 'Your old Ch. With a longer nose than ever'. And in another missal barely a week later:

*Have the grey curtains that were in my study by the piano hung in the hall, put the ones that were in the bedroom in the new bedroom but with pale muslin ones under the grey ones... If the red sofa that stood in the dining-room can have white*

*covers made of the same stuff as the chairs, it could be put
in the drawing-room... Find me a manservant... Write to me
about Probst... Don't forget Wessel... Tell Gutmann that I was
glad he asked after me... And you yourself can take a bath in
an infusion of whales, to restore you after all my commissions;
I give them to you because I know that you willingly do for me
as much as your time permits; and I'll gladly do the same for
you when you marry.*

What Fontana's reward was for all this is uncertain. He was
to live rent free at Rue Tronchet and was given a steady
string of pupils, thanks to Chopin; but the amount he was
expected to accomplish pushed the boundaries of friendship
to its limits. On 4 October, Chopin reeled off a list of clothes
that he wanted bought and made:

*Order a hat for me... Tell [my tailor] to make me a pair of
grey trousers at once. You can choose the shade of dark grey;
winter trousers, good quality, without belt, smooth and
stretchy... Also a plain black velvet waistcoat, but with a tiny
inconspicuous pattern, something very quiet and elegant. If he
has nothing suitable, then a black stuff one, good and plain. I
rely on you. Not very open; that's all...*

Oh – and find an apartment for George. In a further letter
he even drew a plan of the ideal layout for Sand's apartment,
adding that there should be peace and quiet (no whores or
blacksmiths), no neighbors or smells (especially not smoke)
and that it should have a separate entrance for children and
servants.

After a year away from Paris, Chopin arrived back on
10 October. Word had spread and he was once more
inundated with pupils. Soon he was giving up to eight

lessons a day. In his diary, a new pupil, Friederike Müller, described his teacher as: 'Feeble, pale, coughing much, he often took opium drops with sugar or drank gum-water, rubbed his forehead with eau de cologne, and nevertheless taught with patience, perseverance and zeal which were admirable.'

Less than a fortnight later, Chopin met Ignaz Moscheles for the first time. One of the most eminent musicians of the day, Moscheles was Chopin's senior by some sixteen years (and outlived him by over thirty). He was a brilliant and energetic pianist and had been the toast of Europe ever since his debut aged fourteen in his birthplace of Prague. By his mid-twenties, he was sufficiently eminent to have prepared the piano score of Beethoven's *Fidelio*. It is only recently that some of his works have been rescued from the unjustified obscurity in which they have languished since his death. Chopin had long been an admirer; though Moscheles had long had reservations about Chopin. A brilliant improviser with an enthusiasm for the music of Schumann and Mendelssohn, Moscheles' particular method of touch and fingering made it difficult for him to play the music of Chopin and Liszt. Writing in 1833 of Chopin's Études, he confessed:

> A new pupil described his teacher as: 'Feeble, pale, coughing much, he often took opium drops with sugar nevertheless taught with patience, perseverance and zeal.

> My thoughts, and consequently my fingers, ever stumble and sprawl at certain crude modulations, and I find Chopin's productions on the whole too sugared, too little worthy of a man and an educated musician, though there is much charm and originality in the national color of his motive.

Apart from being a celebrated pedagogue, Moscheles was an acutely observant diarist. When he and Chopin met at the home of their mutual friend, the banker Auguste Léo, he recorded his impressions:

> He played to me at my request and now for the first time I understand his music, and can also explain to myself the enthusiasm of the ladies. His ad libitum *playing, which, with the interpreters of his music, degenerates into disregard for time, is with him only the most charming originality of execution; the dilettante-like hard modulations which strike me disagreeably when I am playing his compositions no longer shock me, for he glides over them in a fairy-like way with his delicate fingers; his* piano *is so softly breathed forth that he does not need any strong* forte *in order to produce the wished-for contrasts. It is for this reason that one does not miss the orchestra-like effects which the German school demands of the pianoforte-player, but allows himself to be carried away, as by a singer who, little concerned with the accompaniment, entirely follows his feeling. In short, he is unique in the world of pianists.*

Among the music Chopin played that evening was his B flat minor Sonata. A few days later he and Moscheles were summoned to play at the French court in the Palace of Saint-Cloud and, after each had performed a selection of solos, they played Moscheles' Grand Sonata in E flat, Op. 47 for piano duet. Chopin, as he always did when playing music for four hands in concert, insisted on playing the bass part. 'In the finale,' wrote Moscheles, 'we gave ourselves up to musical delirium. Chopin's enthusiasm throughout the piece must, I think, have affected the listeners, who now burst forth into eulogies.' Chopin was presented with a valuable set of Sèvres, Moscheles with an elegant travelling case – a hint for him to go, Chopin is supposed to have quipped.

In fact, the two pianist-composers got on famously. Moscheles was the joint editor with the revered critic François-Joseph Fétis, one of Chopin's earliest champions in Paris, of a comprehensive piano tutor entitled *Méthode des Méthodes*. He invited Chopin to contribute some studies for the third and final part of the publication. In the late summer of 1841, Chopin's Trois Nouvelles Études appeared along with works by other composers, such as Liszt's Morceau de salon and Mendelssohn's Étude in F minor.

1840 proved to be a comparatively uneventful year. Chopin fell ill with chest pains in April. On his return from Majorca, the doctor's verdict, contradicting the three Spanish physicians, had ruled out tuberculosis and diagnosed a chronic infection of the larynx. Jan Matuszyński, though, was certain that Chopin was consumptive, an opinion made all the more poignant by the fact that Matuszyński himself was now dying of the disease. Today, even a person without Matuszyński's medical knowledge could recognize the symptoms of consumption (the secondary phase of TB) whereby the victim loses weight, feels fatigued, and suffers from shortness of breath, chest pains and a dry cough that produces blood and pus-filled sputum. It is a disease that takes hold slowly, caused by bacteria usually transmitted from one person to another through air. Could Matuszyński have caught his tuberculosis from the friend whose apartment he had shared?

George Sand's play *Cosima* opened and closed within a week.

In the same month, George Sand's play *Cosima* opened and closed within a week. Its costly failure meant that Sand was unable to afford to return to Nohant, where she always kept an open house. Instead, the couple remained in Paris. Sand's new apartment in Rue Pigalle, however, became an attractive alternative to Nohant, with regular visitors including Delacroix (who was helping Maurice to further his painting ambitions), the actress Marie Dorval (some sources hint at a lesbian relationship with Sand) and the extravagantly gifted singer Pauline Garcia-Viardot. Sand would get up at four o'clock in the afternoon, the time at which Chopin generally finished his teaching in Rue Tranchet. He would then invariably make his way over to Rue Pigalle and sleep there.

In this atmosphere of happy domesticity, Chopin took on the role of stepfather to the two children. In September they acquired a puppy called Mops (the Polish for 'Pug'), and Sand applied herself to two new novels (The Journeyman *Carpenter* and *Horace*) while Chopin taught much and composed little. During the whole of 1840 he wrote only three Waltzes, one song, and the (magnificent) Polonaise in F sharp minor. He rarely went to concerts but he did attend one on 15 December when the remains of Napoleon were brought back from the British island of St. Helena to be buried in the crypt of Les Invalides. Chopin heard Viardot, Luigi Lablache and Alexis Dupont, accompanied by a choir of 300, as soloists in Mozart's Requiem. It was the work that Chopin would request to be sung at his funeral eight years later.

In 1841 Liszt returned to the French capital to give a series of concerts which he called piano 'recitals'. The concept was entirely new, dreamt up during his recent appearances in London.

In March 1841 Liszt returned to the French capital to give a series of concerts which he called piano 'recitals'. The concept was entirely new, dreamt up during his recent appearances in London. Here, for the first time, a concert was given by just one artist instead of several. 1839–47 were Liszt's so-called 'years of transcendental execution' in which he toured Europe, conquering all before him. It is reckoned that during this period he earned at least 300,000 francs a year. Chopin's earnings, as we have seen, were very small beer in comparison. If there is no direct evidence of Chopin's jealousy of Liszt's regal status and princely income, it is certain that his relationship with him had cooled dramatically. Chopin had not played in public since the spring of 1838. Financial necessity, as well as a desire to reassert his prominence, allowed him to be persuaded to give a concert. The date was set for 26 April 1841.

Sand wrote jubilantly to Pauline Viardot in London: 'A great, grrrreat piece of news is that little Chip-Chip is going to give a grrrrreat concert.' Chopin, of course, then immediately changed his mind. But it was too late – even before the actual date had been announced, three-quarters of the tickets had been sold: there was no going back. Sand was amused by the spectacle of 'the meticulous and irresolute Chip-Chip obliged not to change his mind any more'. Sand organized what she called 'this Chopinesque nightmare' with calm efficiency. 'He doesn't want posters, he doesn't want any programmes, he doesn't want a numerous audience. He doesn't want anybody to talk about it. He is afraid of so many things that I have suggested he play without candles, without an audience, on a mute piano.' She had once more assumed the role of a mother figure, while Chopin had shut himself away to play Bach fugues in order to calm his nerves.

Unsurprisingly Chopin did not dare risk a Lisztian-style solo recital, but the concert was the first occasion on which he played a large selection of his own music in public. This included a number of the Preludes, the four Mazurkas, Op. 41 and the Third Scherzo, Op. 39. The Ballade in F major, Op. 38 and two Études had to be repeated. Sharing the programme were the singer Laure Cinti-Damoreau and the dazzling Moravian violinist Heinrich Ernst, with whom Chopin played a duo. Chopin

The 300-strong audience, each of whom had paid the extraordinary amount of twenty francs for a ticket, were ecstatic.

ended the evening with the two Op. 40 Polonaises. The 300-strong audience, each of whom had paid the extraordinary amount of twenty francs for a ticket, were ecstatic. The editor's review in *La France Musicale* summed it up:

> *Chopin is a composer of conviction. He composes for himself and performs for himself... In truth nothing equals the lightness, the sweetness with which this artist preludes on the piano; moreover nothing can be placed beside his works, full of originality, distinction and grace. Chopin is a pianist apart, who should not be and cannot be compared with anyone.*

**One unlooked-for outcome of the concert was the end of Chopin's friendship with Liszt.**

George Sand wrote to her half-brother, Hippolyte Châtiron, in triumph:

> *Chopin has put himself in the position of being able to loaf all summer by giving a concert where, in a period of two hours, with a couple of flourishes of the hand, he put six thousand and several hundred francs in his pocket, amid applause, encores and the flutterings of the most beautiful women in Paris – The Scoundrel!*

One unlooked-for outcome of the concert was the end of Chopin's friendship with Liszt. The Hungarian's relationship with Marie d'Agoult had foundered. The Countess and George Sand, too, had had a falling-out and now seemed the ideal moment for d'Agoult to mount a campaign of hatred against the writer, make a move towards Chopin, and spread as many venomous rumors as she could in order to drive a wedge between Chopin and Sand, Liszt and Chopin. She tried to convince Liszt that Chopin's concert was a plot by Sand to destroy Liszt. Liszt was having none of it but, in the event, over-egged the pudding. At the conclusion of Chopin's final selection, Liszt rushed onto the platform in a disgraceful bit of upstaging and, embarrassingly, attempted to carry the exhausted pianist into the wings. Liszt had also persuaded *La Gazette Musicale*, a paper founded by Fétis, to let him cover the concert. In the course of a lengthy review, opening with a vivid portrait of the glamorous mien of the evening, he wrote:

> *Even before the concert began, people were settled and ready to listen, telling themselves they could not afford to miss a chord, a note, a nuance, a thought of him who was about to sit there. And they were right to be so greedy, attentive, so devoutly moved, for he whom they awaited, whom they longed to see and hear, to admire and applaud, was not only a consummate virtuoso, a pianist in full command of the technique of his art, a musician of great renown, he was all this and much more: he was Chopin.*

Whatever the motives for such a fulsome tribute, Chopin thought the review patronizing and offensive. The matter of Liszt abusing his hospitality in order to cuckold Pleyel, the high-handed manner of departing from Chopin's painstakingly considered scores, the malicious gossip that Marie d'Agoult had directed against Sand, and the review of the concert were enough for Chopin to turn his back on his extravagant and generous friend. What need had he of Liszt and his circle when he had George Sand at his side?

# Chapter 11

## The Fading Idyll, 1841–1845

# The Fading Idyll, 1841–1845

*The other day I heard Chopin improvise at George Sand's... it is marvelous to hear him compose in this way; his inspiration is so immediate and complete that he plays without hesitation, as though it had to be thus. But when it comes to writing it down and recapturing the original thought in all its details, he spends days of nervous strain and almost frightening desperation. He alters and retouches the same phrases incessantly and walks up and down like a madman.*

So wrote Josef Filtsch, the brother of Chopin's most brilliant pupil, Carl, in a letter to his parents. A cursory glance at any Chopin autograph reveals the struggles that he endured and the frequency with which he changed his mind. His Polish compatriots might have wished for an opera extolling the land of his birth, and admirers such as Schumann might have hoped for a symphony; but the process of writing a single example in either form would have taken years. The neurotic perfection that he lavished on each short piano work gave him more than enough trouble.

In the case of every other major composer, such lack of range would have been his undoing. For Chopin, it was his hallmark. Liszt argued that Chopin was unable to achieve perfection in any form that he himself had not created.

Whether or not the Concertos and Sonatas are de facto less successful than the Nocturnes, Mazurkas and Ballades is a moot point but it is an extraordinary feature of Chopin's genius that, having alighted on a form that suited him, he could ring so many varied and completely original changes without repeating himself.

At the beginning of June 1841, after an absence of nineteen months, Chopin and Sand returned to Nohant. Far from the distractions of Paris, he was able to settle down and complete a string of works and send them off to Fontana for copying. These included the Tarantella, Op. 43, the Ballade No. 3 in A flat, Op. 47, the great C minor **Nocturne, Op. 48 No. 1** and the **Fantasy in F minor, Op. 49**.

It was not only music that was winging its way from Nohant to Fontana. Chopin penned another series of letters to his put-upon factotum, issuing a whirlwind of fussy instructions: pay the house porter and the flower woman; buy some soap, two pairs of Swedish gloves, a bottle of patchouli, a bottle of bouquet de Chantilly, and one of 'those tiny ivory hands for scratching your head'; make Pleyel do this and Schlesinger do that, send a flat metal flask and an air cushion… Fontana was a willing slave. But the more demands he fulfilled, the more his master asked of him.

The first barely perceptible cracks now appeared in the Chopin–Sand liaison. Marie de Rozières was a pupil whom Chopin had introduced to Sand as a piano teacher for Solange. Not only had this spinsterish lady ingratiated herself into 'The Family' (as Sand called it) but, somewhat unexpectedly, had become the mistress of the feckless Antoni Wodziński, Maria Wodzińska's brother. Chopin was furious, becoming even more agitated when he heard in July that Maria herself had married Józef Skarbek, son of Chopin's

*Portrait of Chopin*
*by George Sand*

godfather (the marriage was a disaster and the couple soon separated). Chopin banned Marie and Antoni from stepping foot inside Nohant. He knew, though Sand seems to have been unaware, that Wodziński was merely using de Rozières before his planned return to Poland, and that the lady's belated discovery of sex was having a dangerous influence on the rebellious Solange.

George Sand simply could not understand Chopin's anger and explained to Marie de Rozières that if she knew what had caused his pique, she would do something about it:

> But with his exasperating nature, one can never know
> anything. He went through the whole of the day before
> yesterday without uttering a syllable to anyone. Was he ill?
> Had someone annoyed him? Had I said something to upset
> him? I searched and searched. I know his sensitive spots as
> well as anyone can, but I was unable to discover anything,
> and I shall never know, any more than I know about a million
> other little things, which he may not even know himself.

The atmosphere was lightened by the arrival of Pauline
Viardot and her husband Louis. Viardot (1821–1910) was
an exceptional talent – wonderful looks, one of the greatest
mezzo-soprano voices of the nineteenth century, as well as a
pianist and composer. She had made her debut in London in
1839 as Desdemona in Rossini's *Otello* and married Viardot,
director of the Théâtre Italien, in 1840, a relationship
engineered by the maternal Sand. Chopin and Sand adored
them, and their own relationship flourished again, for on
their return to Paris they decided to live together in Rue
Pigalle.

Three weeks after leaving Nohant, Chopin was once again
asked to play for the Royal Family. The concert he gave at the
Tuileries on 2 December was before 500 guests who included
not only the King and Queen but Delacroix, Sand and her
erstwhile lover Alfred de Musset. Also on the programme
was Giuditta Grisi, one of the great divas of the day. For some
reason, Chopin, though once more handsomely rewarded
with gifts of fine china, was left depressed by the occasion. It
was the last time that he played at the French court.

Nevertheless, encouraged by the success of his concert
the previous year, he decided to pay a return visit to the Salle

Pleyel. On 21 February 1842 he gave a second triumphant programme of his own works, which included the new Ballade (No. 3), as well as accompanying Viardot in one of her own songs and Franchomme in one of his cello pieces. What could be more satisfying than making music with your friends and getting paid for the pleasure? With the astronomical price of tickets, the evening netted Chopin 'more than 5,000 francs profit, a unique result in Paris,' wrote George Sand to Châtiron, 'which merely proves how eager people are to hear the most perfect and the most exquisite of musicians'.

Less than a week later, Chopin was taken ill and remained in bed for a fortnight with an aching mouth and tonsils. He had not fully recovered when Jan Matuszyński died of tuberculosis on 20 April, at the age of just thirty-three, after 'a slow and cruel agony'. He passed away in Chopin's arms. Sand wrote to Viardot that the strength, courage and devotion that Chopin had shown to his friend during this terrible ordeal were 'more than one could expect from such a frail being, but afterwards he was shattered'. As if that were not enough, news arrived from Warsaw that Chopin's former teacher Żywny had also died, he who had tearfully bade farewell to his pupil on the outskirts of Warsaw by conducting a valedictory cantata.

At the beginning of May Sand took Chopin to Nohant to recuperate. They travelled there for the first time on the new railway line between Paris and Orléans, a journey completed by overnight coach from Châteauroux to Nohant. Here Sand's physician Doctor Pepet determined that Chopin's trouble was simply due to an excess of mucus. Reassured by such incompetence, Chopin slowly regained some measure of health and once more spent the summer months in a phase of concentrated composition. From this period come three important works: the Ballade No. 4 in F minor, Op. 52, the celebrated **Polonaise in A flat major, Op. 53**, and the Scherzo No. 4 in E major, Op. 54.

CD 2
track 8
www.naxosbooks.com

Welcome interruptions came from the poet Stefan Witwicki, who stayed for a few days, and Eugène Delacroix, who stayed for longer (and even brought his cat, a rare dispensation from the châtelaine). Chopin had come to respect his great artist friend but could never quite understand or appreciate his work. While Chopin might urge his pupils to 'be bolder' and 'let yourself go' he was unable to see that these same elements were at the heart of the expressive freedom and abandon of Delacroix's canvases. The finest musical colourist could not relate to the work of his finest visual equivalent. Never mind: the two of them were inseparable. Delacroix was in awe of Chopin, describing him as 'the most real artist I have ever met'. While at Nohant, Delacroix solved a problem that had been vexing him. He had been commissioned to decorate the ceiling of the library in the Palais de Luxembourg and he alighted on the idea of showing Virgil introducing Dante to Homer. Chopin was to be the model for Dante. In a second section, George Sand was the model for Aspasia, the brilliant and influential mistress of Pericles, the fifth-century statesman.

> Delacroix was in awe of Chopin, describing him as 'the most real artist I have ever met'.

In September, Chopin and Sand moved back to Paris into spacious new accommodation in the fashionable Square d'Orléans (the steep staircase outside Rue Pigalle had always left Chopin gasping for breath). Sand had taken an apartment at No. 9 for herself and Maurice, who had managed also to secure a studio in one of the other houses in the Square. Chopin took two ground floor rooms at No. 5. This was to remain his Paris home until June 1849. His neighbours included the Marlianis, Kalkbrenner and his family,

*No. 9, Square d'Orléans, Paris*

Zimmerman and Alkan. In fact, so many artists, musicians and writers lived there that the Square acquired the nickname of 'La Petite Athènes'.

It was not Fontana but Grzymała who had engineered this happy arrangement. There had been none of the usual flurry of commands to Chopin's old school friend when they had arrived at Nohant that May. What passed between the two is not known but a letter written at that time by Fontana to his sister in Poland reveals that he had finally faced up to the truth: he would never be part of the charmed circle of Chopin and Sand. That was what had kept him hanging on – and with ever more smoldering bitterness. Now at the end of his financial and moral resources, he had had enough:

*I always relied on one friend who was supposed to open doors for me but who, instead, lied to me while leading me on... I even left Paris for a while to escape his domination – a move that damaged my career still more. I could only begin composing again on my return.*

Fontana was undoubtedly deluded as far his own musical gifts were concerned and did indeed rely too heavily on one influential friend – Chopin – to further his ambitions. What is equally certain is that Chopin, so famously generous to his friends, allowed the man who had conducted his publishing business and performed so many menial tasks for him, to live in poverty and in the hope that, in some way, he would be rewarded. It is inexplicable why Chopin should give another pupil, Adolf Gutmann, every advantage to which Fontana aspired when Gutmann was generally agreed to be a nonentity.

Fontana gave a matinée concert in Paris in March of the following year. Chopin attended with Thalberg. 'The event did not rise above mediocrity at any point,' read one review. Shortly afterwards, Fontana left for America.

Two months earlier, in January 1843, Chopin had had no qualms about appearing with a truly gifted pupil of his. This was the Hungarian prodigy Carl Filtsch who, as an eleven-year-old, had made a great impression on Chopin. Baroness Betty de Rothschild decided to launch the boy's career and, for months, Chopin coached Filtsch in the solo part of his E minor Concerto. In doing so, he imparted something of himself, which he did only very rarely. It was as though Filtsch had been appointed his heir, as though the secret pianistic ingredients were being handed down from father to son. On one occasion, Chopin burst into tears while listening to Filtsch play his music. 'No one in the world will ever play it like him – except myself,' Chopin declared, the only report of him lavishing such praise on any other pianist.

For the glittering concert at the Rothschilds' splendid mansion at 15, Rue Lafitte, Chopin played the orchestral part of the Concerto from memory. One listener recalled: 'I have never heard anything comparable to that first tutti as he played it himself at the piano. To hear them together was the experience of a lifetime.' Carl, as has been noted, died two years later in Vienna, aged fifteen. The cause of death was tuberculosis.

After his customary February bout of illness, Chopin's health improved dramatically with the prescription of a homeopathic remedy. As a result of this treatment he was able to breathe more easily. In mid-May he went to Nohant once more, this time in the company of Sand and Louise Viardot, the eighteen-month-old daughter of Louis and Pauline. Sand had undertaken to look after her while her mother was away on tour. Sand adored young children, Chopin far less so; yet when the toddler took to calling him 'Petit Chopin' she completely disarmed him, even when she 'took to peeing on every carpet'. 'Chopin loves her,' wrote Sand, 'and spends his days kissing her little hands.' This, surely, must have been the inspiration for the sublime **Berceuse, Op. 57** which, with a handful of Mazurkas, was the only music he produced that year.

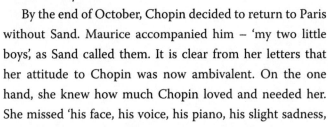

In truth, though, Chopin and Sand were living separate lives under a shared roof. Without guests, Chopin became bored. 'Chopin always wanted Nohant,' Sand later wrote, 'but could never bear Nohant.' Delacroix visited once again; Chopin nipped back to Paris to collect Solange from her boarding school; there were excursions into the countryside on donkeys; the Viardots arrived to collect their infant, their departure prompting Sand to write, 'The house feels so empty and sad without you and our darling Louisette that we can hardly bear it.'

By the end of October, Chopin decided to return to Paris without Sand. Maurice accompanied him – 'my two little boys', as Sand called them. It is clear from her letters that her attitude to Chopin was now ambivalent. On the one hand, she knew how much Chopin loved and needed her. She missed 'his face, his voice, his piano, his slight sadness, and I even miss the heartrending sound of his cough. Poor Angel!' But it was the absence of a sick child she missed – no one to mother – not that of a lover. Chopin had become possessive and jealous. It was this part of the relationship that Sand was slowly beginning to resent, yet she was partly to blame for it. From the beginning she had pampered and mothered him, a role accentuated by his constant ill-health. When things did not go his way, he stamped his foot and screamed. What was she to do? On the one hand, he was a faithful, kind, brilliant, witty,

> On the one hand, he was a faithful, kind, brilliant, witty, considerate man; on the other, 'no temper was more unequal.

considerate man; on the other, as she wrote, 'no temper was more unequal, no imagination more umbrageous and more delirious, no susceptibility more difficult not to irritate, no demand of the heart more impossible to satisfy'. The cause of all this, as she related it in *Histoire de ma vie*, was Chopin's illness.

Among those who turned up uninvited to offer their condolences was Liszt. Chopin had the good grace to receive his old friend cordially.

Despite Sand's imprecations to Maurice to look after Chopin's health and diet, he once again fell ill in November. Sand and Solange returned at the end of that month to find him in a state of nervous depression. Sand ordered some medication. To collect it from the doctor, she sent a new young friend, a promising radical journalist named Louis Blanc.

In February 1844, Chopin was felled again, this time by the influenza epidemic that had hit Paris. Two months later, on 12 May 1844, the news reached him of his father's death in Warsaw nine days earlier. Chopin was stricken with grief and locked himself away in his room, refusing to speak to anyone for days, not even Sand or Franchomme. This was despite the fact that he had not seen his father for nine years; indeed, they had never been particularly close. He had known for some time that his father's health had been failing. He must also have been aware that, since the Tsarist occupation, his parents had been struggling financially; yet he had never offered to help, even at the height of his earning power. Perhaps when his mother wrote in the spring of 1842, asking to borrow 3,000 florins to pay off a personal debt but begging him to keep the matter secret from his father, Chopin did send her money, but his response is not known.

Among those who turned up uninvited to offer their condolences was Liszt. He had seen Chopin's parents in Warsaw during a recent tour and, with typical kindness, had given them box seats for his concert. Mikołaj had written to his son, urging him to make it up with Liszt. Chopin had the good grace to receive his old friend cordially.

Chopin wrote to his brother-in-law Antoni Barcinski, begging to know every detail of his father's last days. Barcinski gave him the usual assurances that the end had been peaceful and that he had died surrounded by his family, but also revealed that he had suffered from a morbid terror of being buried alive. He had extracted from the undertaker a pledge that he would check for any signs of life before being interred. Seeing the forlorn state into which Chopin had fallen, Sand had the inspired idea of inviting Chopin's favourite sister Ludwika and her husband [Josef] Kalasanty Jędrzejewicz to visit them in Paris. She hastened to reassure the visitors that:

> *You are bound to find my dear boy very frail and much altered since you saw him last! But don't be too alarmed about his health. It has continued pretty much the same for the last six years, during which time I have seen him every day. I hope that with time his constitution will be strengthened, but at least I am sure that with a regular life and care it will last as well as anyone else's.*

The couple arrived in Paris on 15 July and, for the next ten days, Chopin devoted himself entirely to showing them the sights, taking them to the opera, and introducing them to the exiled Polish community. It has only comparatively recently come to light that Kalasanty, a dreary former university professor and by this time a judge in Warsaw, was bitterly envious of Chopin's success and fame. Though expected at Nohant on 27 July, he kept his hosts waiting for another two weeks while he investigated all the technological wonders of Paris. When he and Ludwika finally arrived, Chopin was beside himself with joy. 'We've gone mad with happiness,' he wrote to Marie de Rozières, by now reinstated in the inner circle.

Sand and Ludwika hit it off at once. Far from the dour, devout provincial woman that Sand had expected, Ludwika proved to be 'totally superior to her age and her country, and of an angelic character'. Why, Sand asked, could her brother not be more like her? Nohant had worked its magic: Chopin was with the two women he loved, and those two women had established an immediate rapport. Sand was later to describe those few weeks as 'one of the happiest periods in our life'. On 27 August, Chopin and Maurice travelled to Paris to bid farewell to the Jędrzejewiczes and were supposed to return with Pauline Viardot. Young Maurice, however, had other plans: he went off with Viardot to her country house where he proceeded to seduce her.

On 4 September Chopin returned to Nohant alone where he remained for nearly three months, save for a brief trip back to Paris for business and to check up on Grzymała, who had fallen down some stairs and nearly broken his back. This period saw the completion of one of his finest works: the **Sonata No. 3 in B minor**, Op. 58, a work on which, interestingly, he labored while teaching the sixteen-year-old Solange a Beethoven sonata. As usual, Chopin's contentment was tempered by melancholy. On 18 September he wrote to his sister from Nohant:

> Often, when I come in, I look to see if there is anything left of you, and I see only the same place by the couch, where we drank our chocolate, and the drawings that Kalasanty copied. More of you has remained in my room; on the table

**CD 2**
track 10
www.naxosbooks.com

Sand was later to describe those few weeks as 'one of the happiest periods in our life'.

*lies your embroidery – that slipper – folded inside an English blotter, and on the piano a tiny pencil, which was in your pocketbook...*

On 28 November he returned to Paris to face a bitterly cold winter and another season of teaching. Letters to Sand, who had remained at Nohant, are signed off with 'Your most fossilized fossil', 'Always yours, older than ever; very, extremely, incredibly old...', 'Your mummified ancient', as he wrapped himself in a heavy overcoat and three layers of flannel underclothes to ward off the freezing conditions. Pupils often found him perfectly dressed at eight in the morning but so weak that the lesson had to be conducted from the sofa. Karl Halle and Franchomme called one day to find him 'hardly able to move, bent like a half-opened knife and evidently in great pain'. Yet, as soon as he sat at the piano and began playing, 'his body gradually resumed its normal position, the spirit having mastered the flesh'.

To the chores formerly undertaken by Fontana, Chopin assigned Marie de Rozières and Franchomme, the former for his domestic errands and the latter for his professional requirements. In letters from Nohant, Chopin instructed his friend how to negotiate with his publishers – and with generally more concern than he had shown Fontana, notwithstanding the 500 francs he borrowed at this time from Franchomme. Chopin and money soon parted company and he needed to obtain the highest possible prices for his music to keep his extravagant lifestyle afloat. But a man of his eminence and wealth should never have had to ask for money from his cellist friend with a wife and young family to support. Sand, on the other hand, by dint of fearsome hard work, was earning a steady income, with instalments of her latest novel *Isidora*, about to appear in

*La Revue Indépendente* (a journal she had helped to found) and a two-book contract in Louis Blanc's newly founded newspaper *La Reforme*, the first of which would be *The Miller of Angibault.*

Two new pupils joined the roster at this point, both of whom would play an important role in the last few years of Chopin's life. These were the Scottish heiress Miss Jane Wilhelmina Stirling, a forty-year-old spinster of unremarkable ability, and Princess Marcelina Czartoryska. The latter, born Princess Radziwiłł, had married Alexander Czartoryski, nephew of Prince Adam. Marcelina was a genuinely talented pianist who had studied under Czerny in Vienna. With her musical gifts, striking looks and aristocratic background, Chopin was immediately drawn to her. Marcelina in turn drew Chopin into her privileged world. The center of this was the luxurious Hôtel Lambert on the Île Saint-Louis which was home to a kind of Polish court in exile. Here, several generations and branches of the Czartoryski and Radziwiłł families lived in splendor in the various apartments of the huge building.

During the spring of 1845, Chopin played only here and at the homes of friends – with one exception. In April, Louis Blanc appeared bearing the last request of a friend and colleague, the republican journalist Godefroi Cavaignac, that Chopin might play to him on his deathbed. Chopin scarcely knew Cavaignac and had no sympathies with his politics, but he willingly went round and played to him for hours, gratified that his music had consoled the dying man's last moments. He did not know that Blanc had embarked on a brief affair with George Sand.

# Chapter 12

## A Time of Turmoil, 1846–1847

# A Time of Turmoil, 1846–1847

As Chopin and Sand drove down to Nohant in Chopin's new carriage on 12 June 1845, there was no hint of the upheaval that was shortly to engulf them. Their mother–son relationship had mellowed into one of routine and familiarity even if their life philosophies remained diametrically opposed. Chopin's conservative values, his belief in the governing right of the aristocracy and the doctrine of the Roman Catholic Church (even if his marital status put him outside its bounds) was quite at odds with Sand's socialism, reforming zeal and belief in religious freedom. But it was Maurice and Solange who eventually pushed them apart irrevocably.

Maurice was now twenty-two and increasingly unwilling to accept Chopin's place in his mother's affections and his position in the household. The young master began to assert himself and play his role in the full confidence of being his mother's favorite. The first indication of this was when he dismissed Chopin's dim but loyal manservant Jan, the only member of the Nohant household to whom Chopin could speak in his native tongue. He persuaded his mother to get rid of the family's gardener who had been at Nohant since

Aurore Dupin, Sand's grandmother, had lived there. The new servants would now answer to him. Nohant was his domain. Pauline Viardot was his lover. Maurice had come of age.

Solange, five years younger than her brother, had had few of Maurice's advantages. Named after the patron saint of Bourges, capital of Berry, Solange was an unwanted child, the result of a brief liaison between Sand and Stéphane Ajasson de Gransgane,

Solange's tear-sodden letters pleading for her mother's love and attention went largely unnoticed.

her neighbor and childhood friend. Although given Casimir Dudevant's name, Solange had seen little of him, the man she had always known as her father. Before she was three, Sand described her little illegitimate offspring as 'fat and lazy'. It was an antipathy towards Solange that continued throughout her life. Beaten by the servants at Nohant while Sand was canoodling with Alfred de Musset in Venice, Solange was then despatched to a boarding school in Paris when she was just six.

Casimir Dudevant had been forbidden by Sand from taking Solange out on holidays. In the summer of 1837, while Sand was at Nohant, Dudevant abducted Solange from there amid the hysterical screams of servants and her governess, and took her off to Gascony. In return, Sand mounted her own kidnapping but with the help of the Gascon authorities, who surrounded Dudevant's home in the dead of night and demanded that Solange be handed back to her mother. (The official who oversaw this drama, incidentally, was the man who would shortly redesign Paris and turn it into the city of boulevards, parks and bridges that we know today, Georges Haussmann.)

Sand's successful mission instilled in the nine-year-old a sense of her mother's omnipotence. Despite this, Solange's tear-sodden letters pleading for her mother's love and attention went largely unnoticed. When Sand advertised for a tutor, she warned, 'the girl is a demon who requires constant surveillance morally, everywhere and at all times'. When Chopin entered her troubled life, he not only provided calm, constancy and heavenly music on the piano but was able to inspire in Solange a feeling of trust. He gave her what she so badly needed: praise and affection. Their relationship developed into an empathy that went far deeper than the pragmatic demands of a stepfather and stepdaughter, one which practically excluded George Sand and Maurice.

It was ironic, then, that just at a time when seventeen-year-old Solange was enjoying happier relations with her mother than ever before, George Sand turned her world upside down by 'adopting' another daughter. On 10 September, Maurice returned from Paris with Augustine Marie Brault – Titine. Titine was the twenty-one-year-old daughter of Joseph Brault, a cousin of Sand, and was said to be prettier and cleverer than Solange but with the accent and manners of the Parisian working-class. Sand, with all her mothering and socialist credentials on full display, had volunteered to take her in, educate her, and make something of the girl. Titine was made part of the family.

Chopin detested her. She was coarse, ill-bred and yet gave herself the airs and graces of a social equal. It is not hard to guess Solange's reaction. For this vulgar little tart to be preferred to her meant only one thing: escape. Find a husband and escape.

On the surface, the two sides now ranged against each other cohabited peaceably enough. When Chopin made a brief trip to Paris in the middle of September, he and Sand wrote to each other every day. One of the very few of her surviving letters to him was written at this time. 'Love me, my dearest angel,' it ends, 'my dearest happiness, I love you.' But a planned trip to Italy for a year in the sun never materialized. Maurice put a stop to that. He preferred the country, Chopin told Ludwika, 'and so we didn't go.'

With these tensions, his morbid concerns over his health, and a general depressing inertia, Chopin had lost his appetite for composing. He had completed just three new Mazurkas (Op. 59) by July. Yet the small number of works he produced illustrate his determination to experiment and develop: from this period come the ethereal **Barcarolle**, the Cello Sonata (inspired, once again, by his friendship with Franchomme), and the adventurous Polonaise-Fantaisie, a far cry from the polonaises of his youth and even the mature works in this form from the late 1830s and early 1840s.

The winter in Paris passed uneventfully. Succumbing to his annual bout of flu, Chopin's attacks of morning coughing became more extended, often leaving him too weak to walk. When he did venture out into the freezing air, he found it difficult to breathe. He socialized rarely, though he travelled to Tours in April to stay with Franchomme and his family. At the end of May 1846, he returned to Nohant for what would be his last summer there.

Early in 1846, Sand had embarked in earnest on a new novel, though it is fairly certain that she had already been working on it for at least a year. A contract had been signed for its serialization to run in *Le Courier Français* from the last week of June to the end of July. She left Paris ahead of Chopin on 5 May. By the time Chopin arrived at Nohant, she had rewritten and revised the entire book, 'a labor without precedent in her work', according to Benita Eisler. The book was called *Lucrezia Floriani*, the story of two mismatched lovers. Lucrezia is a famous actress and playwright who retires with her children at the peak of her success to a remote lake in the north of Italy. She has never married, her affairs producing the happy outcome of four children by different fathers.

Into this secluded paradise come two travellers: an old admirer, Count Salvator Albani, and his closest friend, Prince Karol de Roswald. The Prince, delicate, melancholy, virginal, falls ill. Lucrezia nurses him back to health, by which time the two have fallen in love. After a period of idyllic bliss the Prince's suffocating passion, jealousy and personal philosophies begin to torment her. 'Of all angers, of all vengeances, the darkest, the most atrocious and the most agonizing is the one which remains cold and polite,' Sand wrote in the character of Lucrezia:

> I prefer the coarseness of the jealous peasant who beats his wife to the delicacy of the prince who rends his mistress's heart without turning a hair. I prefer the child who scratches and bites to the one who sulks in silence. By all means, let us lose our tempers, be violent, ill-bred, let us insult one another, break mirrors and clocks! It would be absurd but it would not prove we hate one another. Whereas, if we turn our backs on each other very politely as we leave, uttering a bitter and contemptuous word, we are doomed, and no matter what we do to be reconciled we will be driven farther and farther apart.

In the end, Lucrezia attempts to flee her captor and dies of a stroke – or was it mental exhaustion? Delacroix was invited down to Nohant with other house guests. During their stay, Sand read aloud some of the installments:

> As [Karol] was polite and reserved in the extreme, nobody could even suspect what was going on inside him. The more exasperated he was, the cooler he grew, and one could only

*judge the degree of his fury by icy contempt. It was then that he was truly unbearable... Then he would find wit, a false and brilliant wit, in order to torture those he loved. He would become supercilious, stiff, precious and aloof. He seemed to nibble playfully, yet inflicting wounds which penetrated to the depths of one's soul. Or else, if he lacked the courage to contradict and mock, he would wrap himself in disdainful silence, sulking in a pathetic manner.*

Delacroix sat open-mouthed 'in agony' as 'victim and executioner' sat perfectly at ease, Chopin hardly stopping in his admiring comments as Sand proceeded to narrate her thinly concealed account of their relationship. At midnight, Chopin suggested that Delacroix accompany him upstairs. The painter could barely wait to discover Chopin's real reaction to the book. Surely he had been putting on a performance as he heard this public dissection of him? Delacroix was astonished at Chopin's reaction. He had not been pretending at all. 'He hadn't understood a single word.'

Why did Sand write such a novel? was it a warning to Chopin? If so, it singularly failed. Chopin seemed not the least concerned.

Karol (a German prince with a Polish name) is six years younger than Lucrezia (the same age difference as between Chopin and Sand); the heroine is small, plump and dark with a string of previous lovers; Karol experiences hallucinations reminiscent of Chopin's on Majorca; Lucrezia scorns Karol's religious beliefs and political philosophy... The similarities between the novelized lives of Lucrezia Floriani and Prince Karol and those of Chopin and Sand are so exact at times that many passages in the novel were later quoted by Sand in her autobiography. Liszt even used passages from *Lucrezia* for his own biography of Chopin without reference to or explanation of their provenance.

Why did Sand write such a novel? To earn money, of course, but was it also a warning to Chopin? If so, it singularly failed. Despite all Paris buzzing with excitement at each new installment, Chopin seemed not the least concerned by their contents. Whether or not the process of writing the book was a cathartic experience for Sand, she vehemently denied that the novel had any connection with the realities of her own life. If Lucrezia Floriani proved anything it was that the two real-life protagonists were no longer able to understand what the other needed. Was it mere coincidence that after the appearance of the book everything went terribly wrong?

'I lost my temper, which gave me the courage to tell him a few home truths and to threaten to get sick of him. Since then he has been sensible.

Towards the end of June 1846, Chopin and Maurice had an argument over some domestic matter. For the first time, Sand took her son's side. Chopin was dumbfounded. Sand confided in Marie de Rozières: 'I lost my temper, which gave me the courage to tell him a few home truths and to threaten to get sick of him. Since then he has been sensible, and you know how sweet, excellent, admirable he is when he is not mad.'

By the end of the summer, Titine and Maurice were having an affair while Solange had become engaged to Fernand de Préaulx, a tall, bearded young man from a neighboring family of the nobility.

Chopin returned to Paris alone on 11 November, clearly glad to be back teaching and enjoying the company of his old circle – Grzymała, Franchomme, Delacroix, Charlotte Marliani (his neighbor in the Square d'Orléans) and Delfina Potocka, newly returned to Paris. Sand and he kept in touch by letter until the beginning of February when Sand, Solange, Titine and Fernand arrived back in the capital to settle the legal arrangements of the forthcoming nuptials.

Eleven days later, on Ash Wednesday, Chopin held a

soirée at his apartment. In the presence of Sand, Delacroix, Grzymała, Baron and Baroness Rothschild, Delfina Potocka, and Prince and Princess Czartoryski, Chopin and Franchomme gave the first performance of the Cello Sonata. The following day, Sand and her daughter visited the studio of the sculptor Jean-Baptiste Auguste Clésinger, to whom Sand had been introduced a few days previously at the Marlianis'. Clésinger was then thirty-three, well-built, ruggedly handsome, with the swagger of the cavalryman that he had once been. Clésinger had requested several times to make a bust of the novelist. Sand assented. In addition, it was agreed that he should also make one of Solange to commemorate her marriage. Over the next few days, a succession of gifts arrived at the Square d'Orléans – flowers, delicacies, even a puppy – and within a matter of weeks Clésinger had seduced Solange. The wedding to Fernand was off.

Sand heard all the warnings but listened to no one.

Chopin was saddened ('I'm sorry for the boy, who is decent and loving, but I suppose it's better before than after the wedding') and began to make enquiries about Clésinger. What he discovered horrified him. The sculptor was in debt to the tune of hundreds of thousands of francs, he was a heavy drinker, rarely delivered his commissions, and was known to be violent towards his mistress. Though pregnant, she had been unceremoniously discarded as soon as Solange and her well-to-do mother entered his life. The Marlianis warned Sand of his bad character. Delacroix disliked him intensely. Chopin, not surprisingly, loathed him. 'I don't give them a year after their first child,' he wrote to Ludwika, 'and the mother will have to pay the debts.'

Sand heard all the warnings but listened to no one. She was enchanted by this 'second Michelangelo'. It was as if she, too, had been physically seduced by the domineering, vigorous Clésinger, so different from the other men in her life. She returned to Nohant with her 'two girls' on 6 April, followed a week later by Clésinger who presented her with an ultimatum: agree to the marriage in twenty-four hours and secure the permission of Baron Dudevant. Sand was enthralled by such boldness and eagerly set in motion all the arrangements for her daughter's marriage to this paragon – without the knowledge of Chopin. 'It does not concern him,' wrote Sand to Maurice, 'and when once the Rubicon has been crossed the "ifs" and "buts" only do harm.' In another letter to Grzymała, she affirmed that 'his interference in the affairs of my family would mean total loss of all my dignity and love both from and towards my children.'

The first Chopin knew of Solange's wedding day was an announcement in a Paris newspaper on 4 May. As Benita Eisler observes, 'For nine years – since Solange was nine years old – he had shared their lives. Now he was being treated like one of the aged domestics, recently dismissed after years of service.' It must have wounded Chopin deeply. 'God support you always in your purpose and your deeds,' he managed to write to Solange on 15 May. 'Be happy and serene. Your completely devoted Ch.'

A few days later, Solange married Clésinger. Barely a week later, Titine announced her engagement to Théodore Rousseau, a young painter friend of Maurice. The honeymooners returned to Paris in late June and Clésinger wasted no time in revealing his true colors. When asked by Sand to rein in the lavish amounts he was already spending on entertainment, flowers and servants, Clésinger roundly abused her, threatening to end the marriage if she refused to subsidize their lifestyle. Sand's response was to invite them down to Nohant with Maurice and Titine in the hope that its tranquil atmosphere might have a calming effect on her new son-in-law.

For her marriage dowry, Solange had been given a valuable Paris property by her mother, intended to provide the couple with an income from its rent. At Nohant, she learned that Titine was to have a cash settlement as her dowry. Solange and Clésinger were furious and demanded a family conference in the front hall of the house. They insisted that Sand arrange to mortgage Nohant in order to provide an allowance, with payments beginning at once. Sand refused, whereupon Solange accused Maurice of seducing Titine – when Rousseau learned of this he promptly broke off the engagement – and her mother of having an affair with another of Maurice's friends. Maurice attempted to punch Clésinger who replied by threatening to hit him with a hammer. Sand intervened, slapping Clésinger in the face; he promptly punched her in the chest. Maurice had meanwhile rushed to his room and returned with a loaded pistol.

George Sand ordered Solange and Clésinger from Nohant, forbidding them from ever returning and saying that she never wanted to see either of them again.

Solange, now in the early stages of pregnancy, wrote at once to Chopin from nearby La Châtre, saying that she was ill and asking him for the loan of his carriage for her return journey to Paris:

*Please answer immediately... I have left Nohant forever, after the most horrible scenes by my mother. <u>Wait for me, I beg you, before leaving Paris.</u> I need to see you urgently. I was positively refused your carriage, so if you wish me to use it, send me a note with your permission which I can then send on to Nohant.*

Knowing nothing of the events at Nohant, Chopin, in all innocence, replied to Solange with customary concern and generosity. His undated letter reads: 'I am much grieved to know that you are ill. I hasten to place my carriage at your service. I have written to this effect to your Mother. Take care of yourself. Your old friend Ch.'

Sand reacted with fury at this apparent betrayal. Chopin had sided with Solange against her. She winged off a long letter to him which left him distraught. We only know part of its contents from Delacroix to whom Chopin read it aloud. The actual document is now lost (or was destroyed by Chopin). In it, Sand decreed that Chopin could only return to Nohant if he promised never to see Solange and Clésinger again, and never mention her daughter's name in her presence. Delacroix noted sagaciously in his diary:

> One has to admit... that [the letter] is atrocious. Cruel passions and long pent-up impatience erupt in it, and by a contrast which would be amusing if it did not touch on such a tragic subject, the author from time to time takes over from the woman and launches into tirades which look as though they are borrowed from a novel or a philosophical homily.

Sand reacted with fury at this apparent betrayal. Chopin had sided with Solange against her.

Chopin did not reply for ten days, no doubt hoping that this was a storm in a teacup and that all would soon be tranquil again. When he did, his polite, level-headed judgement left George Sand seething. Clésinger meant nothing to him, he wrote, but as to Solange, 'she can never be a matter of indifference to me,' reminding her that he had often interceded on behalf of both her children, without preference, when the need had arisen. 'Surely,' he challenged, 'you are fated to always love them, because a mother's feelings are the only ones that never change. Troubles can disguise but never destroy them.' Hitting home, he ventured:

'Your pain must be overpowering indeed to harden your heart against your child to the point of refusing even to hear her name, and on the threshold of her life as a woman, a time more than any other when her condition requires a mother's care.' Excusing himself from mentioning any matters concerning himself in the circumstances, he finished: 'Time will act. I shall wait, <u>always the same</u>, Your wholly devoted, Ch.'

*George Sand*

This, fumed Sand, from the man whose opinion over Solange's marriage had not been sought, who lived in a world of his own and knew nothing of human life, and who was now inferring that the marriage to Clésinger was her fault and questioning her famed maternal instincts: George Sand's reaction was as illogical and self-deceiving as it was dramatic and accusatory. To anyone who would listen, she now ranted her realization that all along Chopin had been in love not with her but with Solange; that Chopin's passion for her had been fueled by hatred; that she had been betrayed first by her daughter and now by Chopin. In a letter dated 28 June 1847, she wrote:

*Look after her, since it is to her that you think you should devote yourself... I shall not hold it against you... It is enough to be fooled and made a victim. I forgive you and will not address any reproaches to you, since your confession is sincere. It surprised me a little, but since you feel more at ease and freer now, I shall not suffer from this volte face. Goodbye, my friend, may you be rapidly cured of your malady, as I believe you will… and I shall thank God for this strange denouement to nine years of exclusive friendship – Give me news of yourself sometimes. It is pointless to ever come back on the rest.*

> But there was to be no reconciliation – it was far too late for that. And that was the last he ever saw of George Sand.

And that was that. It was the last letter that passed between them. Their friends looked on aghast. The Viardots protested to her that she had thoroughly misrepresented Chopin's role in the whole affair, that he was 'as kind, as devoted as ever – adoring you always, rejoicing only in your joy, afflicted only by your suffering'. But there was to be no reconciliation – it was far too late for that. The next time Chopin met George Sand was nearly nine months later. On 3 March 1848, he heard from Solange the joyful news of the birth of a baby girl. The following day he bumped into Sand in the vestibule of the Marliani house. Had she heard any news of Solange, he enquired?

*'A week ago,' she replied. 'You have heard nothing yesterday, or the day before?' 'No.' 'Then I can tell you that you are a grandmother; Solange has a daughter, and I am very glad that I am able to be the first to give you this news.' I bowed and went downstairs.*

And that was the last he ever saw of George Sand. Sadly, the little girl, Jeanne-Gabrielle Clésinger, lived for only five days.

Later, Sand, with the help of Maurice, destroyed almost all the correspondence between herself and Chopin. Chopin, it was discovered, had kept all Sand's letters to him, preserving a lock of her hair in the back of his diary, and carrying everywhere with him until his death the first note that he had received from her.

In a long letter to his sister at Christmas, 1847, Chopin looked back on the course of events with sanguine objectivity. After revealing that Solange's room at Nohant had been converted into a theatre and her boudoir into a dressing-room for actors, he told Ludwika that:

*The mother appears to be more bitter against her son-in-law than against her daughter; yet in the famous letter to me she wrote that her son-in-law is not bad; it is only her daughter who makes him so. It seems as if she wanted, at one stroke, to get rid of her daughter and me, because we were inconvenient; she will correspond with her daughter; so her maternal heart, which cannot do without some news of her child, will be quieted, and with that she can stifle her conscience… A strange creature, with all her intellect! Some kind of frenzy has come upon her; she harrows up her own life, she harrows up her daughter's life; with her son too it will end badly; I predict and could swear to it. For her own justification she longs to find something against those who care for her, who have never done her any discourtesy, but whom she cannot bear to see about her, because they are mirrors of her conscience… I do not regret that I helped her through the eight most difficult years of her life: the years when her daughter was growing up and her son living with his mother; I do not regret what I have suffered; but I am sorry that the daughter, that carefully over-cultivated plant, sheltered from so many storms, has been broken in her mother's hand by a carelessness and levity pardonable perhaps in a woman in her twenties, but not one in her forties. What has been and no longer is, leaves no trace in the register. When, some day, Mme S. thinks the matter over she can have only kind memories of me in her soul. Meanwhile she is now in the strangest paroxysm of motherhood, playing the part of a more just and better mother than she really is: and that is a fever for which there is no remedy in the case of heads with such an imagination, when they have entered into such a quagmire.*

Grzymała had lost his fortune. The Marlianis were in the process of separating. Chopin's friend Stefan Witwicki, the poet, had died, as had Antoni Wodziński, the feckless brother of Chopin's erstwhile love, Maria. In November came news of Mendelssohn's death. 'All Paris is ill,' Chopin wrote to Solange at the end of November. 'The weather is frightful and you do well to be under a clear sky. This <u>hateful year</u> must <u>end</u>.'

# Chapter 13

## London and Scotland, 1848

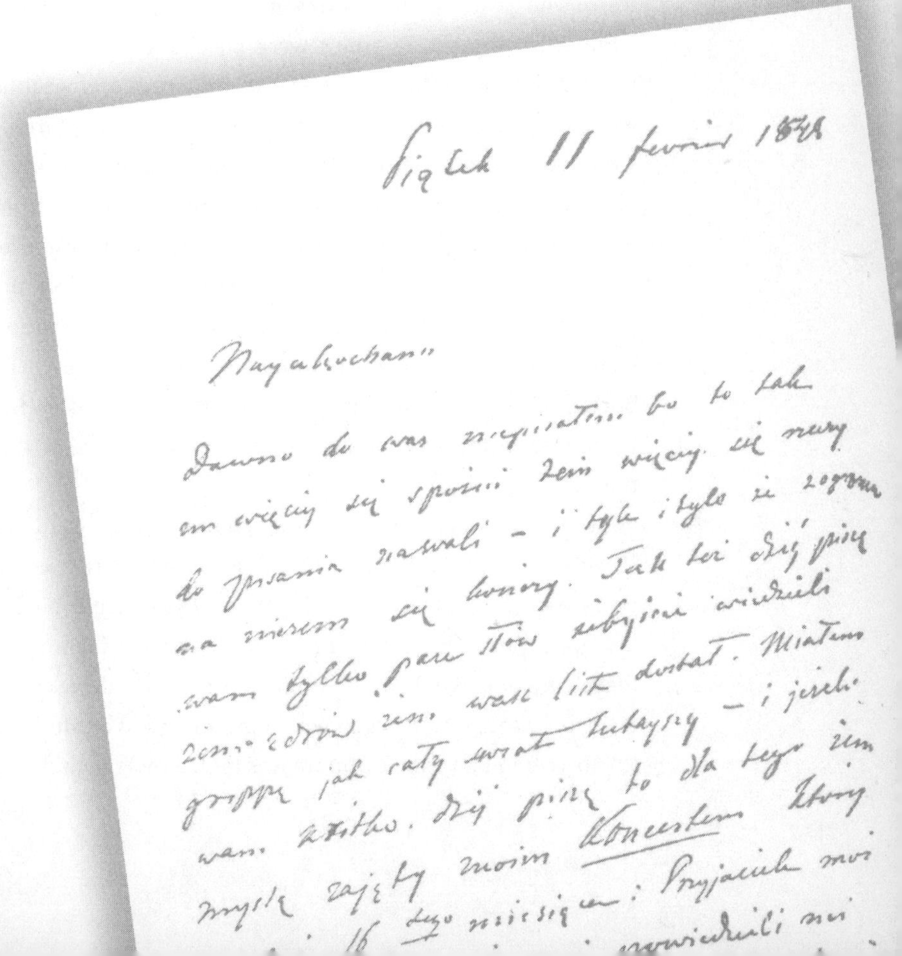
Piątek 11 février 1848

Najukochańsi

# London and Scotland, 1848

1848: the Year of Revolutions. At its dawn, Chopin found himself living on his own and on a much reduced income. His health had impelled him to decrease the number of lessons he gave, and money was in increasingly short supply. Among his remaining pupils were Elise Gavard (to whom Chopin dedicated the Berceuse), the influential and wealthy Russian Princess Obreskoff, Jane Stirling, and the glorious Countess Maria Kalergis – Warsaw-born, twenty-five years old, stunningly attractive, six feet tall, already divorced from her Russian diplomat husband, and a talented pianist. She had enjoyed affairs with Liszt, Musset, Gautier and the future Napoleon III, earning her the immortal description from Heine: 'a Pantheon in which so many great men lie buried'. Chopin enjoyed teaching her; she lifted his spirits as he waited to see what course his life would take at this point.

The next major event was a concert, once again in Pleyel's salon where Chopin had first played nearly twenty years earlier. Wednesday 16 February 1848 would be his last appearance in Paris as a pianist. Organized for him by Pleyel and Auguste Léo, the event was sold out three times over. The programme began with a performance of Mozart's Piano Trio in E in which Chopin was joined by Franchomme

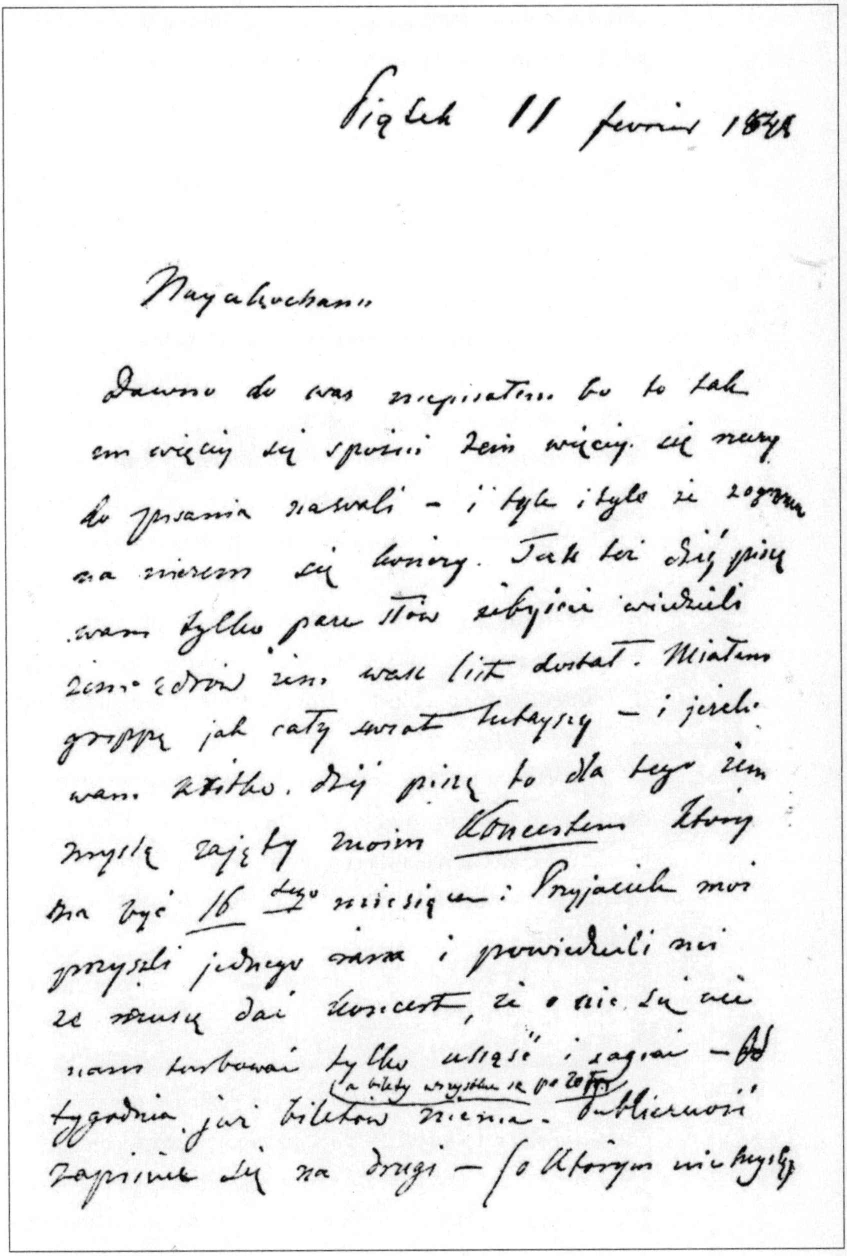

Piątek 11 fevrier 1848

Najukochańsi

Dawno do was nie pisałem bo to tak czem więcej się spóźni tem więcej się nazbiera do pisania nawali — i tyle i tyle że rozum na niczem się kończy. Tak też dziś piszę wam tylko parę słów żebyście wiedzieli żem zdrów żem wasz list dostał. Miałem grippę jak cały świat tutejszy — i jeśli wam krótko dziś piszę to dla tego żem wszystek zajęty moim Koncertem który ma być 16tego miesiąca. Przyjaciele moi przyszli jednego rana i powiedzieli mi że muszę dać koncert, że o nic się nie mam starać tylko usiąść i zagrać — Od tygodnia już biletów niema (a bilety wszystkie są po 20 fr). Publiczność zapisuje się na drugi — o którym nie myślę

*Letter from Chopin to his family, 11 February 1848*

and the violinist Jean-Delphine Allard. Interspersed between some soprano solos sung by a Mlle Molina di Mondi, Chopin played a Nocturne, the Barcarolle, the Berceuse and some Études.

For the second part of the concert, Franchomme and he launched into the second movement (Scherzo) of the Cello Sonata. Why it was decided to omit the first movement of a work being given its public premiere remains a matter of speculation. Chopin had been ill the week before the concert and he certainly would have found the exacting ten minutes of the Allegro moderato physically taxing. He protested that he had not had time to rehearse it sufficiently. But there was something about its opening theme that clearly had a special significance for him. On his deathbed, he asked Franchomme to play it but could not bear to hear more than the opening bars. Were its associations with Nohant simply too painful to put on public display? After an aria by Meyerbeer, Chopin concluded with a selection of Preludes, Mazurkas and Waltzes.

The financial and critical success of the evening encouraged Chopin to give a further concert on 10 March, but on 22 February, six days after his triumph, the so-called February Revolution broke out. Chopin wrote to Solange on 3 March:

> Paris is quiet, from fear. Everyone is enrolled. Everyone is in the national guard. The shops are open, but no buyers. The foreigners are waiting with their passports for the ruined railways to be repaired. Factions are beginning to form.

The people of Paris, angry at the corrupt and autocratic government, had finally risen up against Louis Philippe's July Monarchy with riots ignited by his ban on a meeting for franchise reform. (Louis Philippe fled to England where he died two years later.) In a second Parisian insurrection in June, the new left-wing government, 'the Second Republic', was suppressed; and by the end of the year, Louis Napoleon, the future Napoleon III, was elected President of what would become in 1852 the Second Empire.

Almost overnight, Chopin's society was swept away to be replaced by the beginnings of the new order that George Sand had championed. The last thing people were concerned about was art, literature or music. Piano pupils vanished, to be replaced only by uncertainty, the threat of physical danger, and insecurity. Jane Stirling urged Chopin to come to Britain. There were concerts to be played there, money to be earned, the season to be enjoyed – and she would make all the arrangements for him.

On 19 April Chopin crossed the Channel for only the second time in his life, arriving in London the following day. In his temporary rooms at 10 Bentinck Street, off Cavendish Square, he found Jane Stirling was as good as her word, even down to the detail of supplying notepaper embossed with his monogram and his favourite French cocoa for hot chocolate. A week later he moved into a lavishly furnished apartment at 48 Dover Street, off Piccadilly, large enough to accommodate not only his Pleyel but also the Érard and Broadwood which their respective makers insisted on lending to him.

> Almost overnight, Chopin's society was swept away to be replaced by the beginnings of the new order that George Sand had championed.

He soon found himself surrounded by old friends, relatives and acquaintances of those he had taught in Paris, and a motley selection of amateurs all desperate to be considered 'pupils of Chopin'. His fee was a guinea a lesson. As his rooms cost forty guineas a month, he needed every pupil he could get. He was advised to charge a fee of twenty guineas (much lower than Paris) when invited to play at matinées in the homes of the aristocracy. But competition was fierce. He was not the only foreign musician who had escaped to London. Berlioz, one of those biding his time there, asked in his diary, 'Will the British capital be able to maintain so many exiles?' Also there were Thalberg ('engaged for 12 concerts', Chopin noted), Hallé, Pauline Viardot, and the soprano Jenny Lind – the legendary 'Swedish Nightingale'. Kalkbrenner had recently left, having failed to make a mark.

Chopin, somewhat rashly, turned down the offer to play one of his Concertos for the prestigious Philharmonic Society. The lack of rehearsal time made it impractical for the perfectionist (he had heard the pianist Emile Prudent play his own B flat major Concerto and 'it was a fiasco') and besides he was concerned that he no longer had the physical strength to project the solo part above an orchestra, especially one of which he had no high opinion. 'I prefer not to try, for it may come to nothing,' he wrote to Grzymała. The Philharmonic promoter, none too pleased at this unaccustomed rejection, happened also to be responsible for arranging concerts at the Court.

Nothing daunted, Chopin was delighted to play before Her Majesty – not at Buckingham Palace but at (the much grander) Stafford House, now Lancaster House, St James's, at that time the home of the Duke and Duchess of Sutherland. The occasion was the christening of the Duchess's newest daughter to whom Queen Victoria was to stand as godmother. In this magnificent setting were eighty bejewelled, be-gartered dignitaries, including Prince Albert, the future Wilhelm I of Prussia, and the Duke of Wellington. They heard three fashionable Italian singers: (Giovanni) Mario, Luigi Lablache and Antonio Tamburini. Chopin followed them with some short pieces of his own, and then in a Mozart duet (the Variations in G major) with the German-born English pianist and composer Julius Benedict. The Queen chatted with him (twice) but if he was hoping to be invited to play at the Palace or Windsor Castle he was to be disappointed. He was not to know that the Queen noted in her diary that evening: 'There was some pretty music, good Lablache, Mario and Tamburini singing, and some pianists playing'.

> The English attitude to pianists in particular and music in general was very different from the one he had enjoyed and so long taken for granted in Paris.

The English attitude to pianists in particular and music in general was very different from the one he had enjoyed and so long taken for granted in Paris. At the beginning of June, he wrote to Grzymała with his customary perspicacity on his situation. He was spitting up blood ('often in the morning I think I'm going to cough up my very soul'), worrying about money, and wondering if he had the physical strength for the hectic round of socializing to which he was being subjected:

> *My kind Scottish ladies [Jane Stirling and her sister Mrs Katherine Erskine] show me a great deal of friendliness here... but they are used to jigging about and dragging round London all day long with visiting-cards, and I'm only half alive. After three or four hours of jolting in a carriage, it's as if I had travelled from Paris to Boulogne. [...] I am introduced, and don't know to whom, and am not in London at all. 20 years in Poland, 17 in Paris; no wonder I'm not brilliant here, especially as I don't know the language.*

Money was harder to come by and the only way to make an impact on the 'bourgeois class' was 'to do something startling, mechanical, of which I am not capable. The upper world...[is] so much distracted by thousands of things, so surrounded by the boredom of conventionalities, that it is all one to them whether music is good or bad, since they have to hear it from morning till night.' It is salutary to realize that even in the nineteenth century there was the curse of muzak.

Two private concerts did make him some much-needed money (about £300). The first on 23 June was at the Eaton Place home of Adelaide Sartoris, a celebrated singer and the daughter of the famous actor Charles Kemble. Present among the great and good were Thackeray and Carlyle. Chopin shared the programme with the tenor Mario. The second, on 7 July, was less successful. It was held in Lord Falmouth's mansion in St James's Square where Chopin appeared with Pauline Viardot. She sang, among other things, a selection of her own settings of Chopin's Mazurkas.

The end of July was also the end of the season in London, the time when the aristocracy followed the royal family to Scotland for their holidays and a spot of shooting. Chopin was, once more, abandoned but Jane Stirling came to his rescue again, much against his wishes. If George Sand had mothered him, Jane Stirling smothered him. Ironically, it was she who did more than anybody to undermine Chopin's precarious health over the next few months. An invitation arrived from her brother-in-law Lord Torpichen for Chopin to stay at his home, Calder House, a short distance from Edinburgh. At the beginning of August, Chopin took the train to the Scottish capital – 407 miles away, he noted, travelling via Birmingham and Carlisle on a journey that took twelve hours.

Chopin was vastly impressed by Edinburgh ('the exquisite city' as he described it) and Calder House, the fourteenth-century home of the Sandiwells of Torpichen. With its eight-foot-thick walls, endless corridors of ancestral portraits and resident ghost, his room, he wrote, had 'the most beautiful view imaginable – towards Stirling, beyond Glasgow, and to the north fine scenery... there is nothing I can think of that does not at once appear: even the Parisian newspapers are brought to me every day.'

Yet in the same letter to his family it is clear that he was thoroughly unsettled. After all the financial success of the last eighteen years, he could now hardly make ends meet. He had to give concerts to raise money but these tortured and exhausted him. 'The English... think only in terms of pounds; they like art because it is a luxury.' Those he gave made little impression on the critics. He travelled to Manchester at the end of August where he played before one of the largest audiences of his career: 1,200 people. The *Manchester Guardian* noted that the pianist mounted the platform 'with an almost painful air of feebleness in his appearance and gait' while the Irish pianist George Osborne, who had joined Chopin in the performance of Kalkbrenner's Polonaise, Introduction and March in Paris back in 1832, felt that 'his playing was too delicate to create enthusiasm', adding the heart-breaking admission that 'I felt truly sorry for him'.

> After all the financial success of the last eighteen years, he could now hardly make ends meet. He had to give concerts to raise money but these tortured and exhausted him.

With a substantial fee in his pocket, Chopin returned to Edinburgh where he stayed at the home of a fellow Pole, Dr Lyszczynski, before going on to Johnstone Castle, just outside Glasgow. Chopin had taught the wife of its owner, Ludovic Houstoun, who was Jane Stirling's brother-in-law. The strain of travelling, his feeble health, and the incessant socializing among people with whom he had little in common were taking their toll. Julian Fontana, returned from America, had resurfaced in Chopin's life. The ailing man confessed to him: 'I can hardly get my breath... I am just about ready to give up the ghost... I am vegetating, patiently waiting for the winter, dreaming now of home, now of Rome, now of joy, now of grief.'

To Grzymała on 4 September:

> *I am cross and depressed, and people here bore me with their excessive attentions. I can't breathe; I can't work; I feel alone, alone, alone, although I am surrounded... They are dear people, kind and very considerate to me. There are a whole lot of ladies, 70- to 80-year-old lords, but no young folk: they are all out shooting.*

He gave a further concert in Glasgow on 27 September, his spirits lifted by the presence of the Czartoryskis in the audience, though takings were slim. Then on to Keir House, which had been the ancestral seat of the Stirlings of Keir since the fifteenth century. Next, his besotted pupil whisked him off to Stirling Castle itself, grandest of all Scottish castles. Another letter to Grzymała:

**They are stifling me out of courtesy, and out of the same courtesy I don't refuse them.**

> *I am weaker, I can't compose anything... The whole morning till 2 o'clock I am fit for nothing now; and then when I dress, everything strains me, and I gasp that way till dinner time. Afterwards one has to sit two hours at table with the men, look at them talking and listen to them drinking. I am bored to death... They are stifling me out of courtesy, and out of the same courtesy I don't refuse them.*

He came back to Edinburgh, once more staying with Dr Lyszczynski, and gave another concert, which was again organized by Jane Stirling, on 4 October at the Hopetoun Rooms in Queen Street, Edinburgh. The bookings were so meager the day before, however, that Stirling herself took 100 tickets so that the hall should not be too empty. Here, unusually, Chopin shouldered the bulk of the programme himself: a selection of Études, the Nocturne, Op. 9 No. 2 , the Berceuse, the Grande Valse Brillante, Op. 18 and other pieces – nothing too physically taxing except for the inclusion of the Second Ballade.

His attentive hostess then took him off to Wishaw to stay with Lady Bellhaven, then to Calder House again, before a few days at the magnificent Hamilton Palace, home of the Duke and Duchess of Hamilton. By now he had caught a chill and returned to Dr Lyszczynski. The lengthy close proximity of Chopin and Miss Stirling had by now set tongues wagging. Rumors of their engagement had even reached Paris.

Exhausted, depressed and comprehensively bored, with little money left, Chopin had had enough and left Scotland for London at the end of October. Here he fell ill again. For the first eighteen days after his arrival he did not leave the rooms that had been found for him in St James's Place. He took the time to write to Grzymała and scotch any gossip of forthcoming marriage:

> *There really has to be some kind of physical attraction, and the unmarried one Jane Stirling is too much like me. How could you kiss yourself? Friendship is all very well, but gives no rights to anything further. I have made that clear – Even if I could fall in love with someone, as I should be glad to do, still I would not marry, for we should have nothing to eat and nowhere to live. And a rich woman expects a rich man, or if a poor one, at least not a sickly one... It's bad enough to go to pieces alone, but two together, that is the greatest misfortune... I don't think at all of a wife, but of home, of my mother, my sisters. May God keep them in His good thoughts.*

*Meanwhile, what has become of my art? And my heart,
where have I wasted it? I scarcely remember any more, how
they sing at home. The world slips away from me somehow;
I forget, I have no more strength; if I rise a little, I fall again,
lower than ever.*

On 16 November 1848, Chopin gave a concert in London's Guildhall for 'The Annual Grand Dress and Fancy Ball and Concert in Aid of the Funds of the Literary Association of the Friends of Poland'. His appearance went by almost unnoticed. He played for an hour and then went home. It was especially apt that this concert should have had a connection with his homeland, for it was the last time that he ever played in public.

Jane Stirling arrived in London, still hoping for a betrothal. Accompanying her, as usual, was her sister who had spent many evenings in Scotland attempting to convert Chopin to Calvinism with Bible readings and her own brand of religious fervor. 'My Scottish ladies are such bores that God save me – they've latched on so hard that I cannot get away'. But get away he did on 23 November when he left by train for Folkestone. Seasick all the way to Boulogne, the now fragile little figure arrived back in Paris the following day.

# Chapter 14

## Debt and Decay, 1849

# Debt and Decay, 1849

On his return, Chopin found himself faced with a number of insuperable problems: he had very little money left, even after all his recent concerts; he could not compose, so he had nothing to sell to his publishers; he was too weak to teach on a regular basis (most of his pupils had been taken over by his friend and neighbour Alkan); his breathing confined him to his room at the Square d'Orléans; and his homeopathic Doctor Molin had died (his replacements, some of whom visited twice a day, charged ten francs a visit, putting an enormous strain on Chopin's finances). Pauline Viardot summed up his situation in a letter to George Sand:

> *His health is declining gradually, with passable days when he can drive out and others when he has fits of coughing that choke him and he spits out blood. He no longer goes out in the evenings, but he still manages to give some lessons, and on his better days he can be quite merry.*

Chopin did struggle out one evening in April to hear Viardot in the premiere of Meyerbeer's new opera *Le Prophète*. Its spectacular stage effects made more of an impression on him than the music, which he found a great disappointment.

Grzymała, the Marlianis and many of Chopin's

aristocratic friends had left Paris, but a small coterie of old *Daguerreotype of* friends visited him regularly, including Franchomme, the *Chopin, 1849* reclusive Alkan, Marie de Rozières, Delfina Potocka, Maria Kalergis and, above all, Delacroix – though ill himself, he was frantically putting the finishing touches to the ceiling of the Galerie d'Apollon in the Louvre. None of these, though, could provide Chopin with what he most needed – money

183

and an alternative to the damp ground-floor rooms of the Square d'Orléans with its now unhappy associations. It was Princess Obreskoff, the mother of Princess Soutzo, one of Chopin's pupils, who came to the rescue.

Princess Obreskoff had become a member of Chopin's inner circle. Chopin had asked her, in response to Solange's pleas, about the possibilities of commissions for Clésinger in St Petersburg. The sculptor's inability to find work had been putting a great strain on the couple's marriage, not helped by the arrival of a second daughter: Clésinger had wanted a son. Princess Obreskoff found Chopin a second-floor apartment at 74 Avenue de Chaillot (today it is the site of the Trocadéro) with a commanding view of the Tuileries, Notre-Dame, the Panthéon and Saint-Sulpice. It cost an astronomical 400 francs a month. The Princess told Chopin that the rent was 200 francs: unknown to him, she herself paid the balance.

> Jenny Lind came to see him, and, to his delight, performed an impromptu concert of songs and arias for a small group of friends. It was the last such evening over which he presided.

He moved there at the end of May, his valet Daniel carrying him up- and downstairs whenever he felt able to venture out for a drive. When Daniel left in the evening to go home, Princess Czartoryska sent her daughter's erstwhile nanny to act as a night nurse. A cholera epidemic in June took away Kalkbrenner and Angelica Catalani, the singer by whom Chopin had been so entranced as a boy in Warsaw.

Jane Stirling and Mrs Erskine arrived and took lodgings at St Germain. There are some friends whom one can see too often – and how wretched must Chopin have felt when any visitor would now see him lying in bed dressed in trousers and pumps, his legs and feet swollen, suffering from chronic diarrhea and coughing up copious amounts of blood. But Jenny Lind came to see him, and, to his delight, she and Delfina Potocka performed an impromptu concert of songs and arias for a small group of friends. It was the last such evening over which he presided.

Dr Cruveilhier, the foremost authority on consumption, came to make a diagnosis. Chopin was left in no doubt that he had little time left and wrote to his sister, begging her to come and see him. 'I am ill,' he wrote on 25 June, 'and no doctor will help me as much as some of you.' Ludwika's arrival was delayed by the actions of her husband who, even in this time of his brother-in-law's greatest need, allowed his jealousy and hatred for Chopin to override any compassion. He refused point-blank to pay the travelling expenses, only agreeing to the trip if Chopin's mother footed the bill. Ludwika raised enough to enable herself, her daughter and Kalasanty to go, but was unable to provide funds for either Chopin's younger sister Izabela and her husband or Chopin's mother to make the journey. Princess Obreskoff and Marcelina Czartoryska had anticipated Chopin's wishes and had already used their influence with the Russian authorities to expedite passports for Ludwika's family.

Shortly before they arrived, Franchomme, who had now taken over Chopin's financial affairs, had realized to his horror that the dying man had only a few hundred francs left. He must have told Jane Stirling, who immediately feigned huge surprise. Why, she said, back in March she had left a packet containing 25,000 francs in cash with the concierge at the Square d'Orléans. Had he not received it? A barely plausible stratagem was devised to allow Chopin to believe that this indeed had been the case, and that the concierge, a person of unimpeachable honesty, had simply put the packet of money behind a table lamp and forgotten it. The service of a clairvoyant was employed who miraculously and very quickly found the missing money. Chopin at first refused to accept the sum. Mrs Erskine managed to persuade him to accept 15,000. Chopin agreed – but only as a loan.

On 9 August Ludwika arrived with Kalasanty and their daughter. Chopin's spirits soared. In a long letter to her husband written after Chopin's death but only published in 1968, Ludwika explained her motives for devoting herself to her brother. It is a devastating indictment of Kalasanty's callous treatment of his wife and his despicable behavior towards Chopin:

> *I went there to look after him, to nurse him, to console him, to endure any hardship as long as it would bring him even the smallest relief in his sufferings – and he, poor thing, liked to talk late at night, to tell me all his troubles, and to pour into my loving and understanding heart anything that concerned him most.'*

Her accusatory outpouring concludes: 'Out of a friend you became a tyrant, and I out of a friend became a slave... To all my sufferings one more was added: I ceased to believe in the existence of friendship...'

Kalasanty returned to Poland alone before the end of the month. Almost as incomprehensible throughout the last months of Chopin's life was the attitude of George Sand. On 1 September she wrote to Ludwika enquiring after Chopin's health. 'Some people write that it is much worse than usual, others that he is only weak and fretful as I have always known him. I venture to ask you to send me word, for one can be misunderstood and abandoned by one's children without ceasing to love them.' The letter went unanswered. There was to be no deathbed reconciliation.

In mid-September, Chopin was moved to a new apartment on the ground floor of 12, Place Vendôme, one of Paris's most fashionable addresses. All his possessions

were moved from the Square d'Orléans. A newcomer to his
bedside was Father Aleksander Jelowicki, a childhood friend.
Once a writer and publisher, he had taken holy orders and
was now intent on claiming this lost soul before it departed.
His own protracted account of Chopin's confession and final
agreement to receive the Last Sacrament is as sanctimonious
as it is smug. Chopin, according to Jelowicki, expressed his
gratitude to him with the words, 'Without you, my friend,
I would have died like a pig'. Other accounts insist that the
last rites were forced upon the composer and that he was too
weak and terrified to resist.

*Chopin's salon at 12, Place Vendôme*

In the last week of his life, friends, pupils, acquaintances
and hangers-on crowded into the ante-room to pay their last
respects. In his lucid moments, Chopin managed to speak
to the few visitors allowed into his presence. He was precise
in his instructions: all his unfinished manuscripts were to be
destroyed, only finished works were to be published; Alkan

*Chopin's last*
*handwritten note,*
*asking that he not*
*be buried alive*

was bequeathed the incomplete notes of his Piano Method, sadly a document of little value or insight; Mozart's Requiem was to be sung at his funeral; his heart should be taken from his body and sent to Warsaw. The last note that he wrote (in French) echoed his father's terror at the end: 'As this cough will choke me, I implore you to have my body opened, so that I may not be buried alive'.

Ludwika, Solange, Marcelina Czartoyrska, Franchomme, Thomas Albrecht, Gutmann and one or two others kept vigil as Chopin faded. On 15 October Delfina Potocka arrived from Nice. Chopin asked her to sing for him. The Pleyel was moved to the open bedroom door. What did she sing? There has been much conjecture over the years about this but it has now been established beyond doubt that it was the B minor Largo, 'Dignare Domine', from Handel's Dettingen Te Deum.

On 16 October, Chopin was in agony. He asked for more music. Marcelina and Franchomme played some Mozart. He then asked to hear the opening of his Cello Sonata. They played the opening bars but he began to choke and they stopped.

In the evening, Dr Cruveilhier and a colleague examined him. His face had turned black with suffocation. The doctor bent over and asked whether he was still suffering. Everyone in the room heard the whispered answer: 'Non plus'. That night, Solange was sitting at the bedside when Chopin had a seizure. She called Gutmann. They offered Chopin a drink while Gutmann held him in his arms. But then his eyes suddenly glazed over, his gaze fixed on Solange. It was about two o'clock on the morning of 17 October 1849. He was thirty-nine years old.

---

Before dawn, two photographers arrived. How they managed to slip in unnoticed with their equipment has never been discovered, but they were found attempting to move the bed with Chopin's body nearer to the window for more light. They were quickly expelled.

In the morning, Clésinger was summoned to make a death-mask. His first effort was rejected by Ludwika, for the result betrayed Chopin's last agonized facial expression. He applied another layer of wet plaster and worked to smooth away the evidence of the composer's last struggle. Later, the painter Kwiatkowski drew a beautiful profile of his head. Chopin's heart was removed and, after the body had been taken to the crypt of the Madeleine, the apartment was sealed up. Ludwika took charge of all his possessions, including the casket containing George Sand's letters to Chopin which she returned to the writer. Sand and Maurice, as has been noted, promptly destroyed them. Ludwika wrote to Kalasanty suggesting that Chopin's piano should be kept in the family. His reply ordered her to sell absolutely everything, adding 'do not keep anything, anything at all. Not one rag [of Chopin's] will I let into my house'.

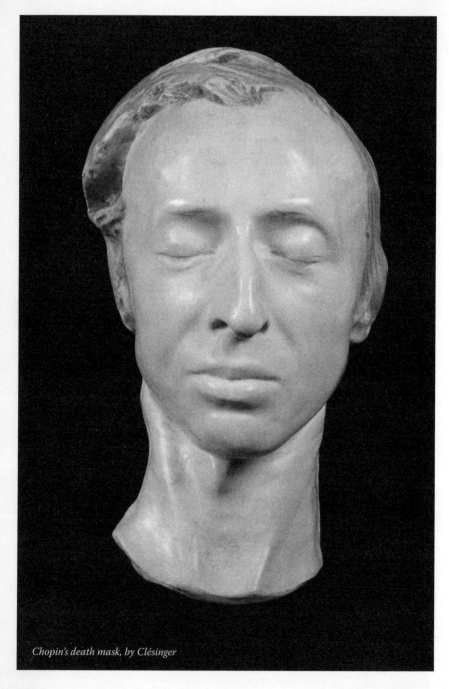

*Chopin's death mask, by Clésinger*

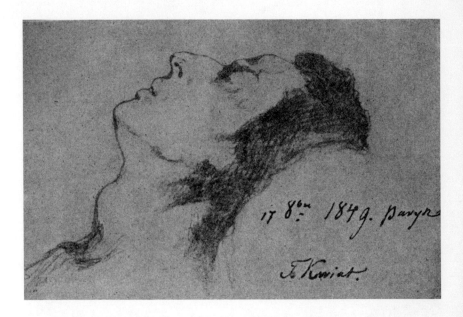

Almost two weeks later, on 30 October, Chopin's
funeral took place in the Madeleine. It was by all accounts
a magnificent and moving occasion. The front of the church
was draped with an enormous black velvet cartouche, the
initials F.C. embroidered in silver upon it. Three thousand
people had been invited. The service began with the orchestra
playing Chopin's Funeral March specially arranged for
orchestra by Henri Reber. Then followed Mozart's Requiem
performed by the special dispensation of the Archbishop of
Paris, for women were not allowed to sing in the Madeleine.
The soloists were Dupont, Castellan, Viardot and Lablache,
the latter having sung the 'Tuba mirum' from the same
work at Beethoven's funeral. During the Offertory, Chopin's
Preludes in E minor and B minor were played by the organist
of the Madeleine, the celebrated Louis Lefébure-Wély.

Prince Adam Czartoryski led the mourners, followed by
the four pall-bearers: Delacroix, Franchomme, Gutmann and
Prince Alexander Czartoryski (some accounts say two of the

*Chopin on his deathbed; drawing by Kwiatkowski, signed 17 October 1849*

191

number were Meyerbeer and Pleyel). Thousands followed the coffin on its three-mile journey to the cemetery of Père Lachaise. It was there lowered into the ground in complete silence, which Chopin had requested. George Sand was not present, but Jane Stirling was. It was she who paid for the entire funeral, at a cost of £5,000.

A visitor to Père Lachaise today will find Chopin's grave adorned by a marble monument designed by Clésinger. It is situated in a crowded enclave near the Carrefour du Grand-Rond that also provides the last resting places of Cherubini, Bellini, Hérold, Méhul, Gossec, Pleyel, Gaveau, Érard, Kreutzer, Grétry, Boïeldieu, Charpentier and Pierné. Their tombstones are silent and empty. Chopin's, no matter when you visit, is adorned with fresh floral tributes.

# Epilogue

Chopin's heart was sent to Warsaw and placed in an urn in the Church of the Holy Cross. Those of his possessions which Ludwika took with her back to Poland were destroyed by the Cossacks in 1863, and during the Second World War.

George Sand continued to live at Nohant, writing and travelling. On 16 December 1854, Solange and Clésinger officially separated. Sand became the official guardian of their second daughter, also named Jeanne-Gabrielle but known as 'Nini'. On 15 January 1855, Nini died of scarlet fever aged six. Sand died in 1876.

Solange was banished from Nohant again after Nini's death and endured her mother's hatred for the rest of her life. She bought her uncle's property in nearby Montgivray with an inheritance from her father and, after a succession of unsuccessful relationships, died in 1899.

Maurice married in 1862. His first son, Marc-Antoine, survived only a year. He then had two daughters, Aurore (b. 1866) and Gabrielle (b. 1868). He became a puppeteer in Nohant's marionette theatre, carving and painting the puppets himself, building the stage scenery and designing the lighting. He died in 1889.

Jane Stirling bought most of Chopin's estate and also collected many autographs, letters, papers and other artifacts

which she then either gave to close friends, kept for herself,
or forwarded to Chopin's family in Warsaw. She remained
on close terms with Ludwika and oversaw the publication
of Chopin's posthumous works. She died just ten years after
Chopin.

Julian Fontana returned to Paris in 1852. It was he who
published (against Chopin's wishes but with the consent of
the composer's mother and sisters) Chopin's posthumous
works, Opp. 66–74. In 1869, twenty years after Chopin's
death, he committed suicide.

Chopin kept in touch with his school friend and confidant
of his youth, Tytus Woyciechowski, all his life but the two do
not appear to have met again after Chopin made Paris his
home. Tytus lived the life of a country squire administering
his estate. Sadly, Chopin's imprecations to Tytus to visit him
as he neared death went unheeded, though his friend was
staying as close to Paris as Ostend. Tytus died in 1879 at the
age of seventy-one.

Ludwika Jędrzejewicz died in 1855 aged forty-eight.
Chopin's mother, Justyna, outlived her by six years, surviving
till the age of eighty-one. Her younger daughter Izabela
Barcinska was seventy when she died in 1881.

As for Chopin's two early loves, Konstancja Gladkowska
died in 1889 aged seventy-nine and Maria Wodzińska in
1896, also aged seventy-nine.

# Music Chronology

Ded. = the dedicatee of the work; Pub. = date of first publication

Where a work has taken a number of years to mature before its final published state (e.g., Scherzo No. 1) or where an opus is comprised of several pieces composed over a number of years (e.g., Études, Op. 10), it is listed under the year of its completion as far as is known.

Space precludes detailed comment on each and every Étude, Mazurka, Song etc. For these, a general note is provided at a key chronological point (e.g., for Études see 1833; for Mazurkas see 1832; for Songs see 1826). Minor compositions are left without comment.

N.B. Works with opus numbers 66–74 were published after Chopin's death by his friend Julian Fontana. All the piano works in this category were composed in Chopin's early years. Not all are of the same high standard as the works he himself authorized for publication.

## 1817
Polonaise in B flat major
Pub. 1947

Polonaise in G minor
Ded. Countess Victoria Skarbek
Pub. privately, Warsaw 1817

## 1821
Polonaise in A flat major
Ded. Adalbert Żwyny
Pub. 1902

## 1822
Polonaise in G sharp minor
Ded. Madame Du Pont
Pub. 1864

## 1824
Variations in E major on a German air, 'Der Schweizerbub'
Ded. Katarzyna Sowińska

Pub. ?1851

'Der Schweizerbub', which translates roughly as 'The little Swiss boy', has all the hallmarks of a Tyrolean folk tune. While its final bars threaten to break into a yodel, the opening bars presage Offenbach's 'Gendarmes Duet' (or 'The Marine's Hymn', as the tune is known in the United States). Katarzyna Sowińska (née Schroeder) was the German-born wife of General Sowiński, who was to achieve fame after the 1830–1 Polish uprising against the Russian Tsar's rule. The Sowińskis were friendly with the Chopin family (Fryderyk wrote his Fantasy on Polish Airs in their house). 'Der Schweizerbub' was a favorite tune of Katarzyna – 'Steh' auf, steh' auf, o du Schweitzer Bub' ('Get up, get up, oh you little Swiss boy') – and it was she who urged her reluctant young friend to write Variations on it. He, it is said, dashed off the piece in under an hour.

It is Chopin's first attempt at variation form and, though a minor work hampered by its repetitive tonic–dominant–tonic theme, it is an attractive piece that shows in its introduction and five contrasted variations the teenage Chopin's natural fluency and inventiveness at the keyboard.

## 1825

Rondo in C minor, Op. 1
Ded. Madame Bogumil Linde
Pub. 1825; arr. pf. 4 hands 1834

To Madame Linde, wife of Mikołaj Chopin's friend, the rector of Warsaw Lyceum, goes the honor of the dedication of Chopin's Op. 1. Chopin used to play duets with her. Opinions are sharply divided over the merits of this Rondo. Schumann could not quite believe that it was an Op. 1: 'I firmly believe that it is his tenth... a lady would say that it was very pretty, very piquant, almost Moschelesque' [i.e., in the style of Ignaz Moscheles]. The voices of Weber and Hummel are present in this piece too, for, unsurprisingly, Chopin had not yet developed the unmistakable voice which would soon be his. Others are less charitable. Moritz Karasowski, an early biographer, thought it Chopin's weakest work; W.H. Hadow, a later critic, found 'passages and even pages through which Elsner ought to have drawn his pencil'. But despite all this, as James Huneker says, 'we cannot help liking the C minor Rondo'.

## 1826

3 Écossaises in D major, G major & D flat major, Op. 72 No. 3
Pub. 1855

The écossaise was originally a quick Scottish dance in 2/4 time, stylized examples of which occur in Beethoven and Schubert. Chopin's three surviving examples may be sawdust from the master's bench but this has not prevented them from being in the encore repertoire of many major pianists. Each lasts under a minute, and all have infuriatingly catchy melodies.

Mazurkas in B flat major and G major
Pub. Warsaw 1826 (2nd versions); 1875 (1st versions)

Polonaise in B flat minor
Ded. Wilhelm Kolberg
Pub. 1879
Wilhelm Kolberg (1807–1891) was a school friend of Chopin. A footnote to this posthumously published work tells us that the Polonaise was composed 'at Chopin's departure for Reinerz' and that some days before his leave-taking, the two friends had been present at a performance of Rossini's *La gazza ladra*. This explains the title heading: 'Adieu to Wilhelm Kolberg' and the Trio's superscription: 'Au revoir! After an air from gazza ladra'.

Precz z moich oczu! (Out of My Sight!), Op. 74 No. 6 (wds Mickiewicz)
Pub. 1857
Chopin composed no more than thirty Songs in his life. Some were never written down, others did not progress beyond a sketch, while a number are spurious or lost. None was published during his lifetime, a fact that may or may not say something about the composer's own feelings as to their merit. If Chopin's instructions had been obeyed, all his song manuscripts would have been destroyed after his death.

In the event, the scattered pages of seventeen songs were collected by Julian Fontana and published, with the family's consent, simultaneously in Warsaw and Berlin in 1857.

All Chopin's Songs are settings of Polish poems, most of them by contemporaries of his acquaintance. Ten of them were written to lyrics by an early-Romantic poet from Warsaw, Stefan Witwicki (1801–1847), from the collection Piosnki sielskie ('Idylls', 1830). Witwicki was a friend of the Chopin family and had strong interests in folklore and Polish nationalism. It was to him that Chopin dedicated his Op. 41 Mazurkas. The soldier-poet Józef Bohdan Zaleski (1802–1886) was the author of three texts set to music by Chopin in the 1840s. Zaleski's folklore stylizations were based on Ukrainian songs and dances. Wincenty Pol (1807–1872), another freedom fighter of the November Uprising, published a collection of highly popular poems of the revolt, Songs of Janusz (1836). According to Fontana, Chopin composed music to ten or even twelve of these on their publication. Only one has survived: Śpiew grobowy ('Hymn from the Tomb').

Poland's leading Romantic poet was another close friend of Chopin – Adam Mickiewicz (1798–1855). Chopin composed two highly expressive love-songs to poems by him, one of which, Precz z moich oczu! ('Out of My Sight!'), was probably the first text put to music by the composer. Chopin's last song (Z gór, gdzie dzwigali, known to us under the title 'Melodya') has words by another great Polish Romantic, Zygmunt Krasiński (1812–1859).

Chopin's Songs fall into two categories: romantic and nationalistic. They seem to have been written in response to poems that described his own mood or feelings at any given moment, and also to satisfy social needs and friendship. There is no record of him ever performing any of his songs in public, reinforcing the suspicion that they were only intended as semi-private creations. They were certainly not designed to be sung as an intégrale. There is no denying the melodic charm and emotional sincerity of Chopin's settings, but none has ever achieved much success with singers and they remain little known.

Ironically, the two known as 'The Maiden's Wish' and 'My Joys' have long been popular encores for pianists in piano transcriptions by Liszt, who arranged six of the seventeen.

Rondo à la mazur in F major, Op. 5
Ded. Mlle la Comtesse Alexandrine de Moriolles
Pub. Warsaw 1828

Chopin's works comprise five Rondos of which Op. 5 is the only one not written in the traditional 2/4 time (a mazur or mazurka being a 3/4 dance step). Its themes and structure are a striking advance on the earlier Rondo in C minor, and it is perhaps the first time in which Chopin's individuality and nationality are unmistakably revealed. 'He who does not yet know Chopin had best begin the acquaintance with this piece,' wrote Robert Schumann, who found it 'Chopin-like throughout, lovely, enthusiastic, full of grace'. It is an entirely individual work, characterized by Chopin's idiosyncratic harmonies and chromatic progressions, as well as his characteristic love of wide-spread chords.

Alexandrine de Moriolles was the daughter of the tutor of the Grand Duke Constantin's illegitimate son.

Variations in D major on a theme of Thomas Moore for piano 4 hands
Pub. 1965

On 10 August 1824 in his first letter from Szafarnia, where Fryderyk was spending his holidays with the family of his schoolmate Dominik Dziewanowski, he asked his father 'to be kind enough, and buy at Brzezina [a book store in Warsaw] some Air Moore varié pour le pianoforte à quatre mains par [Ferdinand] Ries'. Thomas Moore (1779–1852), Ireland's national poet, was a friend of Byron and Shelley as well as being a dab hand as a composer. The air was described as 'one of Thomas Moore's Irish Melodies'. Despite the popularity of Moore's collections in all European countries, including Poland, it is probable that Chopin knew it from Ries.

Chopin's sister Ludwika included the Variations in her list of posthumous works prepared for the publishers in about 1854 and ascribed it to the year 1826. The autograph copy of the duet was unearthed only in 1964. It was missing the Secondo part of the introduction and the Primo part of the finale. Performances today are based on a 'reconstruction' of the missing pages.

The tune remains well known in Poland, despite its alarming lyrics, which translate as:

A small dog got into a kitchen and stole a joint of meat,
And the cook was so ferocious that he chopped him to death.

## 1827

Funeral March in C minor, Op. 72 No. 2
Pub. 1855
This modest offering could be seen as a preliminary sketch of the famous Funeral March from the B flat minor Sonata written ten years later. It has the same dotted rhythm motif as its successor, a feature it also shares with the Marche funèbre from Beethoven's Sonata in A flat, Op. 26, a work that Chopin himself played.

Mazurka in A minor, Op. 68 No. 2
Pub. 1855

Polonaise in D minor, Op. 71 No. 1
Pub. 1855

Variations in B flat major for piano and orchestra on 'Là ci darem la mano' from Mozart's Don Giovanni, Op. 2
Ded. Tytus Woyciechowski
Pub. Vienna 1830; London & Paris 1833
The theme is the famous duet from Act 1 of Mozart's opera. 'Give me your hand,' sings Giovanni to the peasant girl Zerlina. After the brilliantly written introduction and statement of the theme, Chopin writes five contrasted Hummel-inspired variations, each punctuated by an orchestral tutti. One can easily imagine Chopin the improviser at work here, though the layout of the music is similar to many other sets of variations written at the time – one each devoted to triplets, octaves, left-hand bravura, acrobatic jumps, a slow variation in the minor (Var. 5) and a scintillating conclusion, in this case an alla polacca treatment of the tune. The piano writing is undeniably effective, which is more than can be said of the orchestral contribution.

This is the work which Robert Schumann greeted with the now-famous invocation, 'Hats off, gentlemen! A genius!' And while it is undeniably an apprentice work designed as a vehicle for Chopin's virtuoso prowess, Schumann saw through the glitter to end his review of the work, 'I bend before Chopin's spontaneous genius, his lofty aim, his mastership'.

## 1828

Fantasy on Polish Airs in A major for piano and orchestra, Op. 13
Ded. Johann Peter Pixis
Pub. 1834
After Op. 2, a light work for piano and orchestra based on an opera melody, Chopin chose for his next piano-and-orchestra outing a selection of national folk tunes – indeed, he himself referred to Op. 13 as 'the Potpourri on Polish Themes'. After a slow introduction, we hear a plaintive andantino and two brilliant variations, followed by a theme from an opera by Karol Kurpiński (1785–1857) with variations, leading to a rousing conclusion with the kujawiak, a popular dance similar to the mazurka.

Once again, the orchestral writing is incidental, all the focus being centered on the soloist's endeavors, and the different sections are clumsily welded together. However, Chopin was clearly fond of it and kept it in his repertoire for many years. Today, it is rarely heard in concert. The work's dedicatee, Pixis (1788–1874), was a highly esteemed and popular German pianist-composer with whom Chopin became friendly in Paris (also see Liszt's Hexameron). Pixis dedicated a set of his variations to Chopin.

Piano Trio in G minor, Op. 8
Ded. Prince Antoni Radziwiłł
Pub. 1832
This is one of the four chamber works of Chopin which features a cello and the only instance of him composing for the violin. It is a genial work in four movements though not particularly well written for the medium: in the opening Allegro con fuoco, for instance, the violin writing is somewhat banal, and there is little of the true interplay between the three instruments that you find in the piano trios of Beethoven, Schubert and Hummel. Chopin seems to have been aware of the work's shortcomings. In a letter of August 1830, in a rare example of him discussing a technical musical matter, he says that he should have written the violin part for viola, 'as the first string predominates in the violin, and in my Trio is hardly used at all. The viola would, I think, accord better with the cello.' Twelve years after the Trio was written, one of Chopin's pupils, Mme Streicher, tells us that when studying the work with him he drew her attention to some passages which displeased him, saying that he would now write them differently.

Many books on chamber music ignore the Trio altogether, though some commentators are more enthusiastic: 'The inimitable color and variety of the piano writing and the idiomatic use of each instrument pose a mystery as to why so graceful and winning a piece is not more of a staple in the concert hall' (pianist Emanuel Ax).

Polonaise in B flat major, Op. 71 No. 2
Pub. 1855

Rondo à la krakowiak in F major for piano and orchestra, Op. 14
Ded. Princess Anna Czartoryska
Pub. 1834
For his third work for piano and orchestra, Chopin turned from opera and national airs to a folk dance. The krakowiak, indigenous to Cracow, is a lively dance in 2/4 time, with the accent on a usually unaccented part of the bar, especially at the end of a phrase. This is the only time that Chopin was drawn to the krakowiak (his compatriot Paderewski wrote six short examples, including the once-popular 'Cracovienne fantastique'), though the finale of the E minor Concerto resembles the dance. This is another sparkling display piece but more tightly knit and better orchestrated than its predecessors. Chopin frequently played it early on in his career but seems to have dropped it completely after leaving Poland. The work is dedicated to Princess Anna Czartoryska, née Sapieha, (1799–1864), wife of Prince Adam Czartoryski.

Rondo in C major, Op. 73a (orig. version of Op. 73)
Ded. Aloys Fuchs
Pub. ?

Rondo in C major for two pianos, Op. 73
Pub. 1855
'It is full of fire,' writes James Huneker, 'but the ornamentation runs mad, and no traces of the poetical Chopin are present.' In fact the C major Rondo is interesting for its stylistic features as it is a further example of the composer's student years: in the introduction and elsewhere there is the unmistakable voice of Beethoven, a composer about whom Chopin felt ambivalent and whose presence is rarely found elsewhere in his music. No composer of the era entirely escaped Beethoven, of course – nor Hummel and Weber, the other identifiable influences in this piece, particularly evident in the sparkling rondo theme.

Sonata No. 1 in C minor, Op. 4
Ded. Józef Elsner
Pub. 1851
Chopin wrote four Sonatas – three for solo piano and one for cello and piano. This early effort, begun in 1827, is far below the caliber of the others. He sent it to the publisher Haslinger in Vienna together with his 'Là ci darem la mano' Variations. Haslinger was shrewd enough to spot the winner (see below) and pass on the Sonata. It is a student work in which Chopin struggles with the formal sonata structure, resulting in some of his most leaden music. This is especially true of the first movement, which is not only technically awkward to play but, for more than one commentator, the only really dull composition in the whole of Chopin's works. 'A few early pieces may legitimately be termed weak, but they are always brilliant,' wrote G.C. Ashton Jonson. 'This Allegro, however, is tedious.' Interest picks up in the pretty but derivative Minuet, only to be quelled in the meandering Larghetto with its unusual 5/4 time signature, a meter which Tchaikovsky used to incomparably better effect in the second movement of his 'Pathétique' Symphony and Arensky in the finale of his F minor Piano Concerto. The finale (Presto) is the most successful of the four, almost a moto perpetuo in its constant quaver motion, though in the hands of anyone but a first-class pianist it can sound relentless.

## 1829
Concerto No. 2 in F minor for piano and orchestra, Op. 21
Ded. Countess Delfina Potocka
Pub. 1834
'The first allegro [of the F minor Concerto] is accessible only to the few; there were some bravos, but I think only because they were puzzled – What is this? – and had to pose as connoisseurs! The Adagio and Rondo had more effect; one heard some spontaneous shouts.' So wrote Chopin to Tytus on 27 March 1830, five days after the second public

performance of the Concerto. It has been beloved of pianists and public ever since. They have sensibly ignored the pages of abuse poured on it by musicologists and critics who complain about its unconventional structure, its weak development of material, and its pallid orchestration. It could be argued that Chopin's 'barely adequate' orchestration is exactly what his particular style of piano writing requires and that anything more detailed or heavily textured would work against it. In any case, the whole work is really a discreetly accompanied glorious piano solo.

The piano writing in the opening Maestoso movement could only be by Chopin, but he was not writing in a vacuum. He absorbed and adapted many figurations and rhythmical devices used by his older contemporaries in the 'brilliant' style of concerto. Chopin's first attempt at a full-scale work of this kind is in a clear line of development from the concertos of Hummel, Field, Kalkbrenner, Moscheles and others. The haunting second movement was inspired by Konstancja. 'Six months have elapsed and I have not yet exchanged a syllable with her of whom I dream every night,' he wrote in 1829. 'While my thoughts were with her, I composed the Adagio of my concerto.' The main theme, which has the spirit of a nocturne, is interrupted by a striking passage accompanied by tremolo strings (Moscheles had used the same device at a similar point in the slow movement of his G minor Concerto of 1825). In the lively finale, a Hummelesque rondo, Chopin shows further imaginative orchestral touches. For example, the second subject is underscored by the violins playing col legno – i.e., playing the strings with the back of the bow instead of the hair. The coda is announced by another effective gesture – a passage for solo horn which proclaims the key of F major and the Concerto's concluding pages.

The F minor Concerto is dedicated to the Countess Delfina Potocka, one of the very few people to whom Chopin dedicated more than one of his works (Tytus was another). See Chapter 7.

Gdzie lubi (There Where She Loves), Op. 74 No. 5 (wds Witwicki)
Pub. 1857

Jakież kwiaty (Which Flowers) (wds Maciejowski)
Pub. 1856

Mazurka in A minor, Op. 7 No. 2a (orig. version of Op. 7 No. 2)
Pub. 1902

Mazurka in D major
Pub. 1880

Nocturne in E minor, Op. 72 No. 1
Pub. 1855

Polonaise in F minor, Op. 71 No. 3
Pub. 1855

Polonaise in G flat major
Pub. 1870

Waltz in B minor, Op. 69 No. 2
Ded. Wilhelm Kolberg
Pub. 1852

Waltz in D flat major, Op. 70 No. 3
Pub. 1855

Waltz in E major
Pub. 1871

Życzenie (The Maiden's Wish), Op. 74 No. 1 (wds Witwicki)
Pub. 1837

## 1830

Concerto No. 1 in E minor for piano and orchestra, Op. 11
Ded. Friedrich Kalkbrenner
Pub. 1833

The E minor Concerto, though written after the F minor, is designated Chopin's Piano Concerto No. 1 because it was published first. The same criticisms of orchestration, structure and development levelled at Op. 21 have attached to Op. 11, yet both works have stayed great favorites with pianists and the public ever since they first appeared. The reason for this is largely due to the strength of the melodic material and Chopin's idiomatic keyboard expression.

The orchestral opening of the E minor is twice as long as that of the F minor. Until fairly recently, it was common practice to play it with a cut, an approach which is rightly considered heresy today. For all who find the first movement (Allegro maestoso risoluto) too long and repetitive, there are an equal number who find it invigorating and very effective. The touching second subject is quintessential Chopin, its first appearance on the piano a moment of extraordinary beauty. The second movement (Larghetto) is labelled Romanze. As related in Chapter 3, its inspiration was Chopin's Romantic ideal, Konstancja Gladkowska. It consists of a beautiful and melancholy nocturne in E major with a second subject in B major, both of which are heard in highly decorated, quasi-improvisational guises. The finale (Vivace) is one of infectious gaiety, a lively rondo with some resemblance to a krakowiak. Despite the Concerto's key signature, the finale, like the Romanze, is in E major.

Friederich [Wilhelm Michael] Kalkbrenner (1785–1849) was the Concerto's dedicatee. Chopin played a concerto by Kalkbrenner (probably his Op. 61 in D minor) as early as 15 July 1824 during his first school holidays at Szafarnia when staying with the Dziewanowski family. Later, the twenty-one-year-old Chopin met him in Paris (see

Chapters 5, 6 & 7).

Czary (Witchcraft) (wds Witwicki)
Pub. 1910

Grande Valse Brillante in E flat major, Op. 18
Ded. Mlle Laura Horsford
Pub. 1834
Only eight of Chopin's Waltzes were published during his lifetime, and this is the first, composed in Vienna and differing from all the others in that it can actually be danced to. His later essays in the form are more 'dance poems', far away from the world of Strauss and Lanner which this one emulates. It is one of Chopin's most popular works, described by Schumann as, 'Chopin's body- and soul-inspiring waltz', familiar from its appearance in *Les Sylphides*. Some editions name the dedicatee, a Chopin pupil, as Laura Harsford, others as Emma Horsford. The dedicatee of the Variations, Op. 12 was Emma Horsford.

Hulanka (Merrymaking), Op. 74 No. 4 (wds Witwicki)
Pub. 1857

Introduction and Polonaise brillante in C major for piano and cello, Op. 3
Ded. Joseph Merk
Pub. 1831
In a letter to Tytus on 14 November 1829, Chopin reveals, 'I wrote an "Alla Polacca" with cello accompaniment during my visit to Prince Radziwiłł. It is nothing more than a brilliant drawing-room piece suitable for the ladies. I should like Princess Wanda to practice it. I am supposed to be giving her lessons. She's young (seventeen), pretty, and it's a real joy placing her little fingers on the keys.' The Princess must have been an accomplished pianist to negotiate the difficult piano part, though her father would not have found the cello part over-taxing.
The Introduction was added the following year (1830) in Vienna as a result of Chopin's friendship with the Austrian cellist Joseph Merk (1795–1852). Czerny produced a version of Op. 3 for solo piano, but in the 1980s a solo piano version by Chopin himself was discovered by the Polish musicologist Jan Weber.

Lento con espressione in C sharp minor
Ded. Ludwika Chopin
Pub. 1875

Mazurka in C major, Op. 68 No. 1
Pub. 1855

Mazurka in F major, Op. 68 No. 3

Pub. 1855

Waltz in A flat major
Pub. 1902

Waltz in E minor
Pub. 1868

## 1831
Grand Duo concertante in E major on themes from Meyerbeer's *Robert le diable* for cello and piano, Op. posth.
Ded. Mlle Adèle Forest
Pub. 1833
The premiere of *Robert the Devil*, at the Paris Opéra on 21 November 1831, can be accounted one of the most sensational first nights in opera history. It made Meyerbeer's name and fortune. However, despite being widely performed throughout the nineteenth century, the opera is rarely seen today. Thalberg, Herz, Kalkbrenner and Liszt all wrote piano transcriptions and fantasies based on themes from it. Chopin was commissioned to write his Grand Duo by his publisher, Schlesinger. It is the only one of his compositions written in collaboration, in this case with his friend the cellist August Franchomme, who also rewrote the cello part of the earlier Polonaise, Op. 3 and arranged two of the Nocturnes for cello and piano.

One of only four works published without an opus number during the composer's lifetime, it uses a variety of melodies from throughout the opera and is written in the typical salon style of the day. 'A pièce d'occasion,' thinks Huneker, 'the occasion probably being the need of ready money.'

Narzeczony (The Bridegroom), Op. 74 No. 15 (wds Witwicki)
Piosnka litewska (Lithuanian Song), Op. 74 No. 16 (wds Osinski)
Poseł (The Messenger), Op. 74 No. 7 (wds Witwicki)
Smutna rzeka (The Sad Stream), Op. 74 No. 3 (wds Witwicki)
Pub. 1857

Wojak (The Warrior), Op. 74 No. 10 (wds Witwicki)
Pub. 1837)

## 1832
Mazurkas in B flat major, A major, F major, A flat major & C minor,
Op. 7 Nos 1–5
Composed 1830–2
Pub. 1832

Mazurkas in F sharp minor, C sharp minor, E major & E flat major,

Op. 6 Nos 1–4
Composed 1830–2
Ded. Countess Pauline Plater
Pub. 1832

Mazurka in B flat major
Composed 24 June 1832
Ded. Alexandrine Wolowska
Pub. 1909
It has often been said that the Mazurkas are the most characteristic of Chopin's works, revealing all the facets of his personality and emotions more directly than any other of his compositions. It was a form that engaged him from his teenage years until his death.

There are some sixty-two Mazurkas in all (more if one includes doubtful and spurious works). Forty-one were published during Chopin's lifetime. Eight (assigned as Opp. 67 and 68), though the composer directed them to be destroyed, were published posthumously by Chopin's friend Julian Fontana. A further thirteen have no opus numbers: some of these are early works either published separately while Chopin was alive or posthumously, that in A flat major composed in 1834 appearing as late as 1930.

Few last longer than four minutes; most are far shorter. The main characteristics of the mazurka (a dance form that takes its name from the area of Mazovia around Warsaw) are triple time, with the second or third beat strongly accented, and a dotted rhythm. Chopin incorporates elements of other folk dances related to the mazurka, such as the mazur, the oberek and the kujawiak, each with its own subtly different tempos and rhythmic patterns.

Chopin transformed what had merely been a fashionable salon genre into a miniature tone poem – a new, clearly defined genre of piano music. Apart from the extraordinary fountain of melody and emotional expression common to all, his Mazurkas are also marked by abrupt transitions of mood, from melancholy to joyful, from energetic and optimistic to soulful, downcast musings.

It is not only the mood of each piece that is unexpected. Many of the Mazurkas must have puzzled Chopin's contemporaries with their frequently daring and novel harmonies. The predictable and (mostly) unadventurous accompaniments in the Waltzes are rare in the Mazurkas – some boast touches of subtle counterpoint, others have chromatic sequences which flout the conventional rules of harmony, still others feature a simple drone bass, recalling the rustic nature of the dance.

Nocturnes in B flat minor, E flat major & B major, Op. 9 Nos 1–3
Composed 1830–2
Ded. Mme Camille Pleyel
Pub. 1832
The nocturne is a musical form indelibly associated with Chopin. The term 'nocturne' occurs in the preface to the Prayer Book as a service of the Church originally intended

to be celebrated at night. The pianist-composer John Field invented and popularised the nocturne as a piano genre in which a graceful melody would sing over a gentle accompaniment, rather like the long-breathed cantilenas of a Bellini opera.

Chopin took the nocturne into another sphere. By turns his are haunting, sentimental, dramatic, brooding, sensual and melancholy – Chopin at his introspective best, conjuring up music of profound poetic expression. The earliest of Chopin's Nocturnes, eighteen of which were published during his lifetime, is a posthumous one in E minor written in 1827. Another from his earliest youth in C sharp minor (known as the 'Nocturne oublié') turned up in 1895, a beautiful piece but considered by scholars as spurious.

The second of the Op. 9 set is not merely the best-known of all the Nocturnes but of all Chopin's works. It did more for Chopin's popularity in Paris than anything he had published up to that time. Ironically, it is also closer than any others in form and content to a Field Nocturne!

The three Op. 9 Nocturnes are dedicated to the brilliant young pianist Camille Pleyel, née Marie Moke (1811–1875), a pupil of Herz, Moscheles and Kalkbrenner. This was the same Marie Moke who became engaged to Berlioz in 1830 but who, during his absence in Rome, decided instead to marry the piano manufacturer Pleyel. Berlioz records in his memoirs how he started back to Paris in an all-consuming rage, disguised as a lady's maid and armed with a pistol, intent on murdering Marie and her husband. But his luggage went astray, and he calmed down during the consequent delay, meekly returning to Rome.

Nocturnes in F major & F sharp major, Op. 15 Nos 1 & 2
Ded. Ferdinand Hiller
Pub. 1833
The development of the nocturne in Chopin's hands is clearly underway in the three Nocturnes of Op. 15 (No. 3 was composed the following year). No. 1 has a serene and tender Andante followed by a stormy theme marked con fuoco which dies down to return to the opening theme – 'a calm and beautiful lake, ruffled by a sudden storm and becoming calm again' (Theodor Kullak). No. 2 is one of Chopin's most sublime works which 'touches one like a benediction'(Kullak).

Waltz in G flat major, Op. 70 No. 1
Pub. 1855

## 1833
Bolero in A minor, Op. 19
Ded. Countess Emilie de Flahault
Pub. 1834
The bolero is, of course, a Spanish national dance, but this is a Bolero 'à la Polonaise'. Chopin gives it exactly the same rhythm as Poland's national dance though marks it Allegro vivace, somewhat faster and lighter than his genuine Polonaises. In fact, there is

very little that is Hispanic about this piece other than its title. It is possible that Chopin was inspired to write in this form after hearing Auber's opera *La Muette de Portici*, which features a bolero. While hardly a major work of Chopin, it is infectiously lively and elegant, and deserves to be heard more frequently.

The key in which the Bolero is written is given inconsistently by various sources. Some go with C major (introduction), others with A minor (main theme) and still others with A major (final chord). The work is dedicated to Countess Emilie de Flahault, later Lady Shelburne, one of Chopin's aristocratic pupils.

12 Études, Op. 10
Composed 1829–33
Ded. 'à son ami F. Liszt'
Pub. 1833
C major, Op. 10 No. 1
A minor, Op. 10 No. 2
E major, Op. 10 No. 3 ('Tristesse')
C sharp minor, Op. 10 No. 4
G flat major, Op. 10 No. 5 ('Black Keys')
E flat minor, Op. 10 No. 6
C major, Op. 10 No. 7
F major, Op. 10 No. 8
F minor, Op. 10 No. 9
A flat major, Op. 10 No. 10
E flat major, Op. 10 No. 11
C minor, Op. 10 No. 12 ('Revolutionary')

These twelve short Studies, together with the second set of twelve, Op. 25 published in 1837, form the Magna Carta of Romantic piano technique and offer a vade mecum of Chopin's style. Numerous books of piano studies had appeared before these, with each one devoted to a particular aspect of execution – scales, arpeggios, thirds, octaves, etc. Chopin himself must have been familiar with the studies of Czerny, Clementi and Cramer. What makes his stand out is that, although each one poses a particular technical challenge, this is subsumed into the poetry of the music.

Paganini was undoubtedly an influence, with the twenty-year-old Pole seeking the same fusion of bravura technique and lyrical expression as in the Italian's violin Caprices, Op. 1. Chopin's Opp. 10 and 25, as they are known in the trade, extended the range of piano music to the limits of tonality and revolutionized finger technique into the bargain. Some of the audacious harmonies were new concepts in sound, many of them later to become the basis of Impressionism. Of all piano études, Chopin's are simultaneously the most challenging for the player (with the possible exception of Liszt's) and the most rewarding for the listener.

Though they have their moments and are by no means without merit, other near-contemporary sets seem pallid and inconsistent beside Chopin's, among them Moscheles' Studies, Op. 70, published in 1827, Hummel's Op. 125 of 1833, and Henselt's

Opp. 2 and 5 of 1838. Having said that, there are clear parallels between certain earlier Studies and some of Chopin's: the chromatic runs in Moscheles' Op. 70 No. 3 in G major and Chopin's Op. 10 No. 2 in A minor; or the almost identical harmonic progression in Clementi's Gradus ad Parnassum No. 60 and Chopin's Op. 10 No. 6.

Chopin's Études were initially criticized for being too difficult. Moscheles complained that his fingers were constantly stumbling over hard, inartistic and, to him, incomprehensible modulations. The German critic and writer Ludwig Rellstab (1799–1860) remarked: 'Those who have distorted fingers may put them right by practizing these Studies; but those who have not, should not play them, at least, not without having a surgeon standing by.'

Today, Opp. 10 and 25 together form one of the cornerstones of piano literature, de rigueur for every professional pianist to conquer and absorb. The best-known ones of the first set are also known by their nicknames: in 1939 No. 3, 'Tristesse', was turned into the song 'So Deep Is the Night'; No. 5, 'Black Keys', is so-called because the right hand plays entirely on the black keys; No. 12 is the 'Revolutionary', inspired, it is said, by the fall of Warsaw in 1831, though a much later generation got to know it through a 1957 children's record, 'Sparky's Magic Piano'.

Introduction and Rondo in E flat major, Op. 16
Ded. Caroline Hartmann
Pub. 1834
The rather beautiful melancholy in the Introduction gives no hint of the sparky, Weberesque Rondo that follows. Brilliant and graceful though the writing is – and its pages contain some memorable ideas – the Rondo is one of a number of Chopin's concessions to public taste written at this time. Its dedicatee, Caroline Hartmann, one of Chopin's few professional pupils and said to be greatly gifted, sadly died prematurely in 1834.

Mazurkas in B flat major, E minor, A flat major & A minor, Op. 17
Ded. Mme Lina Freppa
Pub. 1834

Mazurkas in G minor, C major, A flat major & B flat minor, Op. 24
Ded. Count de Perthuis
Pub. 1836

Nocturne in G minor, Op. 15 No. 3
Ded. Ferdinand Hiller
Chopin hardly ever revealed the source of his inspiration or the programme behind his music. So it is illuminating to learn that on the original manuscript of this Nocturne he wrote, 'After a performance of Hamlet' but then thought better of it and scribbled, 'No! let them work it out for themselves'. Kullak (see 1832, Op. 15 Nos 1 & 2) once more superbly characterizes the work, seeing in it, 'a picture of grief for the loss of a beloved

one lulled by the consolations of religion.'

Variations brillantes in B flat major on 'Je vends des scapulaires' from Hérold's 'Ludovic',
Op. 12
Ded. Emma Horsford
Pub. 1833
The Variations are based on an air entitled 'I am selling scapulars.' This comes from
the comic opera *Ludovic*, completed by Bizet's father-in-law Fromental Halévy after
Hérold's death in 1833, the year in which the opera was staged in Paris.

This is generally regarded as Chopin's weakest work: 'If ever Chopin is not Chopin in
his music, it is in these variations' (Niecks); 'It is Chopin and water, and Gallic eau sucré
at that' (Huneker); 'Graceful embroideries of an exceedingly poor texture' (Hadow). But
if the music were by any other composer, it would surely be acknowledged as a sparkling
and well-wrought example of tasteful artificiality in the Parisian fashion of the time.
The most remarkable thing about the piece is that Chopin could turn such a dull theme
into such an entertaining confection. One of its peculiarities is a bar on the last page
containing a scale in the key of C flat major, a rare key for any composer.

## 1834
Andante spianato in G major, Op. 22
(see Grande Polonaise Brillante, 1835)

Cantabile in B flat major
Pub. 1931

Fantaisie-Impromptu in C sharp minor, Op. 66
Ded. Baron d'Est
Pub. 1855
This is the finest of all the piano works published posthumously by Julian Fontana,
arguably the best of all the Impromptus and certainly one of Chopin's most popular
pieces. Why he decided to withhold it from publication is a mystery – perhaps he merely
overlooked it – though some of the snootier commentators criticize the outer sections
for being too 'foursquare' and the middle section too saccharine. Such views constitute
an even bigger mystery. It is a wonderful piece, despite the fact that its beautiful central
melody, one of Chopin's finest, was adapted to the words of a popular song penned in
1919 by two Americans, 'I'm Always Chasing Rainbows'.

Mazurka in A flat major
Composed July 1834
Pub. 1930

Presto con leggerezza in A flat major
Composed July 1834

Ded. Pierre Wolff
Pub. 1918

Scherzo No. 1 in B minor, Op. 20
Ded. Thomas Albrecht
Pub. 1835

It is easy to imagine Chopin improvising music like this, late at night, taking out his loneliness and frustrations on 'Graf's dull piano'. It begins with two crashing dissonant chords which, to Chopin's contemporaries, must have seemed very audacious. After the angry and tormented writing of the hectic opening pages, Chopin introduces a Polish Christmas song for the calm central section. It is one of the few instances in Chopin's music where he resorted to direct quotation. The melody is called 'Lullaby, little Jesus' and is still sung today in Poland. The furious coda has a chromatic scale which Liszt (and many virtuosi since) played with interlocking octaves.

Thomas Albrecht was a wine merchant and the Saxon Consul in Paris to whose daughter Chopin was godfather.

## 1835

Ballade No. 1 in G minor, Op. 23
Ded. Baron de Stockhausen

By the beginning of the nineteenth century, the ballad (Fr. ballade) had become both a form of lyric poetry and a type of vocal music. No one is certain how Chopin alighted on the term to describe this new form of piano music. Perhaps it attracted him because the music was of the same hybrid character as the literary ballad, with its contrasting lyric, epic and dramatic episodes. Unlike the Nocturnes, Mazurkas, Waltzes and other small-scale compositions to which Chopin directed most of his energies, his Ballades are more extended works. The inspiration for the four Ballades that he was to write between 1831 and 1842 came from the nationalist poetry of his friend Adam Mickiewicz (1798–1855). Through this new genre, Chopin wanted to create a musical parallel to the literary ballad but, even if the music was inspired by a particular poem, he would never slavishly illustrate its narrative.

The G minor Ballade is justly famous, one of the earliest examples of Chopin moving from the extrovert showpieces of his youth to the emotional works of his maturity. Almost certainly sketched out in Vienna in 1831, it was another four years before it was completed to his satisfaction. Robert Schumann described it as among Chopin's 'wildest and most original compositions'. In a letter to his friend Heinrich Dorne, Schumann said that when he told Chopin that he liked this Ballade best of all, Chopin, after a long, meditative pause, said with great emphasis, 'I am glad of that. It is the one I too like best'.

Baron de Stockhausen was the Hanoverian Ambassador and one of Chopin's closest non-Polish friends in Paris.

Grande Polonaise Brillante in E flat major for piano and orchestra, Op. 22

précédée d'un Andante spianato
Ded. Mme La Baronne d'Est
Pub. 1836
Composed shortly before he came to Paris, this is the sixth and last work of Chopin with an orchestral accompaniment. In 1834 he added an introductory Andante spianato in G major for solo piano. 'Spianato' comes from 'spiana', the Italian for a carpenter's plane, an apt description for this 'planed, level, smooth' music. 'It makes one think of a lake on a calm bright summer day,' wrote one commentator. Today, the two parts are frequently played as a solo, while Chopin himself liked to play the Andante as a separate piece without the Polonaise. In fact, after he once played the Polonaise with orchestral accompaniment in Paris in 1835 there is no record of him ever doing so again.

The Polonaise is a glittering showpiece of no great depth, designed to display Chopin's powers as a virtuoso. That he was successful in this is reflected in the work's enduring popularity with pianists since the day it was published.

Mazurka in G major, Op. 67 No. 1
Ded. Anna Młokosiewicz
Pub. 1855
Mazurka in C major, Op. 67 No. 3
Ded. Mme Hoffman
Pub. 1855

Nocturnes in C sharp minor & D flat major, Op. 27 Nos 1 & 2
Ded. Countess Thérèse d'Apponyi
Pub. 1836
'An entire world separates us here from Field,' writes one commentator (Kleczyński). 'The thought of a poetry profoundly felt, clothes itself in magic form.' The second of these two Nocturnes, embodying surely one of Chopin's most refined and affecting melodies, is much favored by pianists. Op. 27 was dedicated to the Austrian Ambassadress in Paris.

Polonaises in C sharp minor & E flat minor, Op. 26 Nos 1 & 2
Ded. Joseph Dessauer
Pub. 1836
Chopin's earlier Polonaises were concerned with the dance aspects and virtuosity of the form. Here, he has expanded the national dance into a vehicle for subtly expressive emotion. Just as in his development of the waltz, the dance rhythm is subsumed into lyric poetry. The Trio of the C sharp minor Polonaise could almost stand by itself as a nocturne. The second part of the Trio is a duet between soprano and bass, the prototype of the Étude in C sharp minor, Op. 25 No. 7. The fiery E flat minor Polonaise is also known as the 'Siberian' or 'Revolt' Polonaise. There is some melodic similarity between its Trio, the opening of Beethoven's 'Hammerklavier' Sonata and the opening of Tchaikovsky's Fifth Symphony.

Joseph Dessauer was a cellist and composer friend of Chopin who lived from 1798 to 1876.

Waltz in A flat major, Op. 34 No. 1
Ded. Josefine von Thun-Hohenstein
Pub. 1838
Composed on 15 September 1835, this is the first of the three Waltzes, Op. 34 (see 1838 for the others) that were given a warm welcome by Schumann: '[they] will delight above all things, so different are they from the ordinary ones, and of such a kind as only Chopin dare venture on or even invent, while gazing inspired among the dancers... Such a wave of life flows through them that they seem to have been improvised in the ballroom.' There is an intriguing similarity between a passage in the coda of this Waltz (bars 18–24) and one in the 'Préamble' of Schumann's Carnaval. A nod of acknowledgement from Chopin, perhaps?

The dedicatee (1815–1895) was a former pupil of Chopin and the daughter of Chopin's friend Count Franz Anton Thun-Hohenstein (1786–1873) and his family. Chopin stayed with them at their castle at Tetschen on the Elbe in 1835.

Waltz in A flat major, Op. 69 No. 1
Autographs ded. Charlotte de Rothschild, Mme Peruzzi, Maria Wodzińska
Pub. 1855
The original manuscript of this tender, wistful little gem bears the inscription 'Pour Mlle Marie' and is signed 'F. Chopin. Drezno [Dresden], 1835'. It is sometimes known by its nickname 'L'Adieu'.

## 1836
Pierścień (The Ring), Op. 74 No. 14 (wds Witwicki)
Śpiew grobowy (Hymn from the Tomb), Op. 74 No. 17 (wds Pol)
Pub. 1857

## 1837
12 Études, Op. 25
Ded. Comtesse Marie d'Agoult
Pub. 1837
A flat major, Op. 25 No. 1 ('The Shepherd Boy' or 'Aeolian harp')
F minor, Op. 25 No. 2
F major, Op. 25 No. 3
A minor, Op. 25 No. 4
E minor, Op. 25 No. 5
G sharp minor, Op. 25 No. 6
C sharp minor, Op. 25 No. 7
D flat major, Op. 25 No. 8
G flat major, Op. 25 No. 9 ('Butterfly')

B minor, Op. 25 No. 10
A minor, Op. 25 No. 11 ('Winter Wind')
C minor, Op. 25 No. 12

Chopin's earlier set of Op. 10 Études provided a compendium of the contemporary resources of the piano and also a workshop for the preparation of his own later music. Those in Op. 25 consolidate this achievement but, while 'exploring much of the same ground, extend the paths a little and take in some new scenery on the way' (Samson). Some commentators consider the Op. 25 set more original than Op. 10. Schumann, for one, disagreed, though admitted that 'the first in A flat and the last magnificent one in C minor... display great mastership'. While everyone has their personal preferences, no one disputes the importance of the two sets and their contribution to the development of the piano. Among the technical challenges are rhythm (No. 2), staccato (No. 4), sixths (No. 8), octaves (No. 10) and arpeggios (No. 12).

Three of the Op. 25 set are known by their nicknames. Of Op. 25 No. 1 ('The Shepherd Boy' or 'Aeolian Harp'), Chopin once gave some interpretative hints to a pupil: 'Imagine a little shepherd who takes refuge in a peaceful grotto from an approaching storm. In the distance rushes the wind and the rain while the shepherd gently plays a melody on his flute.' This is one of the very few instances in which Chopin provided any sort of programme for an interpreter to bear in mind. No. 9 ('Butterfly') does indeed make the pianist's hands flit over the keyboard like a butterfly; No. 11 ('Winter Wind'), the most extensive of the Études, is more of a winter storm than a wind.

The critic James Huneker summed it up by saying that within the Études, 'is mirrored all of Chopin, the planetary as well as the secular Chopin. When most of his piano music has gone the way of all things fashioned by mortal hands, these Studies will endure, will stand for the nineteenth century, as Beethoven crystallized the eighteenth and Bach the seventeenth centuries in piano music. Chopin is a classic.'

Funeral March
(see Sonata No. 2 in B flat minor, Op. 35, 1840)

Impromptu No. 1 in A flat major, Op. 29
Ded. Countess Caroline de Lobau
Pub. 1837

An impromptu is a short piece reminiscent of an improvisation. The term was first used around 1822, but it was Schubert and Chopin who made it their own. This, the first of three if we exclude the earlier Fantaisie-Impromptu, is considered by many to be one of the most beautiful and spontaneous of all Chopin's works. Caroline de Lobau, its dedicatee, was one of his pupils.

Mazurkas in C minor, B minor, D flat major & C sharp minor, Op. 30
Ded. Princess Maria Czartoryska
Pub. 1837

214

Moja pieszczotka (My Sweetheart), Op. 74 No. 12 (wds Mickiewicz)
Pub. 1857
In Liszt's piano transcription, this is known as 'My Joys'.

Nocturnes in B major & A flat major, Op. 32 Nos 1 & 2
Ded. Baroness Camille de Billing
Pub. 1837

Scherzo No. 2 in B flat minor, Op. 31
Ded. Countess Adèle de Fürstenstein
Pub. 1837
The best-known of the four Scherzos and among Chopin's most popular works, the B flat minor Scherzo used to be disparagingly known as the 'governess's Scherzo' because at one time every well-brought-up young lady seemed to play it. According to Wilhelm von Lenz, the arresting opening bars – an innocent question followed by a decisive answer – could never be played to Chopin's satisfaction. It was never played questioningly enough, never soft enough, never rounded enough, never sufficiently weighted. 'It must be like a house of the dead,' he once said. 'That's the key to whole piece.' And of its lyrical D flat major central section: 'You should think of [the singer] Pasta, of Italian song – not of French vaudeville!'

Dedicated to another of Chopin's pupils, the B flat minor, like the other three Scherzos, has an A–B–A structure but its richness, variety and triumphant coda set it apart.

Variation in E major from 'Hexameron, Morceau de concert – Grandes variations de bravoure pour piano sur la marche des Puritains de Bellini, composées pour le concert de Mme La Princesse Belgiojoso au bénéfice des pauvres par M.M. Liszt, Thalberg, Pixis, Henri Herz, Czerny et Chopin'
Ded. Madame La Princesse Christine de Belgiojoso
To raise money for Italian refugees, Princess Belgiojoso persuaded Liszt to assemble a set of opera variations with contributions from Thalberg, Pixis, Herz, Czerny and Chopin. The chosen theme was the baritone and bass duet 'Suoni la tromba' from Bellini's last opera *I puritani*, and the finished work, with an introduction, interludes and finale by Liszt, was to have been performed by the six pianists on six pianos at the end of March. Some sources say that it did actually take place on 30 March but, according to the diligent research of the pianist and scholar Raymond Lewenthal, the concert never happened. Extracting the manuscripts from each composer proved intractable and by the time Liszt had completed the 'compilation', entitled Hexameron, the moment had passed. The title page of the music gives it away, for it reads 'composed for' and not 'played at' Princess Belgiojoso's concert. The names of Liszt and Thalberg, it might be noted, were printed in large capitals on the music's cover. Chopin and his three peers were given second billing in smaller letters.

The piece provides an omnibus of the musical styles to be found in Paris 1837, an invaluable (and entertaining) illustration of the ways in which six of the greatest pianists of the day thought, composed and played. Every variation is outlandishly difficult and brilliant – except Chopin's, whose quiet, reflective, nocturne-like Variation in E major (all the others are in A flat) achieves its own subtle victory through understatement and refined distinction. Liszt shrewdly gave him the penultimate place in the running order (just before his own flashy finale).

Hexameron became a favorite vehicle for Liszt who thrilled audiences with it from Lisbon to St Petersburg and Stockholm to Constantinople.

## 1838

Andantino in G minor
Arrangement for piano solo of the song Wiosna, Op. 74 No. 2 (below)
Pub. 1968

Mazurkas in G sharp minor, D major, C major & B minor, Op. 33 Nos 1–4
Ded. Countess Roza Mostowska
Pub. 1838

Mazurka in B major, Op. 41 No. 2
Composed 28 November 1838
Ded. Stefan Witwicki
Pub. 1840

Nocturne in G minor, Op. 37 No. 1
Pub. 1840
Schumann, in reviewing the two Nocturnes, Op. 37 (see 1839 for the second of these), wrote of them, 'they are essentially distinguished from his earlier ones by simpler decoration and more gentle grace. We all know how Chopin was formerly strewn with pearls, spangles, and golden trinkets. He has altered and grown older; he still loves decoration, but now of that nobler kind under which poetic ideality gleams more transparently.'

Polonaise in A major, Op. 40 No. 1
Ded. Julian Fontana
Pub. 1840
One of Chopin's best-known works, the so-called 'Military' Polonaise is an unabashed call to arms. It is consistently optimistic, vigorous and brilliant, the composer at his most patriotic with 'the gallantly advancing chivalry of Poland, determination in every look and gesture' (Niecks). Strange, then, that such a heroic work has no coda but simply restates the opening theme before coming to an abrupt conclusion.

24 Preludes, Op. 28

Ded. (Leipzig edition) J.C. Kessler; (London & Paris editions) Camille Pleyel
The set of 24 Preludes form an integrated whole through the sequence of keys in which they are written. This follows the circle of fifths, each major key work paired with its relative minor. For example, No. 1 in C major is followed by No. 2 in the relative key of A minor; the next Prelude must then logically be in a key one fifth higher – G major – followed by No. 4 in the relative key of E minor... and so on. The more remote the key, the more intricate the music tends to become.

Most of the Preludes had been completed prior to Chopin's departure to Majorca with George Sand and her children. Despite the difficulty of his time in Valldemosa, Chopin completed the cycle here. He was fond of creating new forms from old titles. A prelude is normally an introductory piece of music (the opening of a suite, say), but these Preludes preface nothing – they are simply self-contained thoughts, miniature tone poems exploring myriad shades of feelings and moods. Eight of them are less than a minute in length; only three last longer than three minutes.

The cycle contains some of Chopin's most beloved works – No. 15, for example, the 'Raindrop' Prelude; No. 20 in C minor inspired sets of variations from Rachmaninov and Busoni (as well as being used as the basis for Barry Manilow's hit song Could it be magic?); the E minor and B minor Preludes were played on the organ at Chopin's funeral, while No. 16 in B flat minor is, as every professional pianist will confirm, terrifyingly difficult, despite its brevity. Whether or not Chopin intended the entire set to be played straight through is a moot point and a matter of individual taste. He himself presented them as single pieces or in groups.

Even on their own, the 24 Preludes would have ensured Chopin's claim to immortality. Kullak felt that 'in their aphoristic brevity [they are] masterpieces of the first rank'.

Waltz in A minor, Op. 34 No. 2
Ded. Baroness d'Ivry

Waltz in F major, Op. 34 No. 3
Ded. Mlle A. d'Eichtal
Pub. 1838
'The least waltz-like of all the Waltzes', Op. 34 No. 2 opens with a memorable cello-like melancholy air of delicious languor. The story goes that Chopin was at his publisher's, when Stephen Heller called in to order all the Waltzes. Chopin asked him which one he liked best. Heller mentioned this one and Chopin said, 'I am glad you like that one. It is also my favorite.'

The whirling energy of the opening section of its successor in F major could not be more of a contrast. Its central section, complete with right-hand appoggiaturas, gave rise to its nickname, the 'Cat Waltz'. Legend has it that Chopin's cat leapt upon the keyboard while he was improvising, giving him the idea for this particular figure.

Wiosna (Spring Song), Op. 74 No. 2 (wds Witwicki)

(also published as piano solo: Andantino in G minor)
Pub. 1857

## 1839

Ballade No. 2 in F major, Op. 38
Ded. Robert Schumann
Pub. 1840

One of the masterpieces of the piano literature, the Second Ballade is unusual for its time in beginning in one key (F major) and ending in another (A minor). More important is the programme of the music itself. The listener is introduced to an innocent, pastoral scene played sotto voce in a gently rocking siciliano rhythm. This, it seems, is going to be a children's fairy story. But no sooner has the opening theme faded away than a nightmare scenario explodes, marked ff, presto con fuoco. This passage bears a strong resemblance to the 'Winter Wind' Étude, Op. 25 No. 11. Finally the first theme returns, evoking perhaps Othello's line to Iago: 'But yet the pity of it… O, the pity of it'. Its dedicatee regarded it as 'One of his wildest and most original compositions'.

Impromptu No. 2 in F sharp major, Op. 36
Pub. 1840

Though entitled 'Impromptu', there is more than a little of the ballade about Op. 36. After a dream-like opening, it progresses to a march in D major (a modulation over two bars that Huneker describes as 'creaking on their hinges'). But its most celebrated section is the coda, a scintillating example of what the French call 'jeu perlé': the art of playing rapid scale passages with the lightest, most even of touches.

Mazurkas in E minor, A flat major & C sharp minor, Op. 41 Nos 1, 3 & 4
Pub. 1840

Nocturne in G major, Op. 37 No. 2
(see also Nocturne in G minor of 1838)

This Nocturne was completed during Chopin's first stay at Nohant, but probably sketched in Majorca. There is a theory that the music was inspired by the night sea crossing to the island. More than one commentator is of the opinion that its second subject, possibly derived from a Normandy song, is one of the most beautiful of all Chopin's melodies.

Polonaise in C minor, Op. 40 No. 2
(see also Polonaise in A major of 1838)

While the great Russian pianist-composer Anton Rubinstein thought the A major Polonaise portrayed Poland's greatness, he saw in its gloomy companion Poland's downfall. The poignant opening theme (given in the left hand) combines nobility, regret and suffering, emotions that are heightened when it returns embellished towards the end.

Scherzo No. 3 in C sharp minor, Op. 39
Ded. Adolf Gutmann
Pub. 1839
Another cornerstone of the piano repertoire, the Third Scherzo, like the Ballade No. 2, has wildly contrasted sections, though achieved by different means. Its opening theme is a 'peevish, fretful, fiercely scornful' (Niecks) burst of octaves. The central section in D flat major is a serene chorale interrupted every four bars by a delicate fall of broken arpeggios, creating a magical effect. The episode returns after a repeat of the impetuous opening theme, but then Chopin introduces into the chorale an unexpected and heart-catching modulation. It is a passage of the utmost beauty.

This Scherzo is the only one of his works that Chopin dedicated to a male pupil. By all accounts, though Gutmann was one of the earliest to study with him in Paris and remained a faithful friend throughout the composer's life, he was not the most distinguished of players. Chopin, for some reason, was blind to his pupil's shortcomings. '[Chopin] had gone to incredible pains to try and shape an image from this block of wood.' (Lenz)

## 1840
Dumka (Reverie) (wds Zaleski)
Pub. 1910

Mazurka in A minor
Ded. Emile Gaillard
Pub. 1841

Sostenuto in E flat major
Pub. 1955

Trois Nouvelles Études in F minor, A flat major & D flat major
Composed 1839–40
Pub. 1840
Though composed to order (for the Piano Method of Moscheles and Fétis), these three short Studies are worthy pendants to the Opp. 10 and 25 sets, though they would be equally at home among the Preludes. All three elegantly and mellifluously disguise different technical challenges. Interestingly, when set beside the transcendental virtuosity of the studies by Liszt, Mendelssohn, Henselt and Thalberg that were also commissioned for the Piano Method, Chopin's seem like innocent interlopers.

Sonata No. 2 in B flat minor, Op. 35
Pub. 1840
On 8 August 1839, Chopin wrote to Julian Fontana from Nohant: 'At present I am writing a Sonata in B flat minor in which will be found the march that you know [the famous

Funeral March had been composed as a separate piece in 1837]. This Sonata contains an allegro, a scherzo in E flat minor, the march, and a short finale – three pages, perhaps, in my notation. After the march, the left hand babbles in unison with the right.'

Perhaps no work of Chopin's has been discussed more than this extraordinary Sonata, 'one of the priceless possessions of music. It must for ever rank with the masterpieces of all ages,' according to one commentator. To Schumann, 'Chopin has simply bound together four of his wildest children, to smuggle them under his name into a place [i.e., a work calling itself a sonata] to which they could not else have penetrated.'

After a brief introduction marked grave, the first movement opens with an agitated first subject contrasted with one of Chopin's finest, long-spun melodies as a second theme. The whole first section is repeated before a loose development of the themes, culminating in an exciting and forceful coda. The Scherzo, equally impetuous, powerful and sombre at the outset, is set against another of those heavenly melodies for its central section. The Funeral March follows with its grief-wracked tolling – surely one of the world's best-known (and certainly most parodied) themes – and a serene middle trio that brings consolation before the March resumes, taking us 'into the very luxury of woe', its last bars dying away to nothing.

The most talked-about aspect of the Sonata is the finale, marked 'presto, non tanto'. Its seventy-five bars (lasting about one minute and thirteen seconds, compared with the twenty minutes of the three preceding movements) consist solely of the two hands playing in unison an octave apart. Schumann could not understand it ('music it is not… the Sonata ends as it began, puzzling, like a sphinx with a mocking smile'); Kullak suggested that it portrayed 'the autumn wind whirling away the withered leaves over the fresh grave'; many others think the finale is one of the most remarkable movements in the history of the piano sonata. Today, few demur from the view that the Sonata is a highly successful unified cycle. It has always been part of the repertoire of almost every great pianist.

Waltz in A flat major, Op. 42
Pub. 1840
'This waltz,' writes Lenz, 'springing from the eight-bar trill, should evoke a musical clock, according to Chopin himself. In his own performances it embodied his rubato style to the fullest; he would play it as a continued stretto prestissimo with the bass maintaining a steady beat. A garland of flowers winding amidst the dancing couples!' It is one of Chopin's finest examples of the genre, and the only one to bear no dedication.

## 1841

Allegro de concert in A major, Op. 46
Ded. Friederike Müller-Streicher
Pub. 1841
This fascinating work, astonishingly neglected, is dedicated to one of Chopin's most gifted pupils. It is the complete first movement of a Third Piano Concerto that Chopin

began composing in Vienna in 1830. When his attention drifted away from works involving orchestra, it was abandoned, leaving just this extant movement to be revised and extended into its present form– a Concerto without orchestra – before publication. Stylistically, it is similar to the early Concertos combined with the piano writing of the more mature Chopin. It is extremely demanding to play.

Jean-Louis Nicodé (1853–1919) arranged the work for piano and orchestra sometime in the 1880s, adding seventy bars of his own. André Messager made a second version which was played before the First World War by Paderewski. A third was produced in Poland by Kazimierz Wiłkomirski (1900–1995) between the two world wars. This was destroyed during the Second World War, after which Wiłkomirski gallantly set to and made another version. It is highly effective, even though the orchestra is given a prominence far beyond anything that Chopin himself would have written.

Ballade No. 3 in A flat major, Op. 47
Ded. Princess Pauline de Noailles
Pub. 1841
There could hardly be more of a contrast between the preceding Ballade and this heart-warming tone poem. 'The finely intellectual Pole accustomed to move in the most courtly circles of the French capital, will be distinctly recognized in it,' reports Schumann, refusing 'to analyze its poetic atmosphere further'. Quite so.

The work was a favorite of Sir Winston Churchill, who never failed to request his friend the great pianist Benno Moiseiwitsch to play 'the Galloping Horse' (Churchill's name for the piece) whenever they met. Though the Ballade's second theme is surely more of a cantering horse, Moiseiwitsch commissioned a statuette of a horse and rider, the appropriate musical quotation fixed to the plinth, which resided on the mantelpiece of Churchill's home at 28 Hyde Park Gate. The Princess Pauline de Noailles, dedicatee of the Ballade, was a pupil of Chopin.

Fantasy in F minor, Op. 49
Ded. Princess Catherine de Soutzo
Pub. 1841
To another princess-pupil went the dedication of this, 'one of the highest expressions of the composer's genius'.

No one who loves the piano can be in any doubt that the F minor Fantasy is not only one of Chopin's greatest works but one of the greatest masterworks of the piano literature as a whole. It has never achieved the same level of popularity as some of the Ballades which it closely resembles. The music has a story to tell, though it is down to the individual listener to decide what exactly that story is. Liszt (reporting third-hand) said it represented a quarrel and reconciliation between Chopin and George Sand. Certainly it was written at Nohant at a time when the couple were at their happiest – yet the dominant atmosphere of the piece is melancholy, despite passages of nobility, dramatic grandeur and, in its central section, extreme tenderness.

Fugue in A minor
Pub. 1898
A short fugal exercise written at Nohant that sounds very much like Bach and nothing like Chopin.

Mazurka in A minor
Pub. 1841

Nocturnes in C minor & F sharp minor, Op. 48 Nos 1 & 2
Ded. Mlle Laure Duperré
Pub. 1841
The C minor Nocturne is the grandest (and, for this writer, the greatest) of all Chopin's works in this form. Kullak felt that its 'design and poetic contents... make it the most important one that Chopin created; the chief subject is a masterly expression of a great powerful grief, for instance at a grave misfortune occurring to one's beloved fatherland.' He sees the second subject as a band of heroic men gathering solemnly to go forth on a holy war to conquer or die for their native land.

Chopin was particularly finicky about how the haunting first four bars should be played. 'He was never satisfied,' reports Lenz, who finally succeeded 'after long efforts' to play the first two bars satisfactorily for the composer, before being put to the test again over the next two bars.

Its companion is inevitably a slighter work but beautiful nonetheless in its 'tear-laden sweetness' (Niecks). When Gutmann studied it with Chopin, the composer told him that the middle section should be played as a recitative: '"a tyrant commands" (the first two chords), he said, "and the other asks for mercy"'.

Polonaise in F sharp minor, Op. 44
Ded. Princess de Beauvau
Pub. 1841
This and the later Op. 53 are Chopin's greatest essays in the Polonaise form. It opens with 'a rush of exasperation and surprise – and indignant pause – and then a roar of defiance' (Ashton Jonson) before being transformed midway into a tender mazurka of touching melancholy. The whole work is bathed, in Herbert Weinstock's words, in a wonderful 'semi-twilight.'

Prelude in C sharp minor, Op. 45
Pub. 1841

Śliczny chłopiec (The Handsome Lad), Op. 74 No. 8 (wds Zaleski)
Pub. 1857

Tarantelle in A flat major, Op. 43

Pub. 1841

Tarantelle is a Polish translation of the Italian, which exactly describes this music: a transmutation of Rossini into Chopin. There is nothing remotely Neapolitan about this bustling if somewhat severe homage to Rossini's *La danza*. It is a pleasant enough salon piece, another product of Nohant and the summer of 1841. It is extraordinary that in asking Julian Fontana to make a fair copy of the piece, Chopin requested that he check up if Rossini's song was written in 6/8 or 12/8. 'As to my composition, it does not matter which way it is written, but I should prefer it to be like Rossini.' How could he not know that a tarantella is always in 6/8?

## 1842

Impromptu No. 3 in G flat major, Op. 51
Ded. Countess Jeanne Batthyany-Esterházy
Pub. 1843

The least popular of the three Impromptus, Op. 51 has been characterized by more than one commentator as 'morbid' in its sentiment. It is a strange, uncheerful piece for which Chopin had a particular predilection, according to his pupil Lenz.

Mazurkas in G major, A flat major, C sharp minor, Op. 50 Nos 1–3
Ded. Leon Szmitkowski
Pub. 1842

Nocturnes in F minor & E flat major, Op. 55 Nos 1 & 2
Composed 1842–4
Ded. Jane Stirling
Pub. 1844

One of Chopin's most popular Nocturnes, No. 15 in F minor gives the impression of improvisation like few others – Chopin sitting idly at the piano following the impulse of the moment. The critic Hanslick thought it represented 'a sadness which rises by different degrees to a cry of despair, and is then tranquilized by a feeling of hope'. Its companion in E flat, less frequently heard today, is unusual among its companions in having no contrasting middle section.

Polonaise in A flat major, Op. 53
Ded. Auguste Léo
Pub. 1843

Here is the most famous of all the Polonaises and one of the most celebrated pieces of piano music. It is often called the 'Heroic' or 'Military' Polonaise which describes its character perfectly, written as it is in 'a most majestic and finished style... a glorious apotheosis of the past' (Kleczyński). The originality of the themes and the rich variety of ideas are all worked through in a breathtaking epic of just six minutes. To hear it played by a great pianist – such as Arthur Rubinstein, who frequently used to end his recitals with it – can be an unforgettable experience.

The striking central section, with its descending semiquaver octave figure in the bass, is usually said to represent a cavalry charge or the trampling of horses; but if it is played at the correct tempo, as Chopin insisted, it is more like an approaching cavalcade. Hallé recalled how on one occasion he played the work to the composer. 'In his gentle way he laid his hand upon my shoulder, saying how unhappy he felt, because he had heard his "Grande Polonaise" in A flat jouée vite!, thereby destroying all the grandeur, the majesty, of this noble inspiration.'

Waltz in F minor, Op. 70 No. 2
Ded. (different autographs) Marie de Krudner, Mme Oury, Elise Gavard, Countess Esterházy
Pub. 1852
One of three Waltzes, composed at different times, published after Chopin's death as his Op. 70.

## 1843

Ballade No. 4 in F minor, Op. 52
Ded. Baroness Charlotte de Rothschild
Pub. 1843
General consensus puts the F minor Ballade at, or near the summit of, Chopin's art. Here are all aspects of his consummate skill brought together in a tone poem of about eleven minutes in length: the large-scale heroics, the memorable themes, the adventurous, intelligent keyboard writing, the intimate, and the melancholy. 'It is a masterpiece in piano literature as the Mona Lisa and Madame Bovary are masterpieces in painting and prose.' (Huneker)

Its haunting opening was once aptly described by the critic Joan Chisell as bringing the same sense of wonder that a blind person, if granted the gift of sight, might feel on discovering the world's beauty for the first time. The Ballade's concluding pages, with its mini-cadenza, canonic treatment of the opening theme, and coruscating coda, are as remarkable as anything that Chopin wrote.

Moderato in E major
Ded. Countess de Cheremetieff
Pub. 1910

Scherzo No. 4 in E major, Op. 54
Ded. Jeanne de Caraman
Pub. 1843
After the drama and turbulence of the earlier Scherzos, Chopin's final essay in the genre is the only one of the four written in a major key, appropriate for its generally airy, almost Mendelssohnian mood. It is certainly more of a true scherzo than any of its companions. Op. 54 was a favorite of Saint-Saëns, who lifted a passage from it (and also the contrasted duple and triple rhythms of the A flat Waltz, Op. 42) for the Scherzo of

his G minor Concerto. There are moments when the composer seems to be looking back to some of his earlier works, a feeling efficiently dispelled by the scintillating final pages.

## 1844

Berceuse in D flat major, Op. 57
Ded. Elise Gavard
Pub. 1845
Having elevated the Nocturne, Étude, Polonaise and Mazurka into higher art forms, Chopin here works his magic on the cradle-song. It was probably inspired by the small daughter of Pauline Viardot who was left at Nohant to be cared for by Chopin and George Sand while Viardot went on tour. The simple rocking figure remains unaltered throughout the entire course of the piece (about four and a half minutes), every bar beginning with the same low D flat in the bass and, except for two bars towards the end, unvarying in its gently alternating tonic and dominant harmonies while the right hand traces delicate filigree figures above it. One of the composer's biographers, Charles Willeby, makes the charming suggestion that in the last eight bars the nurse, who has been rocking the child, herself succumbs to the drowsy influence of the music.

Mazurkas in B major, C major & C minor, Op. 56 Nos 1–3
Composed 1843–4
Ded. Catherine Maberly
Pub. 1844

Sonata No. 3 in B minor, Op. 58
Ded. Countess Emilie de Perthuis
Pub. 1845
Any amount of scholarly analysis has accrued round Chopin's three Piano Sonatas. The First is far inferior to its successors; the Second has only a very loose connection to Classical sonata form but is, nonetheless, a masterpiece; the Third is closer to sonata form but less successful... To most music lovers, such academic considerations do not matter one jot. The 'ifs' and 'buts' (or should that be 'sniffs' and 'tuts'?) of the professors cannot confine genius to a straitjacket. Is the B minor Sonata a great work? Yes it is.

Perhaps the first movement has an over-abundance of themes, but what themes they are! The scherzo which follows is succinct, dazzling and graceful. The nocturne-like slow movement is the weakest of the three, with a meandering, somewhat self-absorbed melody. That weakness, however, only has the effect of bringing anticipation to the gloriously jubilant finale, a galloping rondo that brings the work to a thrilling conclusion. Technically, it is one of the most difficult movements of all Chopin's music to play. Interestingly, its second subject is one of the few occasions where he writes in scales (other examples are the end of the Impromptu, Op. 36 and the Barcarolle).

225

## 1845

Dwojaki koniec (Death's Divisions), Op. 74 No. 11 (wds Zaleski)
Pub. 1857

Mazurkas in A minor, A flat major & F sharp minor, Op. 59 Nos 1–3
Pub. 1845

Nie ma, czego trzeba (There Is No Need), Op. 74 No. 13 (wds Zaleski)
Pub. 1857

## 1846

Barcarolle in F sharp major, Op. 60
Ded. Baroness de Stockhausen
Pub. 1846
Like the Berceuse, Bolero and Tarantelle, the Barcarolle is Chopin's only essay in this form. The Venetian barcarolles – gondoliers' songs – were an attraction to visitors as early as the eighteenth century with their characteristic lilting 6/8 rhythm (Chopin's is notated in 12/8), mirroring the rise and fall of the boat. The most famous musical barcarolles before Chopin's were Mendelssohn's 'Venetian Gondola Songs' from his Songs without Words. Fauré was to write a set of thirteen several decades later.

Hallé recalls that at Chopin's last Paris concert, 'he played the latter part of the "Barcarolle", from the point where it demands the utmost energy, in the most opposite style, pianissimo, but with such wonderful nuances that one remained in doubt if this new reading were not preferable to the accustomed one. Nobody but Chopin could have accomplished such a feat.'

Galop Marquis in A flat major
Pub. ?

Mazurkas in B major, F minor & C sharp minor, Op. 63 Nos 1–3
Ded. Countess Laura Czosnowska
Pub. 1847

Mazurka in A minor, Op. 67 No. 4
Pub. 1855

Mazurka in F minor, Op. 68 No. 4
Composed ?1846, perhaps later
Pub. 1855
Realised by Franchomme in 1852 from sketch

Nocturnes in B major & E major, Op. 62 Nos 1 & 2
Ded. Mlle R de Könneritz

Pub. 1846

Opinions differ on the merit of Chopin's last two Nocturnes. Niecks thinks 'they owe their existence rather to the sweet habit of activity than to inspiration' and that they reflect the composer's poor state of health. Huneker finds the B major work has 'charm, a fruity charm'. Many find in the final E major Nocturne a valedictory element because of its lingering coda, as if Chopin was unwilling to bid farewell to his last inspiration in this form.

Polonaise-Fantaisie in A flat major, Op. 61
Ded. Mme A. Veyret
Pub. 1846

Having raised the Polonaise to new heights, Chopin here attempts to develop the form further. It is quite distinct from the mood and structure of the earlier works – indeed, it is in more than one sense in a class of its own – and although the distinctive rhythm of the Polonaise is prominent in the opening theme, elsewhere it is often absent altogether. Hence the 'Fantaisie' part of the title.

The structure of the work is tricky to absorb on first hearing, for Chopin seems to want to recreate the feeling of rhapsodic improvisation; but through thematic recall and his subconscious sense of form, pacing and proportion, he manages to achieve a remarkably cohesive whole. The manuscript of the work reveals how difficult Chopin found it to arrive at a satisfactory final version. Perhaps that was inevitable in such an exploratory, original work.

Sonata for cello and piano in G minor, Op. 65
Ded. Adèle Forest
Pub. 1847

This was Chopin's final major work and the last to be published during his lifetime. Some of his contemporaries found it difficult to grasp. Moscheles studied the score and found 'passages which sound to me like someone preluding on the piano, the player knocking at the door of every key and clef, to find if any melodious sounds were at home'. Nevertheless he subsequently arranged the work for four hands, even if he did call it 'a trial of patience'. Anatole Leikin detects in the work's initial phrase a reference to the leading motif of Schubert's Winterreise which first appears in the opening song 'Gute Nacht'. The subject matter of Winterreise, the disappointed lover in despair at leaving his beloved, would seem to reflect the circumstances of Chopin's life when he was writing the Sonata. Leikin has evidence that Chopin turned to Winterreise at the time of his separation from George Sand. Could that be why he omitted the first movement at the work's premiere? Would the Parisian audience have understood the hidden musical reference? Is that why he could not bear to hear the opening phrase when on his deathbed?

The first movement poses a challenge to the players in terms of balance. In the dance-like Scherzo, the contrapuntal Largo and the final Allegro, this is less of a problem. Although it is a score that at times manifests Chopin's doubts and lack

227

of fluency as he composed, this remains at the very least an interesting work, and a notable example of the Romantic cello sonata.

**1847**
Largo in E flat major
Pub. 1938

Melodya (wds Krasiński), Op. 74 No. 9
Pub. 1857

Nocturne in C minor
Pub. 1938

Waltz in D flat major, Op. 64 No. 1
Ded. Countess Delfina Potocka
Waltz in C sharp minor, Op. 64 No. 2
Ded. Baroness Charlotte de Rothschild
Waltz in A flat major, Op. 64 No. 3
Ded. Countess Katarzyna Branicka
Pub. 1847
The Waltz in D flat is the 'Minute' Waltz, the most famous of the Waltzes and one of the best-known works in all piano literature. It is impossible to play in sixty seconds, even if you rush the lyrical central section. On average, it lasts about ninety seconds – the shortest, or 'minute', Chopin Waltz. The story goes that its inspiration was George Sand's little dog that used to run round in circles, chasing its own tail. One evening Sand said to Chopin that if she had his talent she would improvise a waltz for the dog; whereupon Chopin sat down at the piano and improvised the main theme, hence the work's occasional alternative nickname 'Valse du petit chien'. There have been dozens of different arrangements, including at least three song versions, and several piano transcriptions that cleverly combine the two themes played simultaneously (see Appendix).

The popular C sharp minor Waltz alternates between its lovesick opening theme, a whirling dance (though one feels the dancers' hearts are not really in it) and a tenderly consoling third theme. It is a masterpiece of concision and poetry. By comparison, the A flat Waltz, though less well-known than its companions, is a light-hearted pendant, all chandeliers and champagne.

Waltz in A minor
Pub. 1955

**1848**
Mazurka in G minor, Op. 67 No. 2
Pub. 1855

# Personalities

Alkan, Charles-Valentin (1813–1888): Visionary composer of piano and organ works. A lifelong friend of Chopin, and his neighbor in the Square d'Orléans, Alkan was said to be the only pianist in front of whom Liszt was nervous of playing. Chopin bequeathed him his (alas) valueless Piano Method.

Bellini, Vincenzo (1801–1835): Sicilian opera composer (*Norma, La sonnambula, I puritani* and many others) and friend of Chopin whose long-breathed melodies greatly influenced Chopin's writing for the piano.

Berlioz, Hector (1803–1869): The arch-Romantic composer whose turbulent, passionate and egotistical life is mirrored in his music. Paris acquaintance of Chopin.

Białobłocki, Jan (1805–1827): Close friend of Chopin in his youth who died tragically young.

Chopin, Emilia (1812–1827): The composer's youngest sister, who died from tuberculosis aged fourteen.

Chopin, Izabela (later Barcinska) (1811–1881): The composer's younger sister and last surviving member of his immediate family.

Chopin, Justyna (*née* Krzyzanowska) (1780–1861): The composer's mother.

Chopin, Ludwika (later Jędrzejewicz) (1807–1855): The composer's eldest sister.

Chopin, Nicolas (1771–1844): The composer's father. Later changed his name to the more Polish Mikołaj.

Clésinger, Jean-Baptiste Auguste (1814–1883): French sculptor who married George Sand's daughter, Solange. He made Chopin's death mask and the marble monument adorning his grave.

Clésinger, Solange (*née* Dudevant-Sand) (1828–1899): Daughter of George Sand.

Custine, Astolphe, Marquis de (1790–1857): French writer and socialite whose mother, Delphine de Sabran, was the mistress of Chateaubriand. An (homosexual) adornment to Parisian society, Custine was warmly solicitous of Chopin and his music.

Czerny, Carl (1791–1857): Revered Austrian pianist and composer of an enormous number of piano studies plus other works. Pupil of Beethoven, teacher of Liszt.

229

d'Agoult, Marie de Flavigny, Comtesse (1805–1876): French writer (pseudonym Daniel Stern), friend of George Sand and notable beauty. Married Comte d'Agoult in 1827 whom she left in 1834 for Franz Liszt. Their daughter Cosima married Richard Wagner.

Delacroix, (Ferdinand Victor) Eugène (1798–1863): Perhaps the greatest figure in nineteenth-century French art and one of the most accomplished colorists of all time. Close friend of Chopin and George Sand, both of whom he painted.

Dudevant, Casimir, Baron (1795–1871): Husband of George Sand.

Dudevant-Sand, Maurice (1823–1889): Painter; son of George Sand.

Elsner, Józef (1769–1854): Polish (of German descent) composer and teacher of Chopin in Warsaw where he founded a school for organists. This later became the Warsaw Conservatoire. He headed the Opera there for twenty-five years.

Field, John (1782–1837): Irish pianist and composer who wrote almost exclusively for the piano and invented the name and style of the piano nocturne, developed to an elevated degree by Chopin. An alcoholic, Field died in Moscow from cancer.

Filtsch, Carl (1830–1845): Chopin's most gifted pupil, who died from tuberculosis aged fifteen.

Fontana, Julian (1810–1869): Born in Warsaw and, like Chopin, studied with Elsner. Settled in Paris in 1830 and taught piano there and in London. Much put-upon by Chopin, whose affairs he managed when the latter was at Nohant. With the family's permission, he was largely responsible for the appearance of Chopin's posthumous works. Committed suicide four years later.

Franchomme, August-Joseph (1808–1884): Renowned French cellist and long-time intimate friend of Chopin. Taught at the Paris Conservatoire from 1846 and wrote many cello works.

Grzymała, Albert (Wojciech) (1793–1871): Polish patriot resident in Paris and confidant of both George Sand and Chopin. Grzymała was a colorful character who had known the young Chopin in Warsaw. He was a highly cultivated man whose career, which had included two spells in Russian jails for his political activities, was based on his financial acumen. Once he arrived in Paris, he made his living from the Stock Exchange and quickly established himself at the heart of Parisian society.

Gutmann, Adolf (1819–1892): German pianist and one of Chopin's favorite pupils (though many who heard him play wondered why). His album of Études caractéristiques enjoyed a degree of popularity in the nineteenth century.

230

Hallé, Sir Charles (1819–1895): Originally Karl Halle from Westphalia, Hallé was friendly with the Chopin–Liszt circle in Paris before going on to become a renowned pianist and conductor. He settled in Manchester, where he founded the Hallé Orchestra.

Heine, (Christian Johann) Heinrich (1797–1856): German poet and essayist. He went into voluntary exile in Paris in 1830 after his revolutionary opinions made him unemployable in Germany. Here he turned to politics, becoming leader of the cosmopolitan democratic movement. He was later confined to bed with spinal paralysis. Schumann and Schubert set many of his poems to music, and he was a friend and admirer of Chopin.

Herz, Henri (1803–1888): Brilliant Austrian pianist and composer whose music in the 1830s realized three or four times the price of that of his superior contemporaries as well as comprehensively outselling them. Also a successful piano manufacturer.

Hiller, Ferdinand (1811–1885): German pianist (pupil of Hummel), conductor, composer, critic and teacher. A close friend of Chopin, Liszt, Berlioz and many others when he lived in Paris (1828–35), and also of Mendelssohn who greatly influenced his style.

Hugo, Victor (Marie) (1802–1885): French poet and writer, a leading figure of the French Romantic movement whose principle works include *The Hunchback of Notre Dame*, *Les Misérables* and *Le Roi s'amuse* (the basis of Verdi's *Rigoletto*).

Hummel, Johann Nepomuk (1778–1837): Great Austrian pianist and composer (he studied with Haydn and Mozart) who wrote concertos and other works for piano, as well as church music and operas. He and his son showed much kindness to the young Chopin, whose early works show Hummel's influence.

Kalkbrenner, Friedrich Wilhelm Michael (1785–1849): Celebrated German pianist and composer whom the young Chopin greatly admired (he dedicated his E minor Piano Concerto to him but declined Kalkbrenner's offer of piano lessons, despite the latter's urging). Much of his music, though superficial, is well wrought and extremely effective. Also a partner in the piano firm of Pleyel.

Lamartine, Adolphe Marie Louis de (1790–1869): French poet, politician and historian.

Lind, Jenny (1820–1887): Famous soprano known as 'the Swedish Nightingale'. She commanded enormous fees during her long career (she retired in 1870), making generous donations to many charitable foundations in Sweden. She died in Malvern Wells, England. There is a bust of her in Westminster Abbey.

Liszt, Franz (1811–1886): Hungarian composer and pianist, one of the most celebrated, revered and influential figures of the age. His twelve symphonic poems created a new form of orchestral music. He was the first person to give a solo piano recital and was the generous teacher and mentor of generations of young pianists and composers. He abandoned the life of a virtuoso pianist in 1848 and settled in Weimar where he composed, taught and conducted, making the town the musical center of Germany. The works of his last years were experimental and prophetic of much later developments in the twentieth century.

Mathias, Georges-Amédée-Saint-Clair (1826–1910): Important pupil of Chopin who was professor of piano at the Paris Conservatoire from 1862 to 1893. Pupils included Teresa Carreño, Paul Dukas, Isidor Philipp, Raoul Pugno, Erik Satie and Ernest Schelling.

Matuszyński, Jan (1809–1842): Close, lifelong friend of Chopin from their schooldays in Warsaw. Having completed his medical studies in Germany, he took up a teaching post at the Ecole de Médicine in Paris and shared lodgings with Chopin. He died in Chopin's arms from tuberculosis.

Mendelssohn (-Bartholdy), (Jakob Ludwig) Felix (1809–1847): Child prodigy pianist and composer who developed into one of the most original and popular composers of the nineteenth century, combining Romantic ardor with Classical decorum. He settled in Berlin in 1841. In 1843 his new school of music opened in Leipzig. He never fully recovered from the death of his sister Fanny in 1847 and, less than six months later, he too was dead.

Merk, Joseph (1795–1852): Austrian cellist and inspiration for the young Chopin. First cello at the Vienna Opera from 1818 and teacher at the Conservatoire from 1828.

Meyerbeer, Giacomo (originally Jakob Liebmann Beer) (1791–1864): Illustrious German opera composer who wrote in a flamboyant and melodramatic style that made him hugely successful. His best-known works are *Robert le diable*, *Les Huguenots*, *Le Prophète* and *L'Africaine*.

Mickiewicz, Adam Bernard (1798–1855): Considered to be the national poet of Poland. Mickiewicz was arrested and exiled to Siberia for revolutionary activities and, after the failure of the Polish revolt (1830–1), he fled to the West. He taught in Paris from 1840, devoting his life to keeping the Polish spirit alive through his writings.

Mikuli, Karol (1821–1897): Polish pianist and teacher. After medical studies, he turned to music and went to Paris to study with Chopin. Left France after the 1848 revolution, settling as director of the Lemberg conservatory. Produced one of the first authentic editions of Chopin's music. One of his pupils was the great Moriz Rosenthal.

Moscheles, Ignaz (1794–1870): Eminent Bohemian composer, pianist and teacher. After early success in all three fields, he settled in London (1821) before moving to Leipzig in 1846 to join the staff at Mendelssohn's new conservatory. He made valuable contributions to piano technique and was a much-loved mentor to a host of pupils from all over the globe.

Paër, Ferdinand (1771–1839): A significant figure in his day, the Italian-born Paër was a composer and conductor who wielded a certain influence in the musical world of Paris. Except for the occasional performance in France of *Le Maître de chapelle*, his forty-three operas have disappeared from view.

Paganini, Nicolò (1782–1840): Great genius of the violin whose dexterity and technical expertise made him a legend (many believed him to be in league with the Devil). His appearance in Warsaw had an electrifying effect on the young Chopin.

Pixis, Johann Peter (1788–1874): German pianist and composer who settled in Paris in 1825 and became part of the Chopin–Liszt circle. One of the contributors, along with Chopin, Thalberg, Czerny and Herz, to Liszt's Hexameron. His now-forgotten music, mainly for piano, ran to 150 opus numbers.

Potocka, Countess Delfina, *née* Komar (?1807–1877): Celebrated as much for her beauty as her excellent soprano voice, the Countess was a central figure in the salons of the Parisian and Polish aristocracy, famous for her longstanding liaison with the poet Zygmunt Krasiński. She took piano lessons from Chopin and the two remained on the closest terms for the rest of his life. Both the F minor Concerto and the 'Minute' Waltz are dedicated to Delfina Potocka. Among the last music Chopin heard, just two days before he died, was the Countess singing the 'Dignare Domine', from Handel's *Dettingen Te Deum*.

Ries, Ferdinand (1784–1838): German pianist and composer who studied with Beethoven (1801–4), after which he enjoyed a successful career, settling first in London (1813–24) and then, from 1827, in Frankfurt.

Rossini, Gioachino (Antonio) (1792–1868): Great Italian opera composer who lived in Paris from 1824 to 1836, and from 1855 until his death. Chopin knew him well and much admired his music, on at least one occasion sharing a concert platform with him.

Sand, George (pseudonym); Amandine Aurore Lucie Dupin, Baronne Dudevant (1804–1876): French novelist and Chopin's partner for ten years. She married Casimir, Baron Dudevant at the age of eighteen and had two children, Maurice and Solange, but after nine years left him to live the Bohemian life in Paris. Her first lover was the writer Jules Sandeau (1811–1883) from whom she derived her pen name. After affairs with Prosper Mérimée and Alfred de Musset, she lived with Chopin. After several more relationships with various philosophers and politicians she opted for the quieter life as 'châtelaine of Nohant', writing and travelling for the rest of her life. Her principal works include *Indiana* (1832), *Valentine* (1832), *Lélia* (1833), *Jacques* (1834), *Spiridion* (1838), *La Mare au diable* (1846), *Mademoiselle la Quintinie* (1863) and her autobiographical *Histoire de ma vie* (1855). Her complete works amount to over 100 volumes.

Schumann, Robert (Alexander) (1810–1856): One of the greatest composers of the nineteenth century whose music expressed the Romantic era at its most personal. He was the first important critic to recognize Chopin's genius, generously championing his music thereafter, despite Chopin's indifference. His piano suite Carnaval includes a touching portrait of Chopin. Schumann eventually became mentally unstable and spent the last two years of his life in an asylum.

Stirling, Jane Wilhelmina (1804–1859): Forever associated with Chopin's final years, Jane Stirling came from a distinguished Scottish family. She travelled to Paris to have lessons from Chopin late in 1843, though some sources speculate that they may have met some years earlier. She and her elder sister, Mrs Erskine, from whom she was inseparable, organized every aspect of Chopin's stay and concerts in London and Scotland. If her relationship with Chopin was motivated by (unreciprocated) love, generous to a fault during his final illness, Miss Stirling was exceptionally loyal in the work she undertook after his death, buying most of Chopin's estate and then sharing it with his family and close friends.

Thalberg, Sigismond (1812–1871): Hugely celebrated pianist and composer (born in Geneva) whose aristocratic bearing and perfect stillness at the keyboard while performing well-nigh impossible technical feats made him the darling of high society. His speciality was to play a central melody with the thumb of either hand, surrounding it with brilliant arabesques and arpeggios.

Viardot, Pauline, *nee* García (1821–1910): Celebrated French mezzo-soprano of extraordinary compass, and a close friend of Chopin and George Sand. She created the role of Fides in Meyerbeer's *Le Prophète* and the title-role in Gounod's opera *Sapho*. Retired in 1863. She also composed operas and made song arrangements of some of Chopin's works.

Witwicki, Stefan (1800–1847): Polish poet whose work Chopin preferred to that of Mickiewicz (see above), though it was considered far inferior: of Chopin's seventeen posthumously published songs, ten have texts by Witwicki.

Maria Wodzińska (1819–1896): Daughter of a family whom Chopin had known since childhood. The two met and fell in love in 1835 but the relationship faded. Her subsequent marriage to the son of Chopin's godfather was a short-lived disaster.

Woyciechowski, Tytus (1808–1879): School friend of Chopin and landowner. The letters he preserved reveal an intense relationship of platonic love. In his role as confidant to the young Chopin, Woyciechowski provided much-needed reassurance and brotherly advice. They stayed in touch though seem not to have met after Chopin settled in Paris.

Żywny, Adalbert (1756–1842): Bohemian violinist and Chopin's first teacher. He arrived in Poland in the eighteenth century, held a post in a private orchestra, and then became a freelance musician in Warsaw.

# Appendix

The listing below does not pretend to be comprehensive but is an attempt to collate all the most significant films, ballets, operas, songs and plays inspired by Chopin's life and/or music.

Dozens of arrangements of Chopin's music have been made for the piano. For reasons of space, only those of special interest are included here (i.e., the arrangement comes from an unexpected quarter, or is for an unusual combination; makes a noteworthy comment on the original or is simply quirky, witty or curious). A fair number of these have never been recorded.

## Chopin on Film

*La Valse de l'adieu* ('The Farewell Waltz')
France 1928
A silent film based on Chopin's life starring Pierre Blanchar as Chopin and directed by Henry Roussell. For a number of showings in the Paris cinema where it was first seen, the great American pianist Walter Morse Rummel (1887–1953) played live music by Chopin for Blanchar whenever his character sat down to 'play' the piano.

*Abschiedswalzer* ('Farewell Waltz')
Germany 1934
Wolfgang Liebeneiner starred as Chopin in this fictionalized life, a film much favored by the Nazi regime for its ideological and nationalistic connotations. With lines such as 'I love my Fatherland more than life' and 'Your Empire is music!' it is easy to see why. The film ends romantically with Chopin and Sand departing for Majorca.

*La Valse Brillante de Chopin*
France 1936
Directed by the legendary Max Ophüls, this short (six-minute) film has the famous pianist Alexander Brailowsky (1896–1976) playing the Grande Valse Brillante in A flat major, Op. 34 No. 1. Unusual angles, dynamic camerawork and a strong visual setting.

*A Song to Remember*
USA 1945
Directed by Charles Vidor, this was one of the most successful filmed biographies of the 1940s, though – in the grand tradition of the genre – it bears little relationship to the facts. The script was originally written by Ernst Marischka for *Abschiedswalzer* (see above). Paul Muni hams his way through the role of Professor Elsner, Chopin's mentor,

while Cornel Wilde and Merle Oberon make a handsome pair as Chopin and George Sand. Pianist José Iturbi provided the fingers and the soundtrack. His recording of the Polonaise in A flat major, Op. 53 became a million-seller as a result.

*Młodość Chopina* ('Chopin's Youth')
Poland 1952
With Czesław Willejko as Chopin, the film covers the composer's early years against a backdrop of European revolutionary movements – with a heavy dose of Communist ideology thrown in. Chopin is portrayed as 'the great revolutionary musician of the Polish people'.

*Impromptu*
UK 1991
Judy Davis as George Sand pursues Hugh Grant's Chopin in a forgettable romp that nevertheless attracted the talents of Julian Sands (Liszt), Anton Rodgers, Anna Massey and Emma Thompson.

*The Mystery of Chopin – The Strange Case of Delfina Potocka*
UK 1999
The normally astute Tony Palmer directed this dire docudrama. It probes the mystery of some pornographic and anti-Semitic letters supposedly written by Chopin which came to light when Delfina Potocka's great-granddaughter took them to the Polish authorities in 1945. Included is an hour-long recital of Chopin's music by Valentina Igoshina, who also talks about his work. Paul Rhys's Welsh-accented Chopin and laughable attempts at miming at the keyboard add to the project's implausibility.

*Chopin: Desire for Love*
Poland 2002
Piotr Adamczyk and Danuta Stenka star in this lush historical drama produced for Polish television. It focuses on the ill-fated love affair between Chopin and Sand. Yo-Yo Ma, Emanuel Ax, Pamela Frank and others provided the soundtrack.

## Chopin in the Movies

There are too many instances to list in detail but below are some of the more notable.

*Moonlight Sonata* (1936): Polonaise, Op. 53 (played by Ignace Paderewski)
*Blue Lagoon* (1980): Nocturne, Op. 9 No. 2
*Shadowlands* (1993): Prelude, Op. 28 No. 15
*The Truman Show* (1998): Romanze from Piano Concerto No. 1, Op. 11
*The Pianist* (2002): Prelude, Op. 28 No. 4; Ballade, Op. 23

# Chopin in the Theatre

## Operas

*Chopin* by Giacomo Orefice (1865–1922). Libretto by Angiolo Orvieto. First performance: Milan, 25 November 1901. Has selections from Chopin's best-known works mixed with authentic and fictional scenarios from Chopin's life.

*Fuego Fátuo* ('Firefly') by Manuel de Falla (1876–1946). An unfinished three-act opera (1818–19) based on music by Chopin. Its nineteen sections quote Scherzos Nos 2, 3 and 4, the Bolero, Tarantelle, Berceuse, Barcarolle, and a number of Études, Waltzes and Mazurkas. There is also an orchestral suite arranged by Antoni Ros Marbà (published in 1976) featuring nine movements from Fuego Fátuo.

## Ballets

*Chopiniana* (1907), five piano pieces orch. Alexander Glazunov (see Orchestral Works, below); later (1908) version includes additional pieces orch. Maurice Keller
*Les Sylphides* (1909), final version of Chopiniana (Polonaise, Op. 40 No. 1 – some companies substitute Prelude in A – Nocturne, Op. 32 No. 2, Waltzes, Op. 18 No. 1, Op. 64 No. 2 & Op. 70 No. 1, Mazurkas, Op. 33 No. 2 & Op. 67 No. 3, Prelude, Op. 28 No. 7). Igor Stravinsky orchestrated the Nocturne and the Waltz, Op. 18 No. 1. Other pieces arr. Anatole Liadov, Nikolai Sokolov and Sergey Taneyev
*Autumn Leaves* (1918), a vehicle for Pavlova
*La Nuit ensorcelée* (not dated), arr. Louis Aubert (Études Nos 3 & 14, Nocturne No. 14, Preludes Nos 10, 11 & 22, Mazurka No. 17, Waltz No. 4, Rondo, Op. 14)
*Les Sylphides* (1936), arr. Douglas
*Chopin Concerto* (1937), set to Piano Concerto No. 1 in E minor
*Classic Ballet* (1937), set to Piano Concerto No. 2 in F minor, revised as Constantia (1944)
*The Concert* (1956), piano pieces, some orch. H. Kay
*Dances at a Gathering* (1969), selection of piano pieces
*In the Night* (1970), set to four of the Nocturnes
*A Month in the Country* (1976), based on Turgenev's play; music arr. Lanchbery
*The Lady of the Camellias* (1978), includes complete Piano Concerto No. 2 in F minor as well as other solo works
*The Lady of the Camellias* (1990, Ballet Florida), uses sections of Piano Concerto No. 1 in E minor, Fantasy on Polish Airs, 'Krakowiak' Rondo, 'Là ci darem' Variations, and Andante spianato and Grande Polonaise Brillante

## Plays

*The Damask Rose* (1930), book and musical adaptation by George Clutsam. Set in 1764 [sic], the play sought to capitalize on the author's 1923 hit *Lilac Time* (*Blossom Time* in America) which exploited the character and music of Schubert. This later effusion tried to do the same with Chopin's life and loves but did not enjoy the same success.

*Waltz without End* (1942) by Eric Maschwitz, Chopin's music adapted by Bernard Grün. The show ran for a respectable 181 performances in London, though the treatment of Chopin's personality, the facts of his life and the handling of his music were said 'to have been in vigorous competition as to which could achieve the more deadly vulgarization'. James Agate in *The Sunday Times* wrote: 'To alter a composer's rhythms, key and tempi is to murder that composer. To make voices sing words that are the acme of tawdry nonsense is to destroy an exquisite reputation.'

# Chopin Plagiarized

> *'Sooner or later, they're going to steal those melodies.'*
> Elsner to his pupil Chopin in *A Song to Remember*

The following is a selection of vocal works based on Chopin's music:

*Aime-moi* (wds Louis Pomey; arr. Pauline Viardot), based on Mazurka, Op. 33 No. 2
*Aspiration* (not dated), based on Nocturne, Op. 9 No. 2
*Berceuse* (wds Pomey; arr. Viardot), based on Mazurka, Op. 33 No. 3
*Castle of Dreams* (1919), based on the middle section of the 'Minute' Waltz, Op. 64 No. 1
*Coquette* (wds Pomey; arr. Viardot), based on Mazurka, Op. 7 No. 1
*Could It Be Magic?* (Barry Manilow, 1973), based on Prelude, Op. 28 No. 20
*La Danse* (wds Pomey; arr. Viardot), based on Mazurka, Op. 50 No. 1
*Faible cœur* (arr. Viardot), based on Mazurka, Op. 7 No. 3
*La Fête* (arr. Viardot), based on Mazurka, Op. 6 No. 4
*Goodnight, My Beloved* (arr. Maurice Besly), based on Nocturne, Op. 9 No. 2
*'Gypsy Love Song'* (1898) from *The Fortune Teller* (Victor Herbert), based on Piano Concerto No. 1 in E minor
*How Do I Love Thee?* (wds Elizabeth Barrett Browning; arr. Leo Hussain), choral setting adapted from Étude, Op. 10 No. 3
*I Found You in the Rain* (1941), based on Prelude, Op. 28 No. 7
*I'm Always Chasing Rainbows* (1918), based on middle section of Fantaisie-Impromptu, Op. 66
*Inno a patria* (wds Glinski), rec. 1949 by Gigli, loosely based on Mazurka, Op. 67 No. 3

*La jeune fille* (wds Pomey; arr. Viardot), based on Mazurka, Op. 24 No. 2
*Messaggero amoroso* (arr. Buzzi-Peccia, 1919 or earlier), based on the 'Minute' Waltz, Op. 64 No. 1
*Minute Waltz* (?1966), every note of Op. 64 No. 1 sung by Barbara Streisand
*Minute Waltz* (lyrics by Richard Stilgoe, c. 1975), Chopin's life story sung to Op. 64 No. 1
*My Twilight Dream* (1939), based on Nocturne, Op. 9 No. 2
*L'Oiselet* (wds Pomey; arr. Viardot), based on Mazurka, Op. 68 No. 2
*Omaggio a Bellini* (wds Glinski), rec. 1949 by Gigli, based on Variation in E from Hexameron
*Plainte d'amour* (arr. Viardot), based on Mazurka, Op. 6 No. 1
*Play, Fiddle, Play* (1932), based on the first theme of Chopin's Piano Concerto No. 1 in E minor
*Pro peccatis suæ gentis* (arr. Ralph Allwood), choral setting adapted from Prelude, Op. 28 No. 20 with text from Stabat mater, attrib. Jacopone da Todi
*Seize ans* (wds Pomey; arr. Viardot), based on Mazurka, Op. 50 No. 2
*So Deep Is the Night* (1939; wds Miller, arr. Melfi), adapted from Étude, Op. 10 No. 3
*Till the End of Time* (1945; wds Kaye, arr. Mossman), based on Polonaise No. 6, Op. 53

# Selected Arrangements of Chopin's Music

## Orchestral works

Allegro de concert, arr. Nicodé for piano and orch.
Allegro de concert, arr. Messager for piano and orch.
Allegro de concert, arr. Wilkomirski for piano and orch.
Chopiniana, works for, arr. Glazunov (Polonaise, Op. 40 No. 1, Nocturne, Op. 15 No. 1, Mazurka, Op. 50 No. 3, Waltz, Op. 64 No. 2, Tarantelle, Op. 43)
Chopiniana, works for, arr. Rogal-Lewitzky (Étude, Op. 10 No. 12, Nocturne, Op. 48, Mazurka, Op. 33 No. 4, Waltz in E minor (1830), Polonaise, Op. 53)
Chopin Suite (1910), works for, four movts, arr. Balakirev (Étude, Op. 10 No. 6, Mazurka in B flat major, Nocturne, Op. 37 No. 1, Scherzo, Op. 39)
Piano Concerto No. 1 in E minor, orch. Balakirev
Piano Concerto No. 1 in E minor, orch. & arr. Tausig
  Second movt (Romanze), arr. Backhaus (1918) for solo piano
  Second movt (Romanze), arr. Balakirev (1905) for solo piano
  Second movt (Romanze), arr. Bradley-Keeler for solo piano
  Second movt (Romanze), arr. Reinecke for solo piano
Piano Concerto No. 2 in F minor, orch. Charles Klindworth (with amplified piano part)
Piano Concerto No. 2 in F minor, orch. Richard Burmeister (with first-movt cadenza)
Piano Concerto No. 2 in F minor, orch. Alfred Cortot

Variations on 'Là ci darem la mano', adapted for solo piano Julia Rive-King

## Piano works

Ballade, Op. 23, arr. Ysaÿe for violin & piano
Berceuse, Op. 57, arr. Cerné for violin & piano
Étude, Op. 10 No. 6, arr. Glazunov for cello & piano
Étude, Op. 10 No. 10, arr. Ricci for violin & piano
Étude, Op. 25 No. 1, arr. W. Posse for harp
Étude, Op. 25 No. 7, arr. Glazunov for cello & piano
Fantaisie-Impromptu, Op. 66, orch. Farnon
Funeral March from Sonata No. 2, Op. 35, arr. Henri Reber for orch. (it was this version that was played at Chopin's funeral), but innumerable other arrangements for orch., military band, etc. (see also 'Sonata', below)
Mazurka, Op. 7 No. 3, arr. Huberman for violin & piano
Mazurka, Op. 7 No. 3, orch. Balakirev
Mazurka, Op. 17 No. 4, orch. Stokowski
Mazurka, Op. 33 No. 2, arr. Kreisler for violin & piano
Mazurka, Op. 33 No. 4, orch. Stokowski
Mazurka, Op. 67 No. 4, arr. Kreisler for violin & piano
Mazurka, Op. 68 No. 2, arr. D. Abram for four tubas
Mazurka, Op. 68 No. 4, arr. Francescatti for violin & piano
Nocturne, Op. 9 No. 2, arr. Sarasate for violin & piano
Nocturne, Op. 9 No. 2, arr. Popper for cello & piano
Nocturne, Op. 27 No. 2, arr. Sarasate for violin & piano
Nocturne, Op. 27 No. 2, arr. Wilhelmj for violin & piano
Nocturne, Op. 37 No. 2, arr. Huberman for violin & piano
Nocturnes, Op. 55 Nos 1 & 2, arr. Franchomme for cello
Nocturne, Op. 55 No. 2, arr. Heifetz for violin & piano
Nocturne, Op. 55 No. 2, arr. Manén for violin & piano
Nocturne, Op. 55 No. 2, arr. Saint-Saëns for violin & piano
Nocturne, Op. 62 No. 2, arr. Saint-Saëns for violin & piano
Nocturne, Op. 72 No. 1, arr. Auer for violin & piano
Nocturne in C sharp minor, Op. posth., arr. Milstein for violin & piano
Nocturne in C sharp minor, Op. posth., arr. Piatigorsky for cello & piano
Prelude, Op. 28 No. 4, orch. Stokowski
Prelude, Op. 28 No. 4, arr. Liszt for organ
Prelude, Op. 28 No. 9, arr. Liszt for organ
Prelude, Op. 28 No. 15, arr. Sieveking for cello & piano
Prelude, Op. 28 No. 24, orch. Stokowski
Sonata No. 2, Op. 35 (Chopin wrote to his family, 'Franchomme… has arranged my

Sonata with the March for orchestra'.)
Waltz, Op. 34 No. 2, arr. Sarasate for violin & piano
Waltz, Op. 34 No. 2, arr. Lev Ginzburg for cello & piano
Waltz, Op. 34 No. 3, arr. Sarasate for violin & piano
Waltz, Op. 64 No. 1, arr. Maud Powell for violin & piano
Waltz, Op. 64 No. 2, arr. Huberman for violin & piano
Waltz, Op. 64 No. 3, arr. Sarasate for violin & piano
Waltz, Op. 70 No. 1, arr. Huberman for violin & piano
Waltz in E minor, Op. posth., arr. Ysaÿe for violin & piano

## Others

6 Chants polonais from Seventeen Polish Songs, Op. 74, arr. Liszt for solo piano: Mädchens Wunsch ('The Maiden's Wish'), Op. 74 No. 1; Frühling ('Spring'), Op. 74 No. 2; Das Ringlein ('The Ring'), Op. 74 No. 14; Bacchanal ('Merrymaking'), Op. 74 No. 4; Mein Freuden ('My joys'), Op. 74 No. 12; Die Heimkehr ('The Homecoming'), Op. 74 No. 15
10 Lieder von Friedrich Chopin, arr. Kirchner for solo piano: Op. 74 Nos 1, 4, 5, 8, 10–14 & 16
Introduction and Polonaise brillante for cello and piano, Op. 3, arr. Czerny for solo piano
Lithuanian Song, Op. 74 No. 16, arr. Auer for violin & piano
Lithuanian Song, Op. 74 No. 16, arr. Sgambati for solo piano
Lithuanian Song, Op. 74 No. 16, arr. Bendel for solo piano
Largo from sonata for cello & piano, Op. 65, arr. Cortot for solo piano
Polonaise brillante in C, Op. 3, cello part reworked Feuermann
Sonata for cello & piano, Op. 65, arr. Moscheles for piano four hands
The Maiden's Wish, Op. 74 No. 1, arr. MacMillen for violin & piano

## Piano arrangements, paraphrases, etc. of Chopin's piano works

The most prolific arranger of Chopin's works was the Polish-American Leopold Godowsky (1870–1938). He wrote a series of fifty-three studies on all but one of Chopin's Études (fifty-four if we include both A and B 'third versions' of Op. 25 No. 2). The exception is Op. 25 No. 7 (Godowsky's Study No. 37), which was almost certainly written but, for some reason, withheld from publication. The entire set contains much novel and even revolutionary writing that raised piano technique to new heights. Some studies attract as many as three different versions (exceptionally, in the case of Op. 10 No. 5, Godowsky wrote seven!), twenty-two of which assign the work of both hands to the left hand alone. In two cases, this master of pianistic contrapuntal ingenuity combines two studies into a single work. For reasons of space, the list below omits the catalogue of Godowsky's fifty-three Chopin Studies but includes all his other Chopin paraphrases.

Also of some interest is the 2004 recording by the French jazz pianist Jacques Loussier of his semi-improvised treatment of the twenty-one Nocturnes on an album entitled *Impressions of Chopin's Nocturnes*.

Allegro de concert, Op. 46, arr. Mikuli for two pianos
Ballade, Op. 47, arr. Rawicz & Landauer for two pianos
Eighteen studies on Chopin's Études 'in contrary motion', Friedrich Wührer
Étude, Op. 10 No. 2, arr. Philipp (Fifth Étude de concert)
Étude, Op. 10 No. 2, arr. Seutin for left hand (1939)
Étude, Op. 10 No. 5, arr. Joseffy (Concert Study No. 2)
Étude, Op. 10 No. 5, arr. Philipp (Fourth Étude de concert)
Étude, Op. 10 No. 5, arr. Seutin for left hand
Étude, Op. 10 No. 7, arr. Seutin for left hand
Étude, Op. 25 No. 2, arr. Brahms
Étude, Op. 25 No. 2, arr. Philipp for left hand (Third Étude de concert)
Étude, Op. 25 No. 2, arr. Seutin for left hand
Étude, Op. 25 No. 6, arr. Reger
Étude, Op. 25 No. 6, arr. Gregory Stone ('in broken thirds')
Étude, Op. 25 No. 8, arr. Philipp (Concert Study, 1944)
Two Études in G flat major, arr. Maier as study for two pianos
Étude in G sharp minor (Op. 25 No. 6 + Op. 10 No. 12 combined), arr. Tiempo
Triple Étude (Op. 10 No. 2 + Op. 25 No. 4 + Op. 25 No. 11 combined), arr. Hamelin
Triple Étude after Chopin (Op. 10 Nos 1 & 8 + Op. 25 No. 1 combined), arr. Mann
Left-Hand Inversions of Five Études (Op. 10 Nos 1, 2, 5, 7 & Op. 25 No. 9), arr. Carlos Chávez
Fantaisie-Impromptu, Op. 66, arr. Morton Gould for two pianos
Impromptu, Op. 29, arr. Reger
Impromptu, Op. 51, arr. Marschner for four hands
Étude after the Impromptu, Op. 29 (Michałowski)
Mazurkas, Op. 50 Nos 1–3, arr. Czerny for four hands
Nocturne, Op. 9 No. 2, arr. Louis Gruenberg as No. 1 of Jazz Masks (1928)
Nocturne, Op. 9 No. 2, arr. Joe Furst as 'modern paraphrase' (1949)
Piano Sonata No. 2, arr. Saint-Saëns for two pianos
Polonaise, Op. 40 No. 1, arr. Géza Zichy for left hand
Polonaise, Op. 44, arr. Czerny for four hands
Polonaise, Op. 53, arr. Carl Burchard for two pianos, eight hands
Scherzo, Op. 31, arr. Scharwenka for two pianos
Rondo, Op. 16, arr. Godowsky
Waltz, Op. 18, arr. Godowsky
Waltz, Op. 42, arr. Reger
Waltz, Op. 64 No. 1, arr. Joseffy, Schütt, Michałowski, Moszkowski, Reger, Sirota, Sorabji, Godowsky, Philipp, Rosenthal, Ferrata, Laistner, Hofmann, Zadora, Habermann, Pennario; also arr. Louis Rée, Arvid Samuelson for two pianos
Waltz, Op. 64. No. 2, arr. Reger, Gruenberg

Waltz, Op. 64 No. 3, arr. Godowsky
Waltz, Op. 69 No. 1, arr. Godowsky
Waltz, Op. 70 No. 1, arr. Rozyckí
Waltz, Op. 70 No. 2, arr. Godowsky
Waltz, Op. 70 No. 3, arr. Godowsky

## Works inspired by Chopin

Aux mânes de F. Chopin: Elégie et Marche funèbre, Op. 71 (Stephen Heller)
Cho-piano (novelty piano solo, Henry Lange, 1922)
'Chopin' from Carnaval, Op. 9 (Schumann)
Chopinata (Wiener & Doucet)
'D'Edriophthalma', No. 2 of Embryons desséchés, parody of the Funeral March (Satie)
'Grazioso (Hommage à Chopin)' from Deux Contrastes, based on Prelude, Op. 28 No. 7 (Casella)
'Hommage à Chopin' from Suite de morceaux, Op. 46 No. 9 (Leschetizky)
Impromptu on the themes of two Preludes by Chopin (Balakirev, 1907)
'Profil – Chopin', No. 7 of Walzermasken for piano solo (Godowsky), also arr. for violin & piano as No. 2 of Twelve Impressions
Ten Variations on the Prelude, Op. 28 No. 20 (Busoni, 1922)
'Un poco di Chopin', from Eighteen Pieces, Op. 72 No. 15 (Tchaikovsky)
Valse-paraphrase on Op. 64 No. 2 for two pianos (Schütt)
Variations and Fugue on the Prelude, Op. 28 No. 20 (Busoni, 1885)
Variations on a theme of Chopin, based on Prelude, Op. 28 No. 20 (Rachmaninov)

## Chopin's Birthplace at Żelazowa Wola

The site of the building in which Chopin was born attracts a huge number of pilgrims each year, despite the fact that the composer spent only the first seven months of his life there and that his actual birthplace has undergone many changes over the years.

The original estate mansion was documented in the sixteenth century and became the property of the Skarbek family at the turn of the nineteenth. When the Chopins lived there, there were three buildings: the main mansion and two annexes – one on the left built c. 1800 and one on the right. The mansion was burnt down in 1812 during the Napoleonic War and never rebuilt. Of the two surviving annexes, the Skarbeks lived in the right-hand one. It is probable that the Chopins lived in the left annexe. After their move to Warsaw, they returned frequently, with and without Fryderyk, to visit the Skarbeks, spending occasional holidays there until 1834 and even organizing the wedding party for one of their daughters.

In 1834 Michał Skarbek committed suicide. Żelazowa Wola then passed through a number of hands before being bought by Adam Towianski in 1859. He reconstructed both annexes. There were eleven buildings and a water mill on the estate by the time he sold it in 1879 to Aleksander Pawłowski. Pawłowski took no care of 'the Chopins' house' and used it for storage. The right annex was destroyed by fire during the First World War. Thus, by sheer luck, from the three Skarbek dwellings only 'the birthplace' survived, albeit in a poor state. In 1918 the land was divided up among peasant families. Ten years later the buildings, together with three hectares of land, were bought by the Chopin Committee, supported by the Ministry of Education.

In 1930–1, the left annex was rebuilt to look much as it would have done in 1800 but with a raised shingle roof and a porch supported on two columns. Its interior was filled with nineteenth-century furniture, much of which was subsequently stolen by the Nazis. Its present state, including the surrounding parkland, was established between 1945 and 1953.

Long and low, and without the main mansion and the right annex, the birthplace now appears to be the central house of the property. It is situated in a large garden surrounded by trees, with a stream flowing nearby.

# Envoi

*'The light was just failing when they went back into the music-room. And, cigar in mouth, old Jolyon said: "Play me some Chopin."*

*By the cigars they smoke, and the composers they love, ye shall know the texture of men's souls. Old Jolyon could not bear a strong cigar or Wagner's music. He loved Beethoven and Mozart, Handel and Gluck, and Schumann, and, for some occult reason, the operas of Meyerbeer; but of late years he had been seduced by Chopin, just as in painting he had succumbed to Botticelli.'*

*The Forsythe Saga*, John Galsworthy

*'The music teacher came twice each week to bridge the awful gap between Dorothy and Chopin.'*

George Ade

# Selected Bibliography

**Ashton Jonson**, G.C., *A Handbook to Chopin's Works*, London, 1905

**Cortot**, Alfred, trans. Cyril & Rena Clarke, *In Search of Chopin*, London, 1951

**Eigeldinger**, Jean-Jacques, *Chopin – pianist and teacher*, Cambridge, 1986

**Eisler**, Benita, *Chopin's Funeral*, London, 2003

**Ferra**, Bortomeu, trans. R.D.F. Pring-Mill, *Chopin and George Sand in Majorca*, Palma de Majorca, 1974

**Gerig**, Reginald R., *Famous Pianists and Their Technique*, London, 1976

**Hedley**, Arthur, *Chopin*, London, 1947

**Huneker**, James, *Chopin – The Man and His Music*, London, 1903

**Methuen-Campbell**, James, *Chopin playing from the composer to the present day*, London, 1981

**Mikuli**, Karol, ed., *Chopin's Works*, New York, 1989

**Niecks**, Frederick, *Frederick Chopin as a Man and Musician* (third edition), London, 1902

**Opieński**, Henryk, ed., trans. E.L.Voynich, *Chopin's Letters*, New York, 1988

**Orga**, Ateş, Chopin: His Life and Times, Tunbridge Wells, 1976

**Sadie**, Stanley, & John Tyrell, *The New Grove Dictionary of Music and Musicians* (second edition), London, 2001

**Samson**, Jim, *The Music of Chopin*, London, 1985

**Samson**, Jim, ed., *The Cambridge Companion to Chopin*, Cambridge, 1992

**Schonberg**, Harold C., *The Great Pianists*, London, 1965

**Schumann**, Robert, trans. Fanny Raymond Ritter, *Music and Musicians*, London, 1876

**Zamoyski**, Adam, *Chopin, A Biography*, London, 1979

# Glossary

Adagio   Slow.

Allegro   Lively.

Andante   Literally 'going', i.e., at a walking pace.

Ballade   Derived from a medieval French song form, from the nineteenth-century onwards it usually refers to an instrumental composition with a narrative. Chopin's four Ballades are atypical in this respect.

Barcarolle   Originally a boating-song sung by Venetian gondoliers. Now a term applied to any vocal or instrumental piece in a lilting rhythm (usually 6/8).

Baritone   The middle male singing voice (in between bass and tenor).

Bass   The lowest range of male voice.

Bel canto   Literally 'fine singing'. A style of opera that emphasizes long, flowing lines, as espoused by Bellini and Rossini.

Bolero   A Spanish dance in triple time, often featuring castanets.

Cantabile   'In a singing style' – a performance direction to play in a melodious, flowing manner.

Cantilena   A smooth singing line, whether vocal or instrumental.

Chamber music   Music for small groups of players, such as a string quartet or a piano trio; so called because such music was originally played in the 'chamber' or home.

Concerto   An elaborate work for solo instrument with orchestra, often, but not always, in three movements, the first of which is frequently in sonata form. The soloist is pitted against the orchestra, often with highly virtuosic music to play.

Contralto ('Alto')   The lowest range of the female singing voice.

Counterpoint  A style of writing in which each part or 'voice' is independent and has significance in itself, as well as in the context of the whole texture. The supreme contrapuntal form is the fugue.

Étude  French for 'study'. Usually a solo instrumental work designed to focus on a particular aspect of technique. The best Études combine this practicality with music of intrinsic merit, such as those for piano by Chopin, Liszt, Scriabin and Debussy.

Fantasy, Fantaisie  A piece in which familiar forms are either abandoned or treated with striking freedom, as opposed to a work written within the rules of a preconceived formal structure, such as a sonata or symphony.

Finale  The last (final) movement of a work.

Fugue  A work or movement which is entirely built around imitative counterpoint. A fugue will usually consist of three or four instrumental or vocal strands (known as voices), based on a short tune (the 'subject' or theme) which is stated at the beginning by a single voice and then taken up by the other voices and repeated in quick succession throughout the piece.

Harmony  The simultaneous sounding of notes to make a chord. Harmonies often serve as expressive or atmospheric 'adjectives', describing or giving added meaning to the notes of a melody. A composer's unique style can be defined from the way in which he or she builds and uses chords.

Impromptu  A short, song-like instrumental piece (usually for piano) that gives the feeling of spontaneity. Those by Schubert and Chopin are the best-known examples.

Improvisation  To extemporize, to invent on the spot (as opposed to playing from pre-existing music).

Key, key signature  The key of a tonal piece of music is determined by the set of notes chosen as the main material for its composition. The chief note is the 'key' note and all the other notes used have a relation to this one. The key signature indicates the precise tonality of the music – generally this concerns which major or minor scale (and the chords built on it) will be used as a basis for the piece.

Larghetto  Slow, but faster than largo.

Largo    Slowly and with dignity.

Legato    'Bound together' – a performance direction indicating that the notes should be played smoothly, not staccato.

Major    If a work is described as being, for example, in D major, it means that the work is predominantly in that key, i.e., uses the notes in the scale of D major.

Mazurka    Polish country dance usually in 3/4 or 3/8 time. Chopin introduced the form into concert music.

Mezzo-soprano    The middle range of the female singing voice.

Minor    Same principle as major (see above), using the notes in the scale of a minor key (B minor, C sharp minor, etc.). Works in minor keys often sound more melancholy than those in the major.

Movement    Comparable to a chapter in a book; a primary, self-contained division of a larger composition, each movement having a different tempo.

Nocturne    A piece that evokes night, usually tranquil in mood. Although the genre has also been used for symphonic movements (by Vaughan Williams) and a song cycle (by Britten), it is most commonly associated with short lyrical pieces for piano, originated by John Field and perfected by Chopin.

Opera    A dramatic work for stage which combines words, drama, music (with singers and orchestra) and often elaborate scenery.

Opus    Latin for 'work', usually abbreviated to 'Op.'. The system by which a composer's work is identified or numbered (usually, but not necessarily, in chronological order).

Polonaise    A courtly Polish dance in 3/4 time. Most of Chopin's are of an ardent, martial nature.

Prelude    A brief orchestral preface to a longer work – or, in the case of Chopin, Debussy, Scriabin, Rachmaninov and others, a short, self-contained instrumental composition. It can also be paired with a fugue, as in the case of Bach's *Well-Tempered Clavier*.

Romance, Romanze | Sometimes used to describe a slow movement which is tender and intimate in mood. It can also be a freestanding work.

Rondo | A compositional form in which the principal tune occurs at least three times in the same key in the same movement. A standard form for the last movement of a sonata or concerto, it can also be a freestanding piece.

Rubato | From the Italian for 'robbed'. A way of playing or singing in which some of the notes are slightly hurried and others slowed down while the underlying pulse remains constant. It gives a flexible, poetic expression to a piece. Chopin was particularly celebrated for his sensitive use of rubato when at the piano.

Scherzo | Literally 'joke'. Generally the liveliest movement in a symphony or chamber work, with three beats to the bar, developed out of the more stately minuet. Chopin and Brahms both wrote independent solo works for the piano which they called 'scherzos'.

Score | The written copy of all the 'parts' (voices or instruments) of a composition placed systematically one above the other on separate lines of the manuscript paper. 'Scored for x, y & z' means that the music has been written for a particular combination of voices or instruments.

Sonata, Sonata form | Extended instrumental composition, usually in more than one movement, most often for keyboard or another solo instrument with keyboard. A movement in strict sonata form comprises three distinct sections: exposition (presenting the themes), development (extending and varying the themes) and recapitulation (repeating the themes as they first appeared).

Soprano | The highest range within the three categories of female singers.

Subject | A tune or theme.

Staccato | Notes played in a short, detached style.

Symphony | Since the time of Haydn this has described a substantial, serious work in the form of a sonata for orchestra with several (three, four or sometimes more) movements.

Tarantella | Fast Italian dance in 6/8 time.

Tenor   The highest natural male singing voice (the male alto and countertenor voices are higher but are achieved using a particular technique called falsetto).

Theme   A subject or tune that is developed within the course of a work.

Transcription   An arrangement of a piece of music for a different instrument or instruments.

Trio   A work for three performers, usually in three or four movements. Also the name given to the central contrasting section of a minuet or scherzo.

Valse   The French for waltz.

Variations   A set of varied versions of a particular theme, using melodic decoration, alteration of rhythm, key, tempo, etc.

Virtuoso   An instrumental performer who demonstrates exceptional technical and musical attainments.

Waltz   A dance in 3/4 time that became universally popular in the nineteenth century. Although it originated in the ballroom, concert Waltzes such as those by Chopin and Brahms were never intended to be danced to.

# Annotations of CD Tracks

Please note: with the exception of CD 1, track 16, all the music on these two discs is presented in the order in which it was composed.

# CD 1

[1] Variations in B flat major for piano and orchestra on 'Là ci darem la mano' from Mozart's *Don Giovanni, Op. 2*. **Alla polacca**

Chopin was just seventeen when he composed this set of Variations with orchestral accompaniment, and it marked his first major success as a composer. The theme is from the famous duet 'Give me your hand', in Act 1 of Mozart's opera, sung by Giovanni to the peasant girl Zerlina. After the brilliantly written introduction and the theme's statement, Chopin writes five contrasted variations, each punctuated by the orchestra. This extract is the scintillating final variation, marked Alla polacca, in which Chopin turns the tune into a polacca, or polonaise.

When the young Robert Schumann first encountered the work he greeted it with the now-famous invocation, 'Hats off, gentlemen! A genius!' When Chopin first played it in Vienna on 12 August 1829, he wrote to his parents: 'Yesterday... I made my entry into the world!... As soon as I appeared on the stage, the bravos began; after each variation the applause was so loud that I couldn't hear the orchestra's tutti. When I finished, they clapped so much that I had to come out and bow a second time.'

[2] Piano Concerto No. 1 in E minor, Op. 11. **Movement 2: Romanze**

The second movement of Chopin's First Piano Concerto is labelled Romanze. Its inspiration was Chopin's Romantic ideal: his first love, Konstancja Gladkowska. It consists of a beautiful and melancholy nocturne in E major with a second subject in B major, both of which are heard in highly decorated, quasi-improvisational guises. In a letter dated 15 May 1830, while he was still working on the Concerto, Chopin described his thoughts about this movement, one of the rare occasions that he attempted to provide a meaning to any of his music. 'It is not meant to be loud, it's more of a romance, quiet, melancholy; it should give the impression of gazing tenderly at a place which brings to the mind a thousand dear memories. It is a sort of meditation in beautiful spring weather, but by moonlight. That is why I have muted the accompaniment.'

3  Waltz in E minor (1830)

This Waltz is one of a number of pieces that were published after Chopin's death (it did not appear in print until 1868). Even if the composer thought little of it, it has become one of his most popular works, often played as an encore because of its dazzling outer sections. In between comes a lilting melody in E major.

4  Nocturne in E flat major, Op. 9 No. 2
5  Nocturne in F sharp major, Op. 15 No. 2

The nocturne is a genre indelibly associated with Chopin. Although orchestral works had been written in the eighteenth century with the same title (Mozart's suite Serenata notturna, for example), it was the Irish pianist-composer John Field who invented and popularized the nocturne as a work for solo piano. Here a graceful melody would sing over a gentle accompaniment, rather like an aria from a Bellini opera. Chopin took the nocturne into another sphere. By turns his are haunting, sentimental, dramatic, brooding, sensual and melancholy – Chopin at his introspective best, conjuring up music of deep poetic expression.

The Nocturne in E flat is not only one of Chopin's best-known compositions but one of the most popular of all piano works. The Nocturne in F sharp major, written a year or so later, was dedicated to his friend the pianist and composer Ferdinand Hiller. Theodor Kullak described it as one of Chopin's most sublime works, which 'touches one like a benediction.'

6  Étude in C major, Op. 10 No. 1
7  Étude in E major, Op. 10 No. 3 ('Tristesse')
8  Étude in G flat major, Op. 10 No. 5 ('Black Keys')
9  Étude in C minor, Op. 10 No. 12 ('Revolutionary')

Chopin's first collection of short Études (or Studies), Op. 10, together with his second set of twelve, Op. 25 published four years later in 1837, form the Magna Carta of Romantic piano technique. Numerous books of piano studies had appeared before these, with each one devoted to a particular aspect of execution, such as scales, arpeggios, thirds and octaves. What makes Chopin's Studies different from their predecessors is that, although each one poses a particular technical challenge, this is subsumed into the poetry of the music.

Chopin's Opp. 10 and 25 extended the range of piano music to the limits of tonality and revolutionized finger technique. Some of the audacious harmonies were new concepts in sound, many of them later to become the basis of Impressionism. Of all piano études, Chopin's are simultaneously the most challenging for the player (with the possible exception of Liszt's) and the most rewarding for the listener.

Here are four of the best-known Studies from the first set. No. 1 is a spectacular exercise for the right hand, aimed at improving the playing of arpeggios (but listen out, too, for the left hand underpinning the swirling notes!). No. 3 is nicknamed 'Tristesse' ('Sadness') for obvious reasons. An étude is not always concerned with flashy, fast fingers. The beautiful melody here makes one forget that it was intended as a study in expressive playing. Arguably the most famous of all the Studies, it was turned into a popular song in 1939 called 'So Deep Is the Night'. No. 5 is known as the 'Black Keys' Study because the right hand plays entirely on the black keys. No. 12 also has a nickname – the 'Revolutionary'. It was inspired, so it is said, by the fall of Warsaw in 1831; but musically it is a Study for the development of left-hand technique. A later generation got to know the 'Revolutionary' through a 1957 children's record, 'Sparky's Magic Piano'.

[10] Mazurka in A minor, Op. 17 No. 4

The mazurka is a dance in triple time with a dotted rhythm and the second or third beat strongly accented. It takes its name from the area of Mazovia around Warsaw, and it was a form that inspired Chopin from his teenage years until his death. Of his total of fifty-seven Mazurkas, forty-one were published in his lifetime. Few last longer than four minutes; many are much shorter. This one in A minor is one of the most poignant and personal of all. It is a mark of Chopin's genius that he could convey such heart-breaking emotion via such economy and simplicity.

[11] Fantaisie-Impromptu in C sharp minor, Op. 66

It is something of a mystery why Chopin decided not to publish this work. Perhaps he intended to and overlooked it; perhaps he felt that somehow it fell below his own high standards; perhaps he agreed with some of his more severe critics, who suggested that the song-like middle section was too saccharine. At all events, this, one of Chopin's best-known works, was written in 1834 and eventually appeared in print in 1855. In 1919 that beautiful central melody was borrowed by a couple of American songwriters who turned it into the song 'I'm Always Chasing Rainbows'.

[12] Ballade No. 1 in G minor, Op. 23

Chopin composed his four Ballades between 1831 and 1842. The inspiration for this new solo piano form came from the nationalist poetry of his friend Adam Mickiewicz. Through this new genre, Chopin wanted to create a musical parallel to the literary ballad but, even if the music was inspired by a particular poem, he would never slavishly illustrate its narrative. Unlike the Nocturnes, Mazurkas, Waltzes and other small-scale compositions to which Chopin directed most of his energies, the Ballade is a relatively extended form.

The G minor Ballade is justly famous, one of the earliest examples of Chopin moving from the extrovert showpieces of his youth to the emotional works of his maturity. Almost certainly sketched out in Vienna in 1831, it was another four years before it was completed to his satisfaction. When Schumann told Chopin that he liked this Ballade the best of all his compositions, Chopin, after a long, meditative pause, said with great emphasis, 'I am glad of that. It is the one I too like best'.

13. Étude in A flat major, Op. 25 No. 1
14. Étude in A minor, Op. 25 No. 11

Chopin's Op. 25 is his second set of twelve Studies, published in 1837. It consolidates the earlier set of Op. 10, exploring much of the same ground, but 'extending the paths a little and taking in some new scenery on the way' (Samson).

The two Études selected here could not be more different. Op. 25 No. 1 has acquired two nicknames: 'The Shepherd Boy' and 'Aeolian Harp'. It is a study in poetic rubato playing and subtle pedalling. In one of the very rare instances in which he provided a narrative clue for the interpreter, Chopin once explained to a pupil, 'Imagine a little shepherd who takes refuge in a peaceful grotto from an approaching storm. In the distance rushes the wind and the rain while the shepherd gently plays a melody on his flute.'

Op. 25 No. 11 is known as the 'Winter Wind'. It is the longest of all the Studies and simultaneously one of the most difficult to play and exciting to hear. Above the march-like figure in the left hand, the right hand has a tumult of virtually non-stop semiquavers (arranged in groups of six) that makes the Study akin to a toccata.

15. Impromptu No. 1 in A flat major, Op. 29

Another work dating from 1837, this Impromptu is the first of three (if we discount the earlier Fantaisie-Impromptu) and is considered by many to be one of the most beautiful and spontaneous of all Chopin's works. An impromptu is a short piece giving the impression of an improvisation. Although the term was first coined around 1822, it was Schubert and Chopin who made the form their own.

16. Mazurka in C sharp minor, Op. 30 No. 4

In reviewing the set of four Mazurkas, Op. 30, published in 1835, Schumann wrote: 'Chopin has elevated the Mazurka to a small art form; he has written many, yet few among them resemble each other. Almost every one contains some poetic trait, something new in form and expression.' This haunting C sharp minor Mazurka is the last and most important of the set.

# CD 2

1  Scherzo No. 2 in B flat minor, Op. 31

Chopin's four Scherzos have little in common with the scherzos found in Beethoven's symphonies nor with the original meaning of the word: a joke or jest. In adopting this title for a new genre of piano music, Chopin was looking to underline the sardonic, scornful and ironic aspects of humor.

The most celebrated of the four is this one, which used to be disparagingly known as the 'Governess's Scherzo' because at one time every well-brought-up young lady seemed to play it. The arresting opening bars – an innocent question followed by a decisive answer – could never be played to Chopin's satisfaction, according to Wilhelm von Lenz. It was never played questioningly enough, never soft enough, never round enough, never sufficiently weighted. 'It must be like a house of the dead,' he once said. 'That's the key to whole piece.' And of its lyrical D flat major central section: 'You should think of [the singer] Pasta, of Italian song – not of French vaudeville!'

2  Prelude in E minor, Op. 28 No. 4
3  Prelude in D flat major, Op. 28 No. 15 ('Raindrop')

Like 'Scherzo', the title of 'Prelude' was appropriated by Chopin for a new form of solo piano piece. Far from being an introductory piece of music (the opening of a suite, say), these Preludes are Chopin's own self-contained thoughts, miniature tone poems exploring all shades of feeling and mood. Eight of them are less than a minute in length; only three last longer than three minutes. There is one Prelude for every major and minor key. Even on their own, the 24 Preludes would have guaranteed Chopin's immortality.

Most of the Preludes had been completed prior to Chopin's departure to Majorca with George Sand and her children. Despite the aggravations of his time in Valldemosa, Chopin completed the cycle here. The E minor and D flat Preludes are among Chopin's most beloved works. The former reminds us of Shelley's line, 'Our sweetest songs are those that tell of saddest thoughts' and was one of two Preludes played on the organ at Chopin's funeral. The D flat Prelude is known as the 'Raindrop' because of the insistently repeated note of A flat (or G sharp, as it becomes in the sinister middle section).

4  Piano Sonata No. 2 in B flat minor, Op. 35. Movement 3: Funeral March: Lento

Chopin's Second Piano Sonata is known as the 'Funeral March' Sonata because of its celebrated third movement. Heard almost as frequently in its arrangement for military band as it is in its original form, the grief-wracked tolling of the main theme is the most widely played funeral march ever written. The central section has a calm, consoling theme in D flat before the March resumes, taking us 'into the very luxury of woe', its last bars dying away to nothing. It was written as a separate piece two years before making its way into the four-movement Sonata.

Although the whole Sonata is doom-laden and sinister in character, the strange thing is that a performance of it leaves you feeling just the opposite.

5   Waltz in A flat major, Op. 42

The opening E flat trill summons the dancers to the ballroom. Whether by chance or design, what follows, with its combination of duple and triple rhythms, seems to suggest the crowded dance floor with couples whirling round, flirting, hesitating and plunging onward with passion and exuberance. 'A garland of flowers winding amidst the dancing couples!' was how one of Chopin's pupils described it. It is one of the finest examples of the genre, and the only Waltz of Chopin not to bear a dedication.

6   Nocturne in C minor, Op. 48 No. 1

The C minor Nocturne is the grandest and, arguably, the greatest of all Chopin's Nocturnes. In fact, in many ways it more closely resembles a Ballade. Chopin was particularly finicky over how the haunting first four bars should be played. 'He was never satisfied', reports Lenz, who finally succeeded 'after long efforts' to play the first two bars satisfactorily for the composer, before being put to the test again over the next two bars.

Kullak, who felt that 'the chief subject is a masterly expression of a great, powerful grief', saw the second subject as a band of heroic men gathering solemnly to go forth on a holy war to conquer or die for their native land.

7   Fantasy in F minor, Op. 49

The F minor Fantasy is not only one of Chopin's greatest works but one of the greatest of all compositions for piano. Those who feel that Chopin was not at his best when constrained by formal structures, such as sonata form, cite the Fantasy as an example of his genius when unfettered by any such considerations.

It closely resembles the Ballades and, indeed, the music has a story to tell – though what exactly that story is will be different for each listener. Liszt (reporting third-hand) said it represented a quarrel and reconciliation between Chopin and George Sand. Certainly it was written at Nohant in 1841 when the couple were at their happiest, yet the dominant atmosphere of the piece is melancholy, despite its passages of nobility, dramatic grandeur and, in its central section, extreme tenderness.

8    Polonaise in A flat major, Op. 53 ('Heroic')

Often called the 'Heroic', Chopin's most famous Polonaise is written in 'a most majestic and finished style... a glorious apotheosis of the past' (Kleczyński). The originality of the themes and the rich variety of ideas are all worked through in a breathtaking epic of just six minutes. It is a martial tone poem and in the hands of a great pianist can be an unforgettable experience.

The striking central section is usually said to represent a cavalry charge or the trampling of horses, but if it is played at the correct tempo, as Chopin insisted, it is more like an approaching cavalcade. Hallé recalled how on one occasion he played the work to the composer. 'In his gentle way he laid his hand upon my shoulder, saying how unhappy he felt, because he had heard his "Grande Polonaise" in A flat *jouée vite!*, thereby destroying all the grandeur, the majesty, of this noble inspiration'.

9    Berceuse in D flat major, Op. 57

Chopin's Berceuse (the only one of his compositions to bear this title) was probably inspired by the small daughter of Pauline Viardot who was left at Nohant to be cared for by Chopin and George Sand while Viardot went on tour. The simple rocking figure remains unaltered throughout the entire course of the piece, every bar beginning with the same low D flat in the bass and, except for two bars towards the end, unvarying in its gently alternating harmonies while the right hand traces delicate filigree figures above it. One of the composer's biographers, Charles Willeby, suggested that in the last eight bars, the nurse, who has been rocking the child, herself succumbs to the drowsy influence of the music.

10   Piano Sonata No. 3 in B minor, Op. 58. **Finale: Presto, non tanto**

This work is more of a sonata in the strict sense than its predecessor and, some think, a weaker work because of that. The first movement is overflowing with ideas; the scherzo is succinct, dazzling and graceful; the slow movement meanders overlong, with a somewhat self-absorbed melody. But the finale is a triumphant success by any standards. It is a jubilant, galloping rondo and is, practically speaking, one of the most difficult movements in all Chopin. Interestingly, its second subject is one of the few occasions in his music where he writes in scales (other examples are the end of the Étude in A minor, Op. 25 No. 11, the Impromptu, Op. 36 and the Barcarolle). The brilliant passagework of the final pages in B major serves as a thrilling conclusion.

11   Barcarolle in F sharp major, Op. 60

As with the Berceuse, Bolero and Tarantelle, the Barcarolle is Chopin's only essay in this form. What mental pictures does it conjure up for you? A gondola being rowed with rhythmic strokes along Venice's silent canals? A pair of lovers in a gondola, utterly absorbed in each other? The Venetian barcarolles – gondoliers' songs – were an attraction to visitors as early as the eighteenth century, with their characteristic lilting 6/8 rhythm (Chopin's is notated in 12/8), the most famous examples for piano before Chopin's being three of Mendelssohn's *Songs without Words*. The music dies away, but ends with four fortissimo octaves as though Chopin was snapping the lovers out of their dream world and back to reality.

# Index

<cite/>